Nothing to Hide

Edward Hide
with
Mike Cattermole

Macdonald
Queen Anne Press

For Sue, Lizzie and Will

A *Queen Anne Press* BOOK

© Edward Hide and Mike Cattermole 1989

First published in Great Britain in 1989 by
Queen Anne Press, a division of
Macdonald & Co (Publishers) Ltd
66–73 Shoe Lane
London
EC4P 4AB

A member of Maxwell Pergamon Publishing Corporation plc

British Library Cataloguing in Publication Data
Hide, Edward.   Nothing to hide
    1. Flat racing. Jockeys, biographies
    I. Title   II. Cattermole, Mike
    ISBN 798.4'0092'4

Typeset, printed and bound by
Hazell Watson & Viney Limited
Member of BPCC plc
Aylesbury, Bucks, England

Contents

Introduction

One of the difficulties I found in writing this book was trying to imagine the person I was addressing. When you talk to someone, you soon ascertain the extent of their knowledge of a subject, but writing is different. In the end I decided to write for two types of reader: the first has perhaps only a passing interest in racing; and the second is a complete racing buff and probably knows as much about the sport as I do.

I hope I got the mixture right.

Acknowledgements

This book would never have seen the light of day without the assistance of several people whose help I very much appreciate. Many thanks are due to John Francome, for convincing me I was capable of having a go; to Caroline North of Queen Anne Press, for commissioning the book; to Mike Cattermole and Pam Cockerill, my co-writers, who helped me to organise my thoughts and memories into readable form. Finally, to Sue I owe a large debt of gratitude, for the endless hours she spent slaving over the word-processor and for her invaluable advice which, while not always appreciated at the time, usually turned out to be right!

Foreword
Peter O'Sullevan

I have known Edward throughout the 35-year span between his first winner at Chepstow in September 1951 and his last in Hong Kong on 18 May 1986; from being an intensely shy young man to his swift maturity into one of the outstanding tactical exponents of his profession – sixth in the roll-call of all-time winning jockeys in Great Britain in the year of his retirement.

When his studious father, Bill, who turned from farming to training in Shropshire, told me in the early 1950s, with evident concern, that 'the boy' was obliged to spend a night in London, he asked, 'would you please keep an eye on him?' It looked like being heavy going as 'the boy' perched high on the edge of an armchair and twisted his cloth cap between nervous fingers while my wife sought to engage him in conversation with strictly limited success. But once seated at a table in the White City Greyhound Stadium restaurant and refreshed by an apéritif, our no longer silent guest became the entertaining companion he was to remain throughout a career during which, from the age of 20, he was 'Cock of the North' for no fewer than 16 years.

On Friday 13 June 1975 Edward broke a leg in a crashing fall at York at a time when he was three winners clear of Lester Piggott in the Jockeys' Championship. Under a heading 'Title Hopes Shattered by Injury' I quoted his principal employer, Bill Watts, in the following day's *Daily Express*, 'Edward will be especially missed by Northern trainers, not only for his ability but for his fine judgement and readiness to ride work and help at all times'.

Few jockeys have ever devoted so much time to study of both the book of form and the contours of Britain's infinitely varied racecourses or put their knowledge to greater effect.

During the immediate pre-war era Harry Wragg was rightly considered to be the 'brainiest' rider at a time when the number boards featured such names as Michael Beary, Brownie Carslake, Joe Childs, Charlie Elliott, Freddy Fox, Sir Gordon Richards, Charlie Smirke, Rae

Johnstone, etc. Some while after he had turned to training Harry observed, 'In my day the jockeys were always thinking and wondering what the others were getting up to. Today I can think of only one jockey who does the same thinking and that is Edward Hide'.

I can recall only one occasion when I regretted having sought Edward's view before making a selection. Intending to go for Babur to win the Lincoln for the second time in 1958, I quizzed the stable's jockey before racing on the previous day. He suggested with typical thoroughness that I defer my decision until he had ridden the course, after which he gave it as his tentative opinion that the going would be too fast for my prospective choice. He was not to know that it was to rain all night, to 25–1 winner Babur's great advantage.

Ten years later, wearing my colours for the first time, he enquired happily after winning Ayr's Craigmore Selling Handicap by six lengths on Stay Friendly, 'Has that made up for Babur?' It had.

Edward's career has been marked by achievement and integrity. Surely few titles reflect their subject as accurately as the delightfully told story *Nothing to Hide*.

– 1 –

The Establishment

'ANY management that stands still is destined to fail'
Sir Ian MacGregor

To enter the doors of 42 Portman Square, London, the headquarters of the Jockey Club, can be a nerve-wracking experience. But today, despite the date – Friday 13 June 1986 – I entered in hopeful antici-pation. I had not been summoned to face some disciplinary action, but had been invited to attend an interview for the vacant post of Stewards' Secretary. According to Rule 29 of the Rules of Racing, 'The Stewards' Secretary shall give to the Stewards such help and advice relating to the conduct of the meeting and the Rules of Racing as they may require'.

This was the first formal interview I had attended in my life. Before I joined Sir Gordon Richards as his stable jockey in 1969, we met up for a picnic lunch at the roadside near Rugby, and when I was asked to ride for Clive Brittain in 1977, I was offered the job over a glass of champagne with Captain Marcos Lemos in the owners' and trainers' bar at Royal Ascot. My daughter Elizabeth had told me that part of her training at college had involved a staged interview. She had been taught the type of questions that might be asked and the sort of answers that would be expected, even what clothes to wear – right down to the colour of her tights. I had no such preparation.

The interview panel consisted of Charles Weatherby, Deputy Sec-retary of the Jockey Club, Colonel Dick Holland, the Chief Stewards' Secretary, both of whom I knew well, and Miss Barbara Orrett, the Chief Personnel Officer of the Jockey Club, whom I had not met before. Miss Orrett did most of the talking. I recall little of that first interview but I do remember Miss Orrett asking me what I felt my faults were. I replied, 'What makes you think I have any?' which raised a laugh all round. I was told that I was the only candidate to have replied in that vein, but it can't have done me any harm because I was invited back for the final interview 11 days later.

I had been thinking for quite some time of applying for the job of Stewards' Secretary when I finally hung up my riding boots. It was a job that with my background I felt I was well suited to. The duties include advising the stewards on such matters as interference during races, abuse of the whip and when it appears that horses are not being allowed to run on their merits. Who better than a man who has seen it all from the inside to spot such things? At least, that was the way I looked at it.

News spreads quickly in racing circles and during the spring of 1978, after I had ridden Parent to win a Haydock handicap, his owner, Major Michael Wyatt, then Deputy Senior Steward, sent me a thank-you note, mentioning also that a little bird had told him of my interest in becoming a licensed official when I gave up riding. He pointed out that one or two Stewards' Secretaries were due to be trained in the next couple of years and enclosed a form for me to return to Gerald Dawson, who was then Chief Jockey Club Stewards' Secretary. The form I received featured requests such as 'state your regiment and rank'. I felt there was little point in my filling in the form, but I informed Gerald Dawson of my interest and of my wish to have my name put on their files.

When a vacancy for a Stewards' Secretary arose in the late 1970s the advertisement stated that no racing experience was necessary, which caused a furore among those professionally involved with the sport. These people realised better than most the responsibilities that the Secretary's job entailed, and the majority of them thought it was crazy that a complete racing novice might be asked to help adjudicate on matters affecting their livelihood. I suppose I should have had an inkling then that the powers that be had rather eccentric criteria for their appointments. However, I hoped that by the time I came to make my application pressure from some of the press might have helped to have changed things.

About three years later, I got a lift from Newmarket to Pontefract with the trainer William Hastings-Bass. We discussed my interest in becoming a Stewards' Secretary. William, whose opinion I have always respected, was most enthusiastic and felt that it would be good for racing. A little while after that, Sir Jakie Astor, who was then head of the Jockey Club Disciplinary Committee, approached me at Newmarket races and he too gave me the impression that he was in favour of the idea, although at the time I expressed the hope that I would go on riding for a few more years. In 1983 I received a letter from Charles Weatherby. Although at this stage I had not formally applied for the post, the letter pointed out that the main problem in appointing me as a Stewards' Secretary was whether I would be able to distance myself sufficiently from the people against whom I had ridden to present an objective position of authority. He wrote: 'To make the comparison of "poacher turned gamekeeper" would be using the wrong terminology, but I hope that this example explains the problem!' Of course, I understood perfectly what he meant and noted his suggestion that it would be beneficial to take some time away from the English weighing-room. However, he ended the letter by telling me that they could be looking for someone in their early 30s, which would obviously have ruled out a 46-year-old Edward Hide!

At that stage, then, I thought I would have to look elsewhere for an occupation on my retirement. The following summer, 1984, I was asked whether I wanted to be considered for the post of Inspector of Courses, based in the north of England, but I had already committed myself to riding in Hong Kong on an eight-month contract. My supply of good rides at home was dwindling, and furthermore I had considered Charles Weatherby's advice and felt that some time away from the English scene would stand me in good stead if I were to be considered for an official position. Indeed, before I left for Hong Kong I was informed that Colonel Holland would be retiring from his job as Stewards' Secretary in January 1988 and that the post would be advertised in June 1986.

The Jockey Club must have had a rethink about the age and type of person they were looking for as the advertisement now read: 'These are positions of high responsibility, requiring a mature personality. Applicants should be aged from 35 upwards and should have a thorough knowledge and understanding of racing. The successful applicants will be required to attend race meetings throughout the country, advising and assisting the stewards of those meetings on the conduct of racing'.

I received those particulars while I was riding in Hong Kong and my application was one of over 100. These were whittled down to 20 for the first interview and five of us were invited to attend a second and final interview. The other four applicants were former trainer Tony Gillam, a race-day steward at five racecourses under both Rules; former National Hunt rider Jeremy Speid-Soote; a successful amateur rider who ran a stud farm; and Terence Brennan, a former household cavalry officer.

Thus I came to face the five-man panel, nine days after my first interview. Sitting directly in front of me was General Sir Cecil 'Monkey' Blacker, the Deputy Senior Steward. The General had recently completed an in-depth survey on the problems of stewarding. The Blacker Report had not pleased everybody but one of the recommendations was that someone with racing experience, such as a former jockey or trainer, would make an ideal Stewards' Secretary. This report encouraged me to feel that the Jockey Club were now looking for someone with my sort of background. I had met General Blacker socially at Phil Bull's and at the centenary celebrations of the Royal Hong Kong Jockey Club, and on both occasions he had shown a genuine interest in whether I was still intending to apply for the job.

On the General's right was Sir William Dugdale, the Chairman of the Disciplinary Committee. I had gained the impression at disciplinary hearings in the past that Sir William did not have a very high opinion of jockeys. During the interview, I mentioned that there were some trainers who had kindly expressed their hopes that I would get the job, because they would prefer to be judged by someone with first-hand knowledge of the problems involved. I also pointed out that I expected there to be a few trainers who would be against my appointment because they were aware that I knew how they operated. Sir William gave me hope by replying, 'That is why we want you, for your experience'.

Dick Saunders, Chairman of the Licensing Committee, sat on General Blacker's left and completed the line-up at the top table. He had become the oldest jockey to win the Grand National when he partnered Grittar to victory in 1982. The only previous encounter I had had with him was after my last winning ride in England on the Jimmy Etherington trained Hi-Tech Leader at Nottingham. Hi-Tech Leader suffered from intermittent lameness but, unfortunately, Jimmy was not present to inform the stewards of the fact. On leaving the winners' enclosure, the racecourse vet noticed this slight lameness and the stewards held an inquiry into the possibility of my having been too severe on the horse in the finish. Dick Saunders handled it all with sympathy and understanding, and no action was taken.

The other two men present at the interview were Colonel Dick Holland, who sat on my right, and Charles Weatherby, on my left. Both had been at the preliminary interview. Colonel Holland had come to tell me when the panel were ready to see me: he was friendly and courteous but had nothing further to add this time.

General Blacker set the ball rolling by asking for my views of the stewarding situation. I felt that a line somewhere between what is practised in Hong Kong and in England would be the most suitable for racing in this country. In Hong Kong, racing is governed by a panel of five, three of whom are professional stipendiary stewards, each of whom has a vote, and they are thus all-powerful should they wish to band together. The other two are unpaid members of the Jockey Club. This can have its drawbacks (more of this later), but I felt that in Britain, once a suitable person had been appointed as Stewards' Secretary and given the required training, it would be in racing's best interests for him to have a vote at any racing inquiry. The Stewards' Secretary is required to attend, on average, four or five meetings a week throughout the year, both on the Flat and over the jumps. So, with all the experience of viewing races that this gives him, he must have at least as good a chance of getting things right as the race-day stewards who, in view of their other commitments, are able to attend far fewer meetings. I was fully aware that the diplomatic answer to General Blacker's question would have been that everything in the garden was rosy. In spite of this, I felt I had to express my true feelings in the hope that the panel would see that what I had to say made sense.

The General seemed most concerned about whether I would cope, particularly after a year or so, with the travelling involved. I said that as a successful jockey I was accustomed to travelling thousands of miles in a season. I had done it for years and did not see it as a problem. I remember explaining to the panel that although there is a friendly atmosphere in the weighing-room, a jockey's occupation is very much an individual one. Charles Weatherby took me up on this, stressing that a Stewards' Secretary is very much part of a team. He asked me how I would cope if, after a stewards' inquiry, I had to show the press the film of the race but did not agree with the stewards' verdict. I have always believed that he who pays the piper is entitled to call the tune and I explained that in that situation I would do my best to justify the panel's decision.

I felt Charles Weatherby's next question was a little below the belt: 'What do you have to say on the headlines in the papers that you were refused a jockey's licence in Hong Kong?' It was true that at one stage my application had been opposed, but on appeal I had been granted a licence and to the best of my knowledge the affair had never made the headlines in this country. I referred him to General Blacker, who had written to me in July 1985 stating that he had spoken to Sir John Archer, the Royal Hong Kong Jockey Club supremo, and that as far as my application was concerned, the little difficulties that I had had in Hong Kong would certainly not count against me, indeed that they would be ignored.

The background work attended to, imagine my surprise when General Blacker said 'You do not appear to have the references, Edward'. Charles Weatherby jumped in to say that this was due to the shortage of time between the two interviews. I told the General that I had obtained, as requested, the two references and also that I had received a copy of Major Pope's letter five days previously and that if they cared to take another look, I was sure they would find them.

At the end of the first interview I had been told that should I reach the second I would need two personal references, preferably from people connected with the racing industry. I thought of a certain well-respected member of the Jockey Club whom I had first met during my early days riding for Captain Charles Elsey. He had seemed an ideal referee so I had 'phoned him. He was very pleasant but when I explained the reason for my call he evaded the issue – he did not tell me he would not provide me with a reference but said he would speak to Colonel Holland at Ascot where he was to act as a steward in the near future. I had then contacted another member of the Jockey Club, Sir Gordon Richards. I had known Gordon for years, first as a colleague in the weighing-room and more recently as my guv'nor at Whitsbury Stables. Sir Gordon was only too willing to help, although he expressed doubts about being able to do me justice in words.

'Gordon,' I said, 'a few words from you would make all the difference'. Later that day, he rang me to read out his reference over the 'phone. It was most complimentary. He said he was going to post it immediately and he was the sort of person who would have done just that: his word was always his bond.

My second reference had been provided by Major Michael Pope, the former trainer, who was at that time the President of the National Trainers' Federation. The Major had also taken the trouble of having a word with those responsible for interviewing the applicants before he pledged his support and that of the NTF in writing. Major Pope had sent a copy of his letter to me in Yorkshire five days before this interview. As requested, I had informed the Jockey Club of the names of my two referees.

At this point Charles Weatherby left the room, still muttering about the shortage of time, and after a few moments returned with only Major Pope's letter. Whatever happened to Sir Gordon's I do not know. I never saw it but Gordon had assured me that he was going to post it and that was good enough for me.

The interview lasted for about half an hour. The panel must have had a rare old discussion after I left the room because they did not call in the next applicant for another 25 minutes. I was not kept waiting long for the outcome. Only two days later I received a personal letter from General Blacker. It said that the panel were 'mindful of my long and distinguished career as a jockey' and that my application had been given 'a very great deal of thought and discussion'. 'Regretfully' there was no job for me, although they would consider me for the job of an official in another capacity. Naturally, I was very disappointed at the time because I felt that I had something positive to offer to the job. Apart from the normal duties I could, time permitting, have used my experience to help the young jockeys and apprentices with race-riding advice.

The most extraordinary outcome of the whole affair was that, of the final five applicants, not one was considered suitable for the job. I thanked both Sir Gordon Richards and Major Pope for their support. Major Pope was angry when I told him about the incident of the letters and it prompted him to write to General Blacker. He felt that it was most unsatisfactory that the panel apparently had no knowledge of the references prior to the interview. Major Pope had made absolutely certain that his letter of support arrived as early as possible before 24 June but, as it turned out, he need not have bothered to have made the effort.

The press were also up in arms. In London's *Evening Standard* Christopher Poole, who had given me plenty of support in his columns, wrote: 'The Jockey Club, ruler of British racing for more than two centuries, evidently has no serious intention of overhauling the outmoded and unsatisfactory system of local stewarding'. He described their decision as 'quite extraordinary and disgraceful'. Major Pope himself was quoted as saying: 'I personally recommended Edward as highly as possible for the job and I also did the same on behalf of the Trainers' Federation who voted overwhelmingly in his favour and were particularly keen that he should get the job. I was amazed when he was turned down'.

In the *Sporting Life*, Jack Logan's amusing reaction to this was: 'Amazed? It's exactly the sort of class-conscious folly I would have expected'. There was, in fact, so much of an uproar that Monica Dixon, then the Jockey Club's spokeswoman, was instructed to justify their decision. She was quoted in the *Sporting Life*: 'It is not a disadvantage to be a former jockey or trainer. On the contrary, we see it as a definite advantage. We are making a conscious effort to attract people such as former jockeys and we have recently employed Guy Williams, who was a trainer in Ireland. In Hide's case, it was simply felt that although he was a top-class jockey, he would not have been suitable as a Stewards' Secretary . . . Any former jockey or trainer who wants to be considered should not be put off in any way by our decision not to give the job to Hide.' It is typical of the Jockey Club's attitude that the Stewards' Secretary was afforded a Christian name but the ex-jockey was still plain Hide. Could that be the answer?

Howard Wright was another journalist who gave me plenty of backing. In his *Racing Post* column he wrote: 'A re-think by the team of Blacker, Dugdale, Holland, Saunders and Weatherby would not be a step backwards; it would be a positive move. It would show that they are big enough to change their minds for the good of racing'. In the event, the Jockey Club team did indeed change its mind, but not in the way that Howard and I might have hoped. They called back Terence Brennan, one of the original five to have been rejected initially, and appointed him as trainee Stewards' Secretary. I certainly do not think that I should automatically have been chosen: some of the other applicants had equally good, if not better, credentials.

Someone who had been a trainer and is a Steward with a vote at five racecourses was not, amazingly enough, the man they wanted.

Someone who had been a National Hunt jockey, an assistant trainer and who had stipendiary stewarding experience abroad was an also-ran.

Someone who had race-riding and stud experience was also put aside.

The one man who had virtually no racing experience was given the job.

Could it be that the Jockey Club does not want someone with racing knowledge and set ideas, but would prefer to start from scratch and train them to their way of thinking? Yet the original advertisement had been amended and now stressed that applicants 'should have a thorough knowledge and understanding of racing'. Was the Blacker Report just a scrap thrown out to keep the journalists and critics at bay? General Blacker had taken a lot of time and trouble over his report and one cannot help feeling that he must have felt frustrated, angry and maybe even insulted that the Jockey Club had simply ignored his report.

Christopher Poole summed up the situation in his *Pacemaker International* column. 'Yet the selection committee which studied his application – about 100 were received – and subsequently interviewed the sixth most successful jockey in the history of British horse racing turned him down in favour of one Terence Brennan, described as the General Manager of a trading company who has "ridden in a few point-to-points and hunts regularly". Mr Brennan, formerly an officer in the household cavalry, is not known to me personally. He may well be a splendid chap, socially acceptable in every way. But as a potential Stewards' Secretary his qualifications are just about zero and his appointment in preference to Hide is nothing short of a scandal.' He ended his piece by saying that nothing had changed in the 20 years since Fred Winter had had his application for the post of Assistant Starter turned down.

Nothing much seems to have changed since my application either. Only one more vacancy for a Stewards' Secretary has arisen since Terence Brennan's appointment, and in 1988 someone called Geoffrey Forster was selected to fill it. An employee of Weatherby's, he had worked in their offices since 1978. His 'practical' experience of racing consisted of six months helping in a non-riding capacity in John Winter's yard in 1975 at the age of 20 . . .

It was not long before I started to hear various rumours about why I had been unsuccessful. In spite of the support of the Trainers' Federation, there had apparently been strong opposition from two trainers who don't live a million miles from me and for whom I had ridden many winners. Could they possibly imagine that I had cause to doubt that some of their horses ran on their true merits?

I also heard that two northern stewards, both owners, one of whom is not averse to the odd bet, had threatened to resign in the event of my appointment. I can't imagine why, can you? It also seems that Charles Weatherby had his doubts about me. After the first interview he told Geoffrey Summers, then Secretary of the Jockeys' Association, that he was worried about how I would get on socially with the stewards! On top of that, when asked by Christopher Poole to explain why the panel had chosen Terence Brennan his reply was, 'He seems a decent sort of chap, so we thought we'd give him a try'!

Easier to understand was the panel's fear of a clash of personalities had I been taken on, in that if I had not agreed with a certain decision, I would have said so. They were afraid I would make waves, and certainly I would have found it difficult to keep quiet if I had thought the panel were thinking along the wrong lines. One of the biggest problems that the race-day stewards face is the need for a quick decision due to the very limited time between the ending of one race and the start of the next.

I do not want this to sound like sour grapes because I believe that it would have been in racing's best interests if someone like me had been appointed. However, I have to say with hindsight I feel that the panel, far from doing me a disservice, actually did me a favour. I am sure that there are many capable Stewards' Secretaries doing a good job for racing. It is often a difficult and thankless task and it is impossible to please all of the people all of the time. The Secretary is required to be at the course about two hours before the first race and is unable to leave until all the business for the day has been sorted out. He is required to submit a written report on all inquiries and has to take a videotape of the day's racing which he is supposed to study when he returns home. I certainly do not envy him all that.

In Hong Kong, there are only two courses, situated within ten miles of each other, which does away with so much travelling. I am coming round to agreeing with General Blacker's doubts about the travelling. It did not bother me while I was a jockey but had I become an official I might have felt differently returning home on a dark winter's night in adverse road conditions after officiating at, say, Perth or Devon and Exeter.

Not so long ago, my wife Sue and I attended our son William's school prize-giving and during the headmaster's speech Thomas Arnold, that famous headmaster of Rugby School in the earlier part of the 19th century, was quoted. I reproduce the words here as they seem particularly applicable to this whole episode.

'There is nothing so unnatural and convulsive to society as the strain to keep things fixed when all the world is in eternal progress; and the cause of all the evils of the world may be traced to that most natural but most deadly error of human indolence and corruption that our business is to preserve and not improve.'

I was flattered by the support of all my friends and colleagues throughout and I was particularly touched to read what my former weighing-room colleague Johnny Seagrave had to say about the affair: 'It was a surprise to a lot of people high up in racing when he was rejected. Edward was the original "Mr Clean" and if anyone should have got the job, he should. He has done it all and if they can turn him down for a job like that, there's not much hope for any jockeys in the future. He was the complete professional with one of the most unblemished characters you could ever hope to have. Edward is a true diplomat of racing and he would have been ideal for the job'.

Not long after being turned down, I was greeted by the familiar voice of a well-known trainer as I walked into the bar at Doncaster Sales. 'Thank God you didn't get the job,' he said, 'because we've got a much better chance with the c**** that are running the show at the moment!'

– 2 –
A Shropshire Childhood

NESTLING in the Corve Dale in South Shropshire between the Brown Clee Hills and Wenlock Edge stood Lawton. Lawton was home – a rectangular, whitewashed old farmhouse, approached by a mile-long drive from a minor road. With the Pyebrook on one side and the River Corve on the other, its situation was delightfully picturesque but, being three miles from the nearest village and seven miles from the market town of Ludlow, it was isolated.

The 330-acre farm had been in the family since Grandfather bought it in 1910. It was mentioned in the Domesday Book and was the legacy of a township that was devastated by the Black Death. The house was spacious with six bedrooms, a large dining-room and an oak-panelled sitting-room. There was no central heating and the place could be very draughty. I remember waking up on winter mornings to find the windows frozen inside. We had an Aga cooker in the kitchen which was on 24 hours a day, and I often sat on the covers to get warm.

There were large brick fireplaces in the dining-room and sitting-room and, fortunately for us, Father was an excellent stoker and liked to see a good fire. Mains electricity didn't reach us until 1948 and only then because a very large cowshed in the nearby village of Peaton was converted into a metal plate factory. We used candles and paraffin lamps for lighting until Father installed our own generator. Unfortunately, it wasn't powerful enough to run a television and so I used to have to travel by bus to watch the England versus Australia Test matches at my aunt's farm ten miles away.

Father was only three years old when his family moved to Lawton. It wasn't long before he was able to ride and as a young lad he became involved in pony racing in a small way. A local farmer boasted that he had the fastest horse in Shropshire and agreed to give my father and his 11-hand pony a quarter-of-a-mile start in a mile race. The stakes were £5 a side and Father's subscription was on credit – his pocket money at the time was a mere sixpence a week! The start of the race was signalled by a shotgun, and after that the farmer and his 'Pegasus' were treated to a rather distant view of Father and his pony as they galloped away to claim their prize. Perhaps the farmer was unaware of the old racing adage that in short races you can give weight but not a start. Father was given both that day!

It was this equestrian background that led Father to cross paths with a certain Charlie Edwards, a local character who was a farmer and auctioneer by profession. Charlie was a fearless and very good horseman who had also found the time to produce five daughters and one son. The whole Edwards family rode and did exceptionally well with showing ponies. Father was never involved in that scene but became associated with the Edwards family through hunting and participating in point-to-points and he became friendly with one of the daughters, Connie, later to become his wife and, more importantly for me, my mother.

Mother was a slightly-built woman standing just over five feet. She weighed only eight stone when she married; so, at the age of 13, when she first rode one of Grandpa's horses in a point-to-point, she would have been knee-high to a grasshopper. She was an outstanding rider who competed in shows all over the country before she married, winning many prizes including the top rider award at Olympia in 1928. But she was always modest about her achievements and if anyone ever suggested she was brave to ride in point-to-points at such a young age she would dismiss the idea with a shrug and a smile . . . 'There was nothing courageous about it', she would insist. 'I had no choice in the matter. The brave thing would have been to say no when Father told me to get on and ride!'

Meanwhile my father's progress in point-to-points was slow, but his long-held ambition to ride a winner between the flags was achieved in 1933 on Double Domino, and the partnership went from strength to strength after that. My parents married in September 1935 and Father sold Double Domino and settled down to serious farming. I was born in 1937 and my brother Tony two years after that. Our sister Jill came along a few years later.

When war broke out grass farming and cattle grazing had to be scrapped. An Agricultural Committee was appointed for each county and it became compulsory to plough up the land.

I recall haymaking on the farm in the summer when I was a little older. We used an old car with a rake on the front to collect the hay and I helped to load it on to the elevator to make the stack. There is no finer scent than the smell of new-mown hay — I can still smell it now. There were no combines then to do the harvesting: the corn was cut with a binder, which more often than not went wrong. Tony and I used to help stook the corn, eight or ten sheaves together, and lead the stooks to the stack where they were stored until the winter when the threshing machine came round. Neighbours came to help out on threshing days and we would go to their farms when it was their turn to have the machine. As the stack was reduced the dogs would go wild catching the rats which used to shoot out from the bottom of the stack in all directions.

Because we were so far from town, we had bread delivered twice a week and the general groceries once. We also milked two cows and made butter in a large churn in the dairy, using a separator to extract the cream from the milk. Once a year we killed a pig and had some marvellous sausages and pork pies. The hams were hung from hooks in the kitchen ceiling.

Our only experience of war action was in November 1940, when a lone German Heinkel dropped a batch of 500 lb bombs on our neighbourhood. The nearest bomb landed a quarter of a mile away at the top of the orchard, but, even at that distance, the force of the blast blew in a few of our windows. A piece of the bomb lodged itself in the living-room of a nearby service cottage, much to the surprise of the person in the room at the time, but apart from a solitary sheep there were no casualties. It was suggested that the pilot may have seen a light from the pub across the valley when the door opened at turning-out time. The bombing incident is one of my earliest memories. The bomb left a huge crater which soon filled with water and became a natural skating rink when it froze over during the winter. The army Nissen huts on the roadside which stored ammunition also served as a reminder that there was a war going on somewhere.

For as long as I can remember I had always wanted to become a jockey and Grandpa Edwards gave me plenty of encouragement in the saddle. Grandpa had wanted his son Ken to be a jockey and sent him to be apprenticed to George Digby, who trained at Exning near Newmarket. Unfortunately, after only two years Uncle Ken had to accept that he was growing too heavy for his chosen career and he returned home to become a successful farmer instead. He maintained his interest in racing by keeping a few point-to-pointers and most of Mother's family had an affinity with horses.

The first record of me on a horse's back is a photograph of me aged two, astride a hunter called Marigold. Grandpa loaned us a very old pony called Teddy which got Tony and me started. Later he had me trotting around in a circle on my pony with pennies between my knees and the saddle to make sure that I was gripping with my legs. It's a good job it was only pennies or I would have cost him a fortune. A little later, Father bought me a white pony called Sixpence of which I thought the world, and which kindled my love of riding. I was soon out hunting with the Ludlow Hounds with Father, first on a leading rein and then on my own.

In December 1941, Father bought a couple of broodmares at New-market. One of them produced a set of dead twins in each of the next three years, which introduced me early to some of the disasters that can attend the breeding of racehorses. Fortunately the other mare foaled a good, strong colt which Father named Free Etching. He was gelded as a yearling and put into training with Josh Hollowell at Wold House in Malton. By a strange quirk of fate Jimmy Etherington, who trained my last winner as a jockey in Britain some 40 years later, now trains there.

During the war, racing was confined to Windsor, Salisbury and Ascot in the South, Stockton and Pontefract in the North and New-market. Horses were able to race in only one of these three zones as travelling was restricted. Training fees were £3 a week at that time. Josh Hollowell got off to a good start at the beginning of the 1946 Flat season, but then disaster struck. A random dope test produced a positive result for caffeine and that meant curtains for Josh: he lost his licence, and in those days when that happened it was for life. The regulations regarding doping have changed now, but at that time the trainer was held to be 100 per cent responsible. Even if Josh could have proved that some other person had been the culprit it would have made no difference.

It is a sobering thought that had Josh's misfortune not occurred, Father may never have taken up training and I certainly would not have benefited from the early opportunities that came my way. Father decided to bring Free Etching home and was granted a National Hunt licence. He had a team of five horses to begin with and in the first season each of them won at least once. Between them that year they collected a total of seven races. It was a remarkable achievement for a newcomer: Father has always modestly claimed beginner's luck, but it inspired one or two local people to send him horses and gradu-ally the farm at Lawton was turned into a training establishment.

There was nothing fancy about our facilities. Some of our early boxes were made out of disused railway sleepers but we draught-proofed the gaps between the sleepers with strips of tin and when we'd finished they were probably sturdier and warmer than any con-ventional stables. Right from the beginning Tony and I were involved in this venture. At the age of nine or ten I thought it was the most exciting thing that had ever happened on the farm and my interest in racing grew rapidly into an obsession. I started to live and breathe horses and, from the time Father began to train, my ambition to be a jockey hardened into a determination. Relatives tell me I would refuse cream cakes, explaining, 'I want to be a jockey and I mustn't put on weight', and any lessons at school other than those which were of potential use to a jockey simply held no interest for me.

We were lucky to have over 300 acres for the horses to use. Hedges were bulldozed and the ground levelled to construct our own gallops. Unfortunately, the land was clay and therefore not the most suitable for galloping on as it was often too firm in a dry summer (in which case we used a six-furlong plough gallop), or too heavy in a wet one. There were no all-weather gallops in those days, although Arthur Thomas, who trained near Warwick, had the nearest to one. It was made from foundry waste (a sort of sand) from a local factory, and we occasionally took horses to work there. Some winters we kept the horses cantering in the fields, other times they went on the roads. We had the odd steep hill around us, and it was noticeable to me that after the winters on the roads the horses required less galloping to get them race fit.

At the age of 11 I had gained enough experience to start riding out. No doubt Father passed on the odd tip, but I learned a lot from keeping my eyes open on the gallops. We had three good work riders: Sid Francis, who rode the jumpers for us, and was later tragically killed in a road accident outside Newmarket; a lad called Bill Mackie, or 'Mac', who had some rides for us on the Flat; and another very good horseman, Ginger Russell. The jockey Ted Larkin also stayed occasionally and rode work for us. Ted was very successful in the North and had a spell at Newmarket riding for Jack Jarvis. He wasn't there long, and soon faded from the limelight and I haven't heard news of him for years. Jimmy Thompson and Frankie Durr also rode work for us and rode some of Father's early winners. Jimmy later lost an eye in a racing accident at Newcastle, and he and Lester Piggott were the prime movers in the introduction of goggles. Now no jockey would dream of riding without them, and it is difficult to see why it took so long for them to be brought into use.

As the number of Father's runners grew I found myself going racing more and more often. One day when I was nine I went with Grandpa Edwards to see a filly of his run at Wolverhampton. He took me into the paddock to meet his jockey, Cliff Richards, who asked me what I wanted to do when I grew up. To Grandpa's delight I replied 'I'm going to become a jockey and beat Gordon', referring of course to Cliff's brother and my great idol, Gordon Richards.

It didn't take me long to realise that I had a real character as a grandfather. As an 18-year-old in 1890 Grandpa had been to Canada, quite an undertaking in those days. He took a train from Calgary to Edmonton, but found to his dismay that only 60 miles of the line had been constructed. So, stuck in the middle of nowhere, he bought 160 acres of virgin land for ten dollars, built himself a log hut and settled there. He returned home four years later, having sold up for £650, when he was needed by his father to run the recently purchased 500-acre Elsich Manor.

Horses were central to Grandpa's life. He hunted, ran a stud, took his children to all the big shows and produced top-class animals which were then sold on to customers, including the Royal Family, all over the country. In his youth he also had an eye for a pretty girl. On one occasion, when he had dropped one lady for a new love, she wrote him a nasty letter and demanded her photograph back. By return she received 25 photographs, all of different girls, with a note which read: 'Take your pick out of this lot, I really cannot remember which is yours'.

In racing circles Grandpa was best-known for his infamous National Hunt horse, Elsich. Though he hunted him early on, on the racecourse Elsich became a horse jockeys avoided. His brakes and steering were faulty and to call his jumping erratic would be a generous understatement. To qualify for the Grand National in those days a horse had to be placed in a chase of three miles or over. Elsich achieved this at Worcester. There were only three runners, he fell and was remounted, and although down to a walk and a trot at times he eventually completed the course. In the National he got only as far as the first fence. Grandpa maintained that Paddy Balf, his jockey, baled out, never having had any intention of going further!

In 1946 Grandpa was joined by Ren Jenkins, who was with him for four years. Ren later went to John Dunlop, for whom he broke in yearlings. During his 21 years there, these included such well-known horses as Shirley Heights, Ragstone, Scottish Rifle and Ragtime. He now assists his son John at Royston. Prior to Ren's arrival Elsich had run 36 times, seldom completing the course. Ever the optimist, Grandpa always backed Elsich each way and, according to Ren, the horse's record was so abysmal that when he first rode him, at Hereford, the bookies were willing to lay 200–1 on him getting round. All went well until the last fence, which the horse took by the roots. Ren was half off when a helpful jockey upsides him reached over and pulled him back on, and Grandpa won his bet!

To describe him as eccentric hardly does Grandpa justice. Have you ever heard of anybody having his coffin and gravestone delivered before his death? Grandpa stored his in one of his stables. The solid four-ton block of granite was already engraved. It read: 'For the Lord's sake, work as hard as you can, live as long as you can, do all the good you can to all the people you can'. Grandpa wanted to be buried on a hill on his own land and said to one of his workers, 'That's where I'm going to lie, and I've chosen this spot so that I can keep an eye on you lot to see that you get on with your work'. Very quietly, with a twinkle in his eye, the old shepherd remarked, 'We'll fix that, Gaffer. We'll bury thee face down'ards'.

Many years later, Ernie Davey, the Malton trainer, told me how he had once put one over on Grandpa, who was then determined to get even somehow. His chance came when Ernie arranged to send an exracemare to be covered by one of Grandpa's thoroughbred stallions. Ernie was delighted with the grand, good-boned foal that duly arrived the following year. It thrived and grew at an amazing rate and Ernie was as pleased as punch with it until one day he noticed that the foal's legs were becoming hairier and hairier. It gradually dawned on him that Grandpa had used a Shire stallion on his mare!

My school days had begun when I was packed off to a small boarding school in the Hereford area at the age of five. Mother thought it would be nice if my elder cousins Jean and Anne, who were already at the school, could keep an eye on me. I was at the place for two years and the only thing I remember learning was how to tie a bow. After that, both Tony and I went daily to a school in Ludlow before going to Gorleston School, which had been evacuated during the war to Fishmore Hall, a mile our side of Ludlow. Father would take us both on an adapted seat on the back of his motorbike to the end of our farm drive (about a mile) and from there we caught the bus.

My mother had wanted to send me to Ellesmere College, where Grandpa and his brother Tom had been founder pupils. In Grandpa's final year, the headmaster, writing his report, had commented, 'Trying', much to the pleasure of my great-grandparents. But their satisfaction was relatively short-lived, for in the end-of-year report the comment was repeated, only this time the word 'very' preceded it! However, there were no vacancies for me at Ellesmere at the time (though Tony was to attend two years later) and so for a while I was a boarder at Lutwych Hall, Wenlock Edge, a boys' school where I was allowed to keep my pony.

It was at Lutwych Hall that I played rugby, at scrum-half. Not being much bigger than the ball it was difficult to make my presence felt at this particular sport. I was always keener on football, and managed to persuade the sports master to let us play that as well. I was made captain of the school football team, although I don't recall inspiring my side to any great successes. I also ran for the cross-country team. I wasn't very fast but could run a long way in a long time. Despite all this robust activity, my parents were worried about my health and kept me off school for most of one spring term. I had a chest X-ray and returned to have it analysed at the surgery where the doctor held it up to the light. I could clearly see an awful 'S' shape in my abdomen. 'What do you think that is?' asked the doctor. My heart sank to my boots: I thought it was my appendix and that it would have to be operated on immediately. Imagine my relief when the doctor pointed out that it was in fact the snake fastening on my belt!

My parents sent me back to school at the local Fishmore Hall. (No wonder they worried for my health — all that changing of schools must have made me giddy.) The headmaster, Mr Oldcorn, was most considerate later on when I asked for time off to ride in races. To satisfy the local authority he said he would give me out-of-hours tuition, but I can't recall ever being given any. I do remember finding Latin a difficult subject. I wanted to be a jockey not a doctor, and I couldn't see it furthering that career, so I asked if I could concentrate on the 'three Rs' instead.

As my father stood at five feet ten inches I knew that the odds were against me remaining short enough to become a Flat race jockey and I tried to frustrate nature as far as I could. Every morning when I woke up, instead of stretching as most people do, I would tighten up and make myself as small as I could in the hope that it might stop me growing. In the end it was Mother's contribution to my genes that probably kept me small but for years I continued to do this 'inward stretching' as well as watching very carefully what I ate. For school lunch we would sit down at long tables with a teacher at one end. I used to sit as far away from the teacher as possible so that I could stuff anything I didn't want to eat into a bag under the table.

Away from school there was always plenty to keep Tony and me occupied. Uncle Phil lived just across the valley and he used to come over for fishing and shooting and Tony and I would try to learn from him. I only ever got as far as using a worm (no fly) to fish. Before going to lunch one day I left my line in the river and on returning found it stuck fast. It wouldn't budge until I gave it an almighty pull and out popped a large eel. What skill! We also caught some nice trout in that river. I was lucky to have a brother of similar age with whom I shared a liking for most things, especially sports, for as we were so isolated there was no other young company for me. We got into trouble together as well. We tried smoking in the barn one morning while Father was away, with Georgina, whose father worked on the farm. As we sat down to lunch in the kitchen we saw smoke drifting across the yard. I had a dreadful sinking feeling in my stomach because I knew very well what the cause was. The barn was indeed on fire, but luckily Grandpa Hide was over for the day and was able to organise a production line of buckets of water. We got it under control before any lasting damage was done. It was certainly a good lesson because neither Tony nor I have smoked since.

In spite of the mutual infliction of injuries that characterise most brotherly relationships, Tony and I got on very well. We played football, tennis (we had our own grass court), table tennis, snooker and darts together. Occasionally, being right-handed, I threw the darts with my left hand in the hope that it would help me to use the whip better in that hand. We also played golf at Ludlow racecourse, on the course in the middle. We were both about the same standard except that Tony once achieved a hole in one – I have still to match that. At one of the holes at Ludlow the players tee off close to one of the steeplechase fences. To prevent balls lodging in it, fine wire mesh was laid along the take-off side of the fence. On one occasion some-one forgot to remove the wire before the races. The first two horses jumped safely but kicked the wire up, which brought down the remainder of the runners. I watched in horror as the horses tumbled down as though they were in a Western film.

Not all jockeys start riding young – Geoff Lewis was a page boy at the Waldorf Hotel in London before joining Ron Smythe – but it certainly can't have been a disadvantage to have been given the opportunity to ride from an early age. So much still had to go right for me and I did have luck on my side. I could suddenly have grown heavy, like Uncle Ken, and what if Father hadn't decided to take up training? This was certainly to my advantage, but although it would have taken me longer to get started, I like to think that I would still have made the grade had I been apprenticed to another trainer.

Father certainly made sure that I did my share. He was a disciplinarian, like most fathers in those days, and I didn't get a chance to argue. He used to remind me that his father had made him milk the cows before he rode his horse six miles to school, so in comparison perhaps my duties weren't all that burdensome. When I was away at school I obviously couldn't be called on to help, but from the age of 11 during the holidays I had to get up at six o'clock and make a large pot of tea before calling the lads, who lived in because of the farm's situation. After that I rode out two lots, mucked out, swept the yards, cleaned my tack and helped tread the divots in the gallops and, like the other lads, 'did' my two horses. I haven't forgotten how tiring it was dressing a horse over. The winter was the worst time: after going round the fields, you came back often freezing and wet, but you still had to clean up your horse before you could go in for breakfast.

When Lester Piggott, a year and a half my senior, rode his first winner on The Chase at Haydock at the age of 12 in August 1948, I very much hoped that I would be able to beat that. I nagged at Father almost non-stop for the next 18 months, but in spite of my badgering he was determined that I wouldn't ride before I was ready. He didn't feel that day had arrived until I'd reached the ripe old age of 13. He announced my big moment during the school summer holidays of 1950. 'Right, Edward,' he said out of the blue one day as I came into the yard on a big mare called Copper Wire, 'you've been going on at me long enough. If you really prove to me by the end of the month that you can manage this mare then you can ride her at Birmingham before you go back to school.'

I must have satisfied Father's requirements because a few weeks later he confirmed that the ride was mine. So at the start of my professional career I was 13 years old, a little under four feet six inches tall and weighed just over four stones.

– 3 –
At the Start

IT was with an uneasy mixture of apprehension and anticipation that I entered the weighing-room for the first time on 29 August 1950. The atmosphere of the racecourse itself was already familiar to me from numerous visits with Father and Grandpa but somehow it felt completely different now I was here to compete. This was the day I had been looking foward to for so long. No longer an onlooker, I suddenly found myself rubbing shoulders with jockeys who, up to now, had been just names. Everyone seemed to be riding at Birmingham that day: Scobie Breasley, Lester Piggott, Doug and Eph Smith, Tommy Lowrey, Manny Mercer and even the Champion Jockey himself, Gordon Richards, my inspiration. I gazed round the weighing-room, awestruck, a small boy in a man's world.

The first problem I faced was finding a valet to look after me and to supply all the gear I would need since Father didn't have an established valet for his apprentice at that stage. I was wandering round the weighing-room looking lost when a valet named Fred Dyer took pity on me and offered to take me on. It was a lucky encounter for me – although not in the first flush of youth Fred continued to valet me until his death shortly before I retired, and over the years he was to become my friend and confidant.

Fred's first task was to search out breeches and boots to fit me and a saddle on which I could ride. Because I weighed over two stones less than the seven stones that Copper Wire had been allotted I was given a big saddle. The breeches and boots were found and finally I put on Father's silks of royal blue with bronze hoops (the blue to be patriotic and the bronze because Father, with typical pessimism, never expected to make any money out of racing). Then, having weighed out, I set off with the other jockeys on the 100-yard uphill walk from the weighing-room to the paddock.

Birmingham was a right-handed course with a good level galloping track. It was a good place to be introduced to race-riding. The race I was to ride in was two miles five furlongs, which was an unusual distance for a small 13-year-old having his first ride. With hindsight it was almost certainly too far, but Father had justified his choice to me beforehand: 'A longer race will give you more time to learn something, Edward. If we put you in a sprint it will be over before you know what's happening'. Another contributing factor in his decision was that Copper Wire was undoubtedly the most suitable horse in the yard for me to start on. She was a big, sensible mare, but she had very limited ability on the Flat and probably needed every furlong of the distance. She later went on to win 19 point-to-points under Ted Greenaway, the racecourse vet.

Instructions in the paddock were kept to a minimum. I was too nervous and excited to have taken them in anyway. Father gave me a leg-up and walked with me down the long lead-out to the racecourse. Due to the distance there was no hurry to go on and the start was straightforward, except that I wasn't strong enough to prevent my mount from making the running. Due to my inexperience, I was pulling her about trying to restrain her and we collided with the rails after six furlongs. This had the desired effect of steadying her but probably winded her as well, as she gradually dropped away, finishing last.

It was hardly the most promising start to a racing career but I was undaunted. As I slipped off and unsaddled the mare I knew that I had found my vocation. The race had been every bit as exciting as I had dreamed it would be, and I was already looking forward to doing better next time. After Copper Wire I had two more rides that season, including Ritornello, a two-year-old chestnut filly, also owned and trained by Father. One of the horses I looked after, she was very soft and gentle and I admit I made too much of a pet of her, which is not a good thing for a racehorse. She came nowhere on that occasion, but she was backward and we hoped that with maturity she'd improve.

As a three-year-old she showed little on her first four starts, and so on her next appearance at Bath, we fitted a pair of blinkers and tried her at a new distance, six furlongs. The blinkers were tried in the hope that she would concentrate on her racing, but they didn't help — we were outpaced and finished seventh of the eight runners. On dismounting I explained to Father what had happened and ended my summary with 'Don't worry, Dad, she'll win a race'. I suppose it was not entirely surprising that he should blow his top. Thrusting his binoculars towards me, he told me in no uncertain terms: 'Don't you think that I can bloody well see through these?'

A month later at Chepstow we tried again. This time we left the blinkers off, as they had made no difference. While travelling to the races with Father in the car, he explained that he had come to the not-so-surprising conclusion that Ritornello would never win a race, and was only costing him money. He was aware of how much I cared for the filly but as today's race was a seller, he had entered her to be sold, something that could be done in those days. It meant that she would be put up for sale after the winner had been auctioned. In this case the minimum bid was 100 guineas and father made it clear that if anyone bid then she would have to go.

Chepstow is an attractive, undulating park course. Ritornello's race was run over the straight mile. We led to halfway, and then, as was usually the case, the rest of the field slowly overtook us. Desperately, I kept on pushing, and suddenly she began to pick up. I can't explain why, as I can't recall ever going for my whip, but maybe my unhappiness at the prospect of losing her got through to her, and one by one she slowly wore down the opposition, getting up in the final strides to win by a short head. One's first winner has to be a momentous occasion, but to have achieved this on a horse that I loved so dearly and which had been valued so little that her owner would have accepted a bid of 100 guineas – that has to be a memory that will last forever. Partly through sentiment and partly in the mistaken belief that what she had done once she would perhaps do again, Father actually retained the filly at the auction for 260 guineas!

My diaries and scrapbooks have been a big help to me in writing this book. My first scrapbook, on my first winner, is a treasured possession. It's a bit tattered now and held together by some sticky tape, but it contains a few strands of hair from Ritornello's tail, stuck in with some old elastoplast, a selection of photos, the racecard and six telegrams. There are also a couple of cuttings from the *Sporting Life*, one a summary of the race and the other a write-up under the heading: 'Boy won with the coolness of veteran'. 'Ritornello, ridden with exceptional judgement and ability . . . got up 20 yards from the post to beat Tormavito by what looked a comfortable short head at 20–1.' The writer added, 'Young Hide never lost his head or his horse's balance, and was content to make up his ground gradually, riding with hands and heels alone, and with Tormavito weakening a little in the last 100 yards, the boy won his first race in really grand style'.

The reporter should have given less of the credit to me and more to my filly, as the main reason that I rode such a cool race was that, at that stage of my career, I wasn't capable of doing much else to help. Had I tried to use the whip, it is most likely that I would have unbalanced the filly and been beaten. Later, Father gave me a pair of binoculars, which I still have, to celebrate the occasion. It was the best present I could have been given. Whenever possible, I made a practice of watching the races in which I didn't have a ride. Most courses now have closed circuit television so that jockeys can view the races with ease. I was continually surprised at the number of jockeys that weren't interested or couldn't be bothered – there was always so much to learn.

In the autumn of the 1951 season I was due to ride Ritornello in a small Northern race when she had to be pulled out having gone 'amiss' a few days beforehand. Father had another horse, a filly called Fast Run, entered at the same meeting and couldn't decide whether or not to let me ride that one instead. She was a bit of a handful, and tended to 'lean on the bit'. He decided that an initial trial at home would be necessary to see if I was up to riding her on the racecourse. To give me a little extra help in controlling Fast Run Father fitted her with a gag, which is quite a severe bit that is often used on hard-pullers and has an effect that is somewhat comparable to that of the handbrake on a car – it gives you extra stopping power in emergencies!

Unfortunately, despite the gag, the filly took charge of me going down to the start of our gallop. The bottom of the main gallop at Lawton adjoined the farm drive which was fenced all along with posts supporting seven strands of plain wire. With the bit between her teeth Fast Run headed straight for this fence, saw it at the last minute, made an incompetent attempt at jumping it, caught her feet in the wire and crashed heavily on to the drive on the other side. Luckily the drive was covered with ashes which lessened the impact a little, and both horse and rider were able to limp away from the scene. My memory of the incident is understandably rather blurred, but Father recounts that my only comment as they all rushed to pick up the pieces was: 'She cleared three of the strands all right, Dad!' Not surprisingly it was decided to postpone our proposed racecourse partnership for a while.

It wasn't until May of the following year that I rode my second winner, Precious Gold, at Haydock. Many people in racing are superstitious and I was no exception. It all started that day at Haydock. As I was leaving the paddock Jimmy White, who was with father for years, said, 'Green for go, red for stop; you'll win today'. Jimmy was referring to the green colour of the bands he had used to plait up the mane. In those days, coloured bands were used a lot more often than they are now. Sure enough we won, but what problems Jimmy's observation caused me after that! From then on, it seemed impossible for me to win if the dreaded red bands had been used. After meeting the connections in the paddock, my first thought was not to look at the horse's fitness and well-being, but to see if it had been plaited up, and if so, in what colour. It really was amazing how often the horse in green bands won and the horse with the red ones finished second. The jinx continued for four years.

In 1955, George Boyd engaged me to ride Persepolis in the Northumberland Plate, the Pitman's Derby, at Newcastle. The horse had been bought at the end of his three-year-old career from Captain Boyd Rochfort with this race specifically in mind. But regardless of my superstition red bands had been used. Of course, I couldn't say anything in the paddock beforehand – it would have been inconceivable to try to explain. Well, the inevitable happened. We did not have the best of luck on the bend into the straight and ran on to finish second to Little Cloud, trained by Noel Murless and ridden by Lester Piggott.

It wasn't until 12 months later at Carlisle that the spell was finally broken. I rode Great Rock in a race for which he was 3–1 on and looked a good thing to win. However, the horse had the almost impossible penalty of the red bands and I remember thinking in the paddock of all the things that could possibly go wrong. To my surprise, the race went according to plan and we won by ten lengths. After that the colours of the bands ceased to matter to me.

Many jockeys are superstitious. No matter how stupid you tell yourself those feelings are, it is difficult to ignore them in a business like racing in which so much depends on luck. Most jockeys consider it a good omen to see a wedding on the way to the races but dread seeing a funeral. A black cat heralds success, of course, but magpies have to be in pairs if they are to bring you luck, and for good measure you have to salute and say 'Good Morning, Mr Magpie'. A new set of jockeys' colours would be trodden on before being worn. Some superstitions have built up rhymes around them: 'See a load of hay and you'll pay, a load of straw and you'll draw'. Others are very individual. Sam Hall, the Middleham trainer, liked by everyone and regarded as being very down-to-earth, always believed that if he had to stop at a level crossing to wait for a train he may as well return home because there was no way he was going to have a winner! There is no chance of suffering that fate these days on motorways and dual carriageways.

The number 13 has always had some sort of significance for me. I broke a leg on Friday 13th in an accident at York, but I have also ridden a double there on the same date. Friday 13th was also, of course, the date of my first Stewards' Secretary interview. Morston was my 13th ride in the Derby and also number 13 on the racecard. Both my brother and grandfather were born on the 13th. The instances seem a little too frequent to be mere coincidence.

Although Ludlow was the nearest National Hunt course to us, Wolverhampton and Worcester, both about 30 miles away, were the closest Flat courses. Racing on the Flat finished at Worcester in 1966. It was an attractive, left-handed riverside course, a pleasant track to ride on, but I shed few tears at its demise as I never regarded the course as lucky. Little went my way there – I only ever managed to ride six winners. Wolverhampton, on the other hand, was the opposite. Up to 1966, I had ridden 55 winners there, including my first treble and my first four-timer.

It was at Worcester in 1952, in a six furlong race for two-year-olds, that I was beaten by a short head in a race that I could and should have won. I was aged 15 and the race resulted in my first appearance in front of the stewards. I was riding Elite, a filly trained by Father who was making her debut. We had two more runners in the race, Choir Master, another debutant, who was ridden by my fellow stable apprentice, Jimmy White, and Eastern Love, who had won her previous race at Edinburgh and was ridden, as she had been on that occasion, by the Australian jockey Bill Evans. In those days we were still a long way from overnight declared runners – the morning newspapers listed a probable field of 15.

On arrival at the course, we made it our practice to go straight to the racecourse stables to check that the horses had arrived safely. The arrivals board in the stableyard was consulted with great interest, as it was a more accurate indication of what was actually going to run. This was always scanned in the hope that the main dangers had not arrived. Horse and jockey had, and still have, to be declared at least threequarters of an hour before the race, usually by the travelling head lad. When the declaration sheet for our race was finally pinned on the noticeboard, we were surprised to see there were only seven runners, including our three. The reason for the field cutting up so badly was almost certainly due to the prevailing hard ground. In those days, of course, if you didn't like the look of the race after studying the opposition in the morning newspaper, you could decide not to run. Nowadays, unless you are able to produce a vet's certificate, it is a costly business to change your mind.

On the strength of her win, for which she had to carry a 7 lb penalty, Eastern Love opened in the betting at 5–4 but she hardened to 8–11, mainly due to the lack of support for any of the others. Elite and Choir Master were among the 100–8 outsiders. We had galloped the three together about a week before and I told father that with my 7 lb allowance and Eastern Love's penalty, there would be little between them. He didn't agree, feeling that with our combined inexperience, Elite and I wouldn't pose a threat.

Elite jumped away from the gate smartly enough and with our light weight we were soon in front. After two furlongs there was a fairly sharp left-hand bend. It was the filly's first attempt at cornering at racing pace. She ran wide, allowing Eastern Love to make up some ground on the inside rail and to dispute the lead. With half the race over I was merely niggling at Elite and I looked across at Bill who was working hard to hold his position. He was using his hands, heels and whip; in fact before long he was throwing everything at his filly bar the kitchen sink! By now we had two furlongs to go and I was in a quandary. The result the stable connections were expecting was a win for Eastern Love. With this thought in mind I dithered. It takes a horse travelling at 35 miles an hour just 12 seconds to cover a furlong, so I had precious little time to come to a decision. As one gains experience, this comes automatically, but at 15, experience was the one thing I lacked.

We flashed past the post together, Bill going all out and me just niggling at Elite. There was no photo finish in those days and the judge gave the verdict by a short head to the favourite. As the numbers were hoisted into the frame, there was booing and catcalling from the bookmakers but I wasn't afraid of them. It was the prospect of facing Father and the stewards that terrified me, for I knew I had done wrong. I may have been doing a man's job but suddenly I felt like a small boy in trouble with the headmaster and I reacted like many small boys had before and have since. After dumping my saddle on the valet's table, I locked myself in the toilet. It shows how naive I still was, despite being in my mid-teens, that I imagined I could find sanctuary there!

Years later, Fred Dyer reminded me that it was only after much persuasion from him that I came out to face the music. Nervously, with father alongside me, I stood before the stewards. Father explained that Elite was unsold as a yearling due to lameness in her shoulder and that consequently she had been difficult to train. Her owner had been anxious to get her on a racecourse but, in view of the state of the ground, he had obviously not wanted her to have a hard race. The stewards accepted our explanations and discharged us from the room.

Later on Father and I were collared by the Stewards' Secretary, Brigadier Roscoe Harvey. The Brigadier was a kindly, sound man who stood no nonsense and whom everybody respected. He combined common sense with compassion and would often take someone aside for a quiet word of advice and warning. But woe betide him if he made the same mistake again. The Brigadier gave me a severe dressing-down and told me not to be such a bloody fool again. He made it abundantly clear that if I should ever find myself in a similar situation in future, I should make sure of only one thing – that I did my best to win. I heeded his advice for the rest of my career.

I rode six winners in my third season and three of those were provided by a horse that could not have been better named: Remember Me. The last of those victories was my seventh winner and so I lost my 7 lb allowance. Remember Me was a special favourite. He came to us as a four-year-old maiden in 1952, and although he remained a full horse he was as kind as a pet dog and never coltish. If you gave him a sweet, he would take it gently from your hand, nuzzling with his lips and never using his teeth as you'd expect a full horse to do. In the stable he would stay lying down while you patted him and fondled his ears. Later, when I enjoyed the odd day's hunting on the old horse, if he heard the rustle of a sweet paper he would turn his head, expecting his share. For a horse that hadn't been gelded his behaviour was remarkable.

Halfway through the following season, despite the horse's further success, Remember Me's owner had a difference of opinion with Father and sent the horse to another trainer. We were all very upset and I'll admit to a few tears. As luck would have it, though, he came up for sale at Newmarket at the end of the next season and Father bought him back for 100 guineas. He remained with us for the rest of his days and gave 16-year-old Tony his first winner in 1955, by coincidence also at Chepstow.

After his treble, Remember Me won a race a season for the next four years — not bad for a horse who came to us as a four-year-old maiden! We kept him on to give the other stable apprentices a ride and later Father used him as a hack. It was a sad day when we had to have him put down. The only other time in my life that I recall shedding tears over a horse was when I held my wife's favourite hunter, Fred, when he had to be put down because of a twisted gut. We had been up throughout the previous night with the vet trying to save him to no avail. Generally, although I feel an affinity with all animals, I try not to become attached to horses or sentimental about them, but when you see a horse every day, feed him and get to know him as a character you can't avoid building up a relationship with him.

- 4 -

Leading Apprentice

DRIVING long distances is a routine part of a jockey's life but these days motorways and ring roads have made travelling to racecourses a lot easier than it was in the 1950s, when journeys often took twice as long as they do today. To travel from Ludlow to any of the Yorkshire meetings usually meant an overnight stay. Later, when I moved to Malton, a journey to Newmarket was an epic voyage. By-passes were a thing of the future, so en route you had to pass through the town centres of York, Tadcaster, Doncaster, Bawtry, Retford, Newark, Grantham, Stamford, Huntingdon and Cambridge; all real bottlenecks. The Great North Road from London to Edinburgh was nearly all single carriageway. Sitting in a long, slow queue of traffic following a heavily-laden lorry, continually pulling out and cutting back in the face of oncoming traffic was both tiring and stressful. By the time you got to the racecourse you often felt more like falling asleep than riding.

Improvements in transport have of course kept pace with better roads and now most cars are both fast and comfortable and make the job of travelling from A to B far less of an ordeal. One of the problems of living near Ludlow was that I was out on a limb and rarely had the opportunity to share transport as the other jockeys at the big training centres were able to do. There was a great advantage in sharing as you were able to relax or even sleep as a passenger, although it depended on who was doing the driving!

I passed my driving test when I was 17 but until then, and for some time afterwards, I used to travel to the races with Father when he had runners. Otherwise our travelling head lad, Dennis Willcocks, drove me. He was exceptionally good company and looked after me well. He joined us upon his de-mob from the services shortly after Father started training and remained until Father retired in 1968. The first decent car I had was a Jaguar to which I treated myself in the late 1950s after a particularly good season. Like most jockeys, I have always enjoyed driving fast cars and am all too often in a hurry – someone always seems to phone just as you're about to set off or else you have to lose the last few ounces to make a low weight so you give yourself an extra ten minutes in the sauna. There is always a good excuse for why you find yourself driving rather faster than is advisable although whether the police agree is another matter.

Not long after I bought the Jaguar I was staying near Epsom and had set off a bit late for Goodwood where I was booked to ride a horse of Phil Bull's in the first race. Afraid of missing the ride, I put my foot down and tried to make up the lost time. Unfortunately, my use of the rear view mirror was far from adequate and I had just negotiated a roundabout when a policeman on a motorbike drove up beside me and waved me down.

The cop leaned in at the window. 'That's the best bit of driving I've seen for a long time', he remarked sarcastically. 'Not only were you exceeding the speed limit but you chopped someone off going into the roundabout as well.'

'I'm sorry, officer, I'm riding in the first race at Goodwood', I pleaded, without much hope.

The policeman raised his eyebrows. 'Really?' He stood back and cast his eye over my Jaguar. 'Nice car. Must have cost you a lot of money.' I nodded uncertainly. He leaned in towards me confidentially, 'Well, bugger off and take more care before it costs you a lot more.'

I drove off cautiously, unable to believe my luck, and was in time to be able to repeat the story in the weighing-room before the first race.

I didn't have many brushes with the law in my riding career although on average I travelled 40,000 miles a year to and from meetings. I prided myself on being a reasonably careful driver despite a tendency to be fast and, touch wood, I never had a really serious accident. Probably the nearest I came to a bad crash was when I was driving with Bill Elsey to Scotland. When I was riding for him we often used to travel together to race meetings. Bill was an excellent driver who never took unnecessary risks, but on this occasion we found ourselves travelling behind a lorry-load of logs. Bill had just moved up to overtake when one of the logs fell off the back of the lorry where it wedged against the chassis of the car, jacking the car violently up in the air. He lost all control of the steering, and we veered off the road and shot up an embankment where the log disengaged itself and Bill found the car responding once more to the wheel. He guided it back on to the tarmac and we continued with our journey, almost as though nothing had happened. However, I think both our faces were a couple of shades paler when we got out at the races.

As more money came into racing it became quite common for jockeys based in Newmarket to fly to meetings. These days Pat Eddery and Willie Carson have their own 'planes. We lesser mortals, particularly in the North, seldom flew, except when it was necessary to arrive in time for an evening engagement after riding first at an afternoon meeting.

Travelling was always going to occupy a large part of my life. Whenever I was a passenger I would try to use the time productively. Many jockeys catch up on their sleep while being driven to meetings but I used the passenger seat to study form. Fortunately I never suffered from the travel sickness that prevents many people from reading in a car, and while Father or Dennis drove I would read the Racing Calendar, the sporting newspapers and form books. That way I was able to weigh up the opposition and sort out possible tactics for that day's racing and the future. In fact those few hours were often the only chance I had to do this. Especially later on in my career, when riding work in the mornings, a spell in the sauna and an afternoon's race-riding meant that by the time I arrived home and had eaten what was often my only meal of the day I was ready for bed rather than study.

Nevertheless I realised very early on that if I wanted to succeed in my chosen career I had to go about it in a methodical, business-like way. My motivation was to ride winners and studying the calendar and form book was a challenge to me in the same way that difficult crosswords engross other people. I passed thousands of miles in cars oblivious to everything except the question of which of my possible future rides had the best chance. It is little wonder that today's jockeys employ agents. Had they been in vogue in my day it is almost certain I would not have ridden so many winners, but at that time I was probably one of the few jockeys who bothered with this detailed analysis of races. Trying to be one step ahead of the rest was my forte.

Since the involvement of the computer all handicaps are now based on the same ratings. Previously there were different handicappers for different meetings, and quite often there was a wide variation in how they individually interpreted the form book. There were dividends to be gained by those who were prepared to study and seek out the best opportunities for their horses. The same still applies but not to such a degree as far as handicaps are concerned.

Trainers are busy people, and when those for whom I rode gained confidence in my judgement of form it was a help to them and to me. From time to time, when I asked a trainer whether he would run a horse in a certain race, he would intimate that if I felt he should run there, then that is where he would go. Later on some trainers told me they liked it if I asked for a ride on a particular horse, as it showed I thought it had a good chance.

To travel from Ludlow to any of the Yorkshire meetings was both a long and tedious journey. Early in my career, after a particularly tough and exasperating journey, Father and I arrived at Pontefract races on a cold October day. My mount in the seller had run three times in similar races, ridden by another jockey, without getting near enough to trouble the judge. On this occasion she was backed from 10–1 to half those odds and won comfortably. As we were in the car park preparing to leave, the successful trainer approached and handed Father a present for my win. 'Here's £15', he said. 'It's half the ten per cent. I'm giving the other half to the jockey who looked after her before.' I remember Father's words as if it was yesterday: 'Mr so-and-so, we all have to live, and if that's the best you can do, you had better put it back in your pocket.' With that, he handed back the money.

The following season I was asked to ride the same horse in a similar race. She had run once since Pontefract and had been well beaten. In the paddock before the race, the trainer spent ages telling me what a good thing she was – all I had to do was to steer her round. I then noticed someone hurrying across the paddock towards us. He beckoned to the trainer, who returned a few moments later saying that the horse was a much shorter price than had been anticipated. Would I give it a run? Although still young, I had learned a lot since Worcester and remembered Brigadier Harvey's words of warning. It didn't take any thinking about: the answer was no. The trainer conveyed my answer to his confederate and then told me that he was pleased that I had said that! Like hell, I thought. Mind you, I did ride winners for him later on. Meanwhile the supposedly 'good thing' was beaten a head – for fourth place.

Geoffrey Willcocks, the brother of my driver, Dennis, lived near Manchester and we used to stay with him for the meeting there which always closed the season (fog permitting). This usually coincided with the televised Miss World contest. After studying the field, Geoffrey and I used to select a filly for a side bet and for years after the course closed we would still ring each other up and continue the practice. One of us usually picked the winner.

Later, when I drove myself, I preferred when possible to go home rather than staying away on my own. This often meant a late journey from the Northern meetings. I knew I was extra tired when the oncoming headlights started to streak. I told myself that home wasn't far away when I reached Wolverhampton, but the last 35 miles often seemed endless. To keep awake I would stick my head out of the window so that the cold air would refresh me. It was exhausting, but I was doing what I had always wanted to do – it would have been much harder if I had not been so keen. More importantly, I was riding some winners which encouraged me and made the long journeys worthwhile. Throughout the season when I woke in the mornings my first thought was 'where am I riding today?' If I wasn't going racing I was most disappointed. It was many years, if ever, before I appreciated the odd day off.

I sympathise with the National Hunt jockeys. Apart from having to negotiate obstacles and the ground coming up to meet them far more often than their Flat racing counterparts, they have to cope with shorter daylight hours and adverse weather conditions which make travelling more onerous and often cause the cancellation of race meetings. Although they have a higher scale of weight many find their battle with the scales just as arduous as we do, in fact more so, as it is very difficult to lose weight and keep it off in the colder weather. Whereas we have to allow 3–4 lb for saddle, boots, breeches, etc., they need to make a greater allowance to cover their woollen colours and bigger saddles.

At best, jump jockeys can expect to ride until their mid-30s. On the Flat, if you stay clear of serious injury, do not have too much of a problem with weight and don't lose your nerve and incentive, you can go on until you are over 50. There are many examples: Sir Gordon Richards, Scobie Breasley, Charlie Smirke and Frankie Durr to name but a few. Alec Russell, who rode mainly in the North, was still going strong until a riding accident on the road put a halt to his career at the age of 55. Davy Jones, who won on the Flat, over hurdles and over fences in this country, was still riding in his 60s in Africa. My own career lasted 36 years, about two decades longer than that of, for example, John Francome, who rode his first winner in 1969 and his last in 1985.

When an apprentice neared the end of his claim, some trainers did not allow him to ride for outside stables for the obvious reason that they wished to keep his valuable allowance for their own horses. To enable me to progress, Father let me ride for anyone that asked as long as I was available. At one time, although it was never compulsory, some jockeys tried to charge travelling expenses. This did not last long because it became apparent that unless you were one of the top few, you found yourself short of rides! When I started riding the fee was £5 for a ride and £7 for a winner with a gentleman's agreement of ten per cent of the first prize-money. Out of that you paid your travelling expenses, your valet and gave a present to the lad who looked after the horse.

In 1969 I attended a meeting at the Jockey Club rooms at Newmarket at which it was decided that the winning percentage should be seven and a half per cent, paid through Weatherby's. I pointed out that we seemed to be the only body of men who would tolerate what amounted to a reduction in our earnings. I was told that the Jockey Club were actually guaranteeing jockeys that amount. There was nothing to stop owners from making it up to ten per cent should they wish. However, before the introduction of the rule only a handful of owners didn't give a present. Afterwards, there were very few who gave any extra. In November 1973 it was agreed that five per cent of the place money should be given to jockeys, which was a terrific boost, especially when the stake money increased.

At the end of the 1953 season I had ridden 25 winners, a large increase on my total of six the previous season. I was a month past my 17th birthday when I lost my 3 lb allowance on Scone at Thirsk. The winner was owned and trained by Captain Charles Elsey, who that year had second claim on me after Father. Scone was my 40th winner overall, and in those days that was the point at which you lost your claim. Nowadays an apprentice doesn't lose his allowance until he has ridden 75 winners, apprentice races excepted, or has reached the age of 24.

Nevertheless, 1954 was a highly satisfactory year for me. I more than doubled my score to become leading apprentice for the first time. I had my first taste of Irish racing at the end of the season on Limereagh in the Naas November Handicap for trainer Kevin Bell. Apprentices occupied the first eight places and Limereagh and I came out best in a tight finish. The Irish press had this to say: 'Honours went to 17-year-old Shropshire lad Eddie Hide, whose timing and handling of Limereagh was indicative of the ability that gave him 53 winners in England this year'. In fact, overall, I received such a good press that Father was quoted as saying 'Don't write the boy up too much – don't want to spoil him'.

But winning is never easy, and I was always grateful for any good publicity.

It is not ideal to rely on old and cast-off saddles borrowed from your valet. I bought my first saddle prior to the start of the 1955 season. As I was so light, I thought it best to buy a heavy one but, unknown to me, the saddle didn't fit well because it was bulky. Pat Eddery never rides on a saddle heavier than 4 lbs because a light one fits closer to the horse. I had a nasty experience at Beverley in May when the saddle slipped and I came off inside the final furlong. Luckily there was no harm done, and I was able to ride again that day.

Two months later at Lanark, I was riding a two-year-old filly called First Aid in the five-furlong seller. I had ridden her at Ayr only three days previously with the same saddle and there had been no problems. This time, however, she was sweating and by halfway I knew I was in serious trouble with the saddle, which was slipping back and round. I just had time to get my feet out of the irons before baling out. This was where a course of parachute training would have come in useful as the prevalent hard ground provided by no means a smooth landing and I sustained serious damage to my left shoulder. After an examination by the course doctor I was taken by ambulance to the nearby Carluke Hospital. The driver's clutch control left a lot to be desired as we kangarooed towards our destination. On arrival he felt the sharp edge of Father's tongue. 'Don't get at me, guv'nor,' he retorted, 'I'm only a garage mechanic hired for the day'!

I was in a ward of about a dozen patients who were highly amused to hear that the horse I had been riding was called First Aid. The diagnosis was a broken bone in the shoulder joint. This in itself was not too painful but the pulled chest muscles were giving me a lot of gyp and, with my sense of humour deserting me, I found it difficult to share their amusement. I have since broken both legs but the pain on those occasions was nothing compared to this. I remember wondering what those who are seriously injured must go through. However, all of this paled into insignificance when I was told that I would never ride again. Fortunately a second opinion was more hopeful: I wouldn't be able to ride again that year but my prospects of resuming the following season were good. That was a great relief and made the pain much easier to bear.

I was in hospital for five days and instructed to report to my local hospital ten days later, when I was given a further X-ray. A pad was placed under my arm which was strapped to my side. I was asked if I was comfortable and told to return in a fortnight. It was Father who persuaded me to visit an osteopath in spite of my arguments that there was no point and that it was just a matter of time. I can't stress how important this was. The osteopath explained that although the bone was broken, had I left the shoulder joint immobile I may well never have ridden again. A build-up of callous bone in a broken arm or leg is fine. However, in a joint it can lead to a restriction of movement, the last thing anybody wants. The osteopath devised an exercise which entailed walking my fingers up the wall, a little at a time, gradually increasing the movement. He also placed an ultrasound disc on either side of my shoulder to help keep the joint mobile. Thanks to his help and advice I responded so well that after six weeks I was optimistic of proving the experts wrong. Far from waiting until the next season to ride again, I planned an imminent return to the saddle.

The first horse I rode at home was a quiet filly called Midair who couldn't pull the skin off a rice pudding. Even so it was apparent that my injured arm was still weak. With more riding out and extra hard work on my punch ball, I was able to resume race-riding just over seven weeks after my accident. I gave myself the go-ahead following an afternoon on my local golf course. Nowadays it is compulsory to have the all-clear from the course doctor before you can return to race-riding after an accident.

We had a couple of suitable horses that were able to take me down and back in the first two races at Wolverhampton. I had already changed afterwards when Fred Clark, the trainer, asked me if I would ride his filly, Nautical Pride, in the last. She had been a doubtful runner due to the hard ground but as there were only two opponents, Fred had decided to let her take her chance. We were the 8–1 outsiders but got up in the final strides to win by a short head from Peter Robinson (the father of Philip). I was happy enough to be back in the saddle but to return with a winner, particularly on such an unexpected chance ride, was very sweet.

As I have said, Wolverhampton was always a lucky track for me. At an earlier meeting in the middle of May, the weather had been most un-spring-like. The sleet, snow and pools of water on the course put prospects of racing in grave doubt. Nevertheless, the stewards gave the all-clear, although they advised jockeys to race on the usually unfavoured far side as the ground near the stand rails was underwater. Not everybody was pleased about this and Harry Carr, for many years the Queen's jockey, described conditions as the worst he had ever encountered. I had three rides, all of which revelled in the swamp-like conditions, resulting in a near 1,100–1 treble, my first-ever. Two of the horses were trained by Father and the other by Sol Parker, trainer of First Aid.

Willie Carr was another trainer who gave me the odd ride. He was a remarkable man. He was tall and used to walk with his feet turned out at ten to two, almost on his ankles due to a point-to-point accident. Eventually he had an operation in which both feet were broken and re-set at the correct angle! Willie trained at Bolton, Lancashire, principally for John Hamer, a brewer who was well-known for his tilts at the bookmakers. He prepared his horses in such a way that they were unlikely to be involved in the finish unless he wanted them to be.

Towards the end of the 1955 season, I rode Cover Plan for him in a six-furlong handicap at Liverpool. He told me to let the horse run along with the leaders but said that if he tired I was not to be hard on him as it was his first race for a few months. The horse showed early speed but was a spent force well before halfway and beat only a handful of the 21 runners. On dismounting, he informed me that the horse was in at Manchester in six days' time and asked if I could take the ride. I doubted whether even his magic wand could bring about the necessary improvement in such a short space of time, so I said I would let him know. When I got back to the weighing-room, I went through the race in my *Sporting Chronicle* Handicap Book, and as I was unable to find another possible mount, I informed him that I could accept his ride.

At Manchester, admittedly on softer ground and over five furlongs, the horse was again with the leaders from the start and battled on to success over the 22-runner field, coming out best in a three-way photo finish. I didn't ride very often for Willie Carr but he put me on a few winners and impressed me with his shrewdness.

Because of the time that I was out of the saddle I finished the season ten wins down on the previous year. However, having thwarted the doom-laden prophecies for the future I was far from disappointed. It was great to have proved the experts wrong. Instead of fretting and wondering, I was able to dream the winter away with hopes of more successes to come.

– 5 –

Great Oaks from Little Acorns Grow

WHEN you see how the whole direction of people's lives can be decided by what seem to be chance events it is tempting sometimes to believe in fate. Probably the most significant encounter of my life happened when I was just 14 years old. I was riding a filly named (rather aptly as it turned out) Hope Dawns on the July course at Newmarket. She was a two-year-old owned by my Uncle Ken and trained by Father. She had only 7 stones 8 lb to carry. At the time I weighed less than 5 stones wet through, and as Hope Dawns was rather a small filly Father had sought the advice of my valet, Fred Dyer, on whether it was safe to burden her with 2½ stones of dead weight.

Most English trainers, Father included, disliked giving a horse too much lead to carry in the belief that putting up a heavier and stronger jockey gives a horse a better chance. Strangely, the opposite view is held in America, where they argue that since the dead weight lies motionless on the horse's shoulders it doesn't unbalance the animal. This is why lightweight jockeys like Willie Shoemaker are so successful there. Fortunately for me, Fred persuaded Father into the American way of thinking on this occasion and I was given the go-ahead to ride Hope Dawns.

You would think putting a saddle and weight-cloth in the correct place on a horse was just a matter of common sense, but it's surprising how many people make a bodge of it. It makes such a difference to the horse and to the comfort of the jockey. The front of the cloth needs to be three or four inches in front of the pommel of the saddle (always assuming that this has been put on correctly). Most jockeys leave it to their valet to put the lead in the weight-cloth but I always made a habit of doing this myself, at the ratio of two in the front pocket to one in the back.

Hope Dawns, normally quiet at home, was on her toes in the paddock and I had to sit tight until I was able to settle her. In the race she came third. It was my first placed ride and I was pretty elated at finding myself in the unsaddling enclosure for the first time. As I dismounted Father caught sight of an onlooker who was studying me with interest. What he had especially noticed, he told me afterwards, was the man's beaming smile as he watched me struggling to unsaddle the filly. It was a struggle, too – I stood only 4 feet 7 inches high then and, with my knees still wobbly after the race, it was quite a fight to undo the girths.

Father recognised that my observer was none other than the great Northern trainer Captain Charles Elsey, one of the most respected men in the racing world at that time. Father didn't say a word to me but after seeing that I had passed the weighing-in scales went and spoke to the great man in an attempt to find out what his interest in me was.

In the car on the way home Father told me that Captain Elsey had watched me closely, both before and during the race, and that he had been impressed by my handling of Hope Dawns. Excited as I was over my third place I was still able to appreciate the compliment I'd been paid. I knew that Captain Elsey was one of the most success-ful trainers that the North of England had ever produced. He was always in the list of the country's top six trainers at the end of the season and only two years previously had trained Musidora to win both the 1,000 Guineas and the Oaks. In those days his string was one of the largest in the country – he had 80 horses in training that year – and among his owners he numbered Lord Allendale, Sir Victor Sassoon and Mr Jim Joel, three of the most important figures on the turf.

Years later Father told me that he always had it in the back of his mind that something might come of that meeting at Newmarket. So when the following year he received a telephone call from Captain Elsey asking if I would ride Firethorn for him in the Cesarewitch, he was probably not as surprised as I was. The chance to ride any horse in the Cesarewitch, which in those days was one of the most popular races in the calendar, would have been thrill enough for me at that stage of my career, but to be asked to ride for the Highfield Stables was extra special. During the 1952 season Captain Elsey had gone from strength to strength, winning the Oaks for a second time, on this occasion with Captain Keith's filly Frieze, and also training what was reckoned to be the best two-year-old colt in the country in Nearula, who had just won the Middle Park Stakes. As often happens, my opportunity was due to someone else's misfortune: in this case that of Ted Carter, Captain Elsey's apprentice, who had been taken ill and was unable to ride.

When the day came, Firethorn finished a respectable ninth of the 36 runners and the Captain must have been satisifed, because he offered me another ride before the season ended, this time on a two-year-old filly called Myron in a back-end nursery at Liverpool. He owned the filly himself in partnership with Miss Jane Clayton, the sister of the Newmarket trainer, so it was a real vote of confidence in me. There was no win on this occasion either but the following season, 1953, I rode Myron to victory at Nottingham on All Fool's Day. I would never have believed it if someone had told me then that Myron was to be the first of 472 winners I would ride for the stable.

1953 was another great year for the Captain. Nearula, ridden by his Australian stable jockey Edgar Britt, won the 2,000 Guineas and might have confirmed his brilliance in the Derby but for a foot infection which interrupted his training. Once again at the end of the season Captain Elsey was high up in the leading trainers' list and this time three of the winners that put him there had been ridden by me. My second winner for the Captain was Tourinta, and it helped me complete my first-ever double at Pontefract on 18 June. My final win for him that season was on the old grey gelding, Crusader's Horn. He was probably my most popular winner with the racegoers up to that point in my career. The horse had been at Highfield since 1947 when he had arrived as a four-year-old. He was a really honest, consistent horse who always tried his best and won at least twice every year. He became a real crowd-puller on Northern racetracks, and when he eventually retired he had 18 races to his credit.

It was possibly my success on this old favourite that brought me the Captain's seal of approval. During the winter I received a letter from Highfield saying that he would like to take a claim on me. It was an offer I'd hardly dared hope for. A claim means that the trainer has the right to have a jockey ride his horses when and where he wishes. To compensate for his loss of independence the trainer pays him an agreed retainer each season. It wasn't the money that interested me as much as the opportunities I would now have to ride really good horses on a regular basis. The stable's first jockey, Edgar Britt, would still get the plum rides but I was certain to get some good mounts whenever Edgar wasn't available. Captain Elsey came to an amicable agreement with Father, to whom I was still technically apprenticed, that if interests ever conflicted then Father should have first call on me. I was to ride for the stable until I joined Sir Gordon Richards in 1969.

During the 1954 season I visited the Highfield Stables near Malton quite frequently to ride work and got to know the Captain much better. It was the start of a professional relationship which probably meant more to my career than any since, and certainly I have never learned so much about racing from one man.

The Captain was a stocky figure who observed the world shrewdly through twinkling brown eyes. A genial man, he was rarely seen without his beaming smile even though in later years he was crippled by arthritis and often in pain. But the aspect of his character that impressed me more than any other was his utter dedication to the job of training winners. I soon discovered that whenever a horse of the Captain's ran it was 100 per cent fit and was always trying its best.

He used to invite me into the house between lots and during our many conversations together I learned of his early background. He had been born at Baumber in Lincolnshire and helped to run the family farm until his father, who had a small stud, failed to sell some yearlings at the Doncaster sales. Having brought them back home his father decided to train them himself and made a great success of it despite his lack of experience. In 1905 he broke all North Country records by saddling 63 winners of 124 races. His story of becoming a trainer almost by accident was similar to my own father's.

Captain Elsey started training in his own right at Middleham in 1911. Later he moved to Ayr and trained on the beach there, although he always had reservations about using that surface, feeling that it jarred the horses' legs. 'It sounded like a machine gun rat-a-tatting when a horse galloped past you', he used to say.

The Captain moved to the Highfield Stable at Malton in 1926. One of the great advantages was that it had its own private gallops, which are now among the best in the country. Originally, however, these gallops were far from ideal as the depth of soil was too close to the underlying chalk to stand a prolonged dry spell. An extra layer of turf was lifted from the fields in the centre and placed on top of the gallops to make a double-turfed surface which lessened the jar. This surface could still be used by the Highfield horses when the other Malton trainers were forced to stop because the public gallops were too hard to risk their horses on. Not unnaturally the Captain made the most of the fitness advantage this gave his horses, especially during a long, dry summer. I'm sure that a lot of his success with moderate horses lay in his skill at reaping the benefit of these gallops at just the right time. It wasn't until many years later that the public gallops at Malton acquired two all-weather surfaces, one of six furlongs and the other over one and a quarter miles.

Between first and second lots there would usually be an hour to kill and I would always be invited into the big lounge at Highfield to have a cup of coffee and discuss the way the horses had worked. Sometimes the Captain would have owners over and during these informal coffee-breaks I met for the first time people like Phil Bull, already a well-known figure in racing, who up until then had been just a name to me.

Phil Bull was one of the most innovative personalities on the turf and his *Timeform* publications were already widely respected. If he or one of the other owners were present to watch some work the

Captain would always make sure I was present at the discussions afterwards to benefit from whatever might be said. I listened all the time, trying not to miss a word as they talked over the future running of horses and their most suitable distances. There was so much to discover. The more I learned the more I realised how far I still had to go.

Mr Bull in particular gave me a good grounding in his theories of race-riding technique. In later years I acquired a reputation for giving careful thought to tactics and it is fair to say that much of that was due to the ideas I first heard in the lounge at Highfield from Mr Bull. One of his favourite words was 'enterprising': if a horse was short of pace he insisted that it must be 'enterprisingly' ridden. By this he meant that the jockey had to react to the way the race was run rather than follow a set plan decided on before the race. If a horse was one-paced he believed it was essential that the race be run at a true pace, otherwise one would be beaten in a slow-run race by a horse with a turn of foot. So if no one else wanted to go on then you had to be the one to do it. On the other hand, if someone else set a sensible pace then you just kept yourself handy.

Mr Bull wasn't content simply to let me absorb his lessons over coffee, though. Whenever possible he would see his horses run and would repeat his instructions in the paddock beforehand, but if for any reason he couldn't make it to the races I would often find a telegram addressed to me stuck on the notice-board of the weighing-room, impressing on me his last-minute thoughts on the tactics that would suit the horse in question. I stuck one in my scrap-book: 'You are by no means a good thing. Forcing tactics again absolutely essential. Good Luck. Bull'. On that occasion the forcing tactics worked and the horse concerned, Carteretta, won by three parts of a length.

If Edgar Britt was riding work he too would come in for coffee, and his opinion would be sought on various topics. He was a friendly person with a lot of experience. Edgar would have been around 40 years old when I joined the stable and had ridden many winners in Australia and India as well. He was, I suppose, everyone's idea of what a jockey should look like – a perfectly proportioned miniature man. He was under five feet in height and I didn't get many rides through his inability to do the weight since he rode at 7 stones 10 lb. In spite of his size he was extremely strong in a finish and rode five classic winners for Captain Elsey before he retired. He soon became a good friend as well as a colleague and I knew I could always turn to him for advice if there was a problem with a horse I was to ride. He had a dry sense of humour. One day, down at the start, I told Edgar 'The Captain says this horse doesn't go very well around the bends'. He replied, in his slow Australian drawl, 'The bastard doesn't go very well down the straight, either'!

Mr Bull thought particularly highly of Edgar and was instrumental in his appointment as first jockey at Highfield. He always credited Edgar rather than Lester Piggott with introducing the really short-leather, monkey-up-a-stick style to English racing. In fact, in his *Best Horses of 1946* Mr Bull wrote a little essay in tribute to Edgar's style which I think is worth quoting here since apart from anything else it illustrates how far ahead of its time Mr Bull's thinking often was:

'I have been impelled to the conclusion that Britt's style, short leathers and very short hold on the rein, is, in general, distinctly advantageous to the horse, and I put it down to the fact that the weight of the rider is thrown further forward over the horse's withers than is the case with what is now the normal jockey's seat in this country. I am well aware that this style of riding is not effective on all horses: it is not effective on the big, long-striding horse who needs to be driven along, to be bashed along if you like, because a jockey perched up on his neck, with his hands close to the ring of the bit, is not in the best position to bash him along. But it is effective on all horses which are in any degree free runners. Though I write only as a layman on the subject, I am very much persuaded that, in general, Britt's seat on a horse is worth in the region of 5 or 7 lb weight.'

When I recently discussed this with Mr Bull he pointed out that once the others copied that style there was very little to choose between the top jockeys. Edgar had acquired this praised seat during his years spent riding abroad. He had come to England in 1945 to ride for the Maharajah of Baroda, who had his horses with Sam Armstrong at Middleham, and he used to swear that the cold of a North Yorkshire spring after years in India nearly killed him.

One of the things that sticks in my mind about Edgar was that he was the only jockey I ever met who always carried his own surcingle with him whenever he came to ride work. He told me that the reason for this sensible precaution was that he had had a couple of nasty accidents with old saddles and girths snapping.

In 1954 I rode 11 winners for the Captain which helped considerably towards making me leading apprentice. In 1955, thanks to my broken shoulder, the number fell to four, but, as if to compensate, 1956 turned out to be a season to remember. Captain Elsey had a fine record in the big handicaps which, in the days before racing became big business, were far more important than they are today, but he usually managed to produce a classic candidate each year, too.

These days, there is seldom a horse trained in the North that is good enough to run in a classic, let alone to win one — the last Northern-bred and trained success was my mount Mrs McArdy, trained by Mick Easterby, who was successful in the 1977 1,000 Guineas. Thirty years ago, however, before the big owner-breeders were taxed out of the game and before the advent of the Arab and business interests that concentrated the best horses down in the South, the situation was quite different.

In 1956 Captain Elsey ran two fillies in the 1,000 Guineas; Honeylight, owned and bred by Sir Victor Sassoon, and Arietta, owned and bred by Mr Bull. Edgar had first choice and won the race on Honeylight but I was thrilled to finish third on Arietta. It was the first time I had been placed in a classic – a real honour, and a rare one for a jockey riding at only a little over 7 stones. Once again it proved that carrying deadweight – in this case nearly 2 stones of it – was not as much of a disadvantage as some people thought. Highfield hit a real purple patch that year. Two days before Honeylight's victory the stable had produced Chantelsey to finish a close second to Gilles de Retz in the colts' classic, the 2,000 Guineas. Just a length that day prevented the Captain achieving the classic Guineas double.

Only weeks later I went on to win on Arietta at the Epsom Derby meeting where, in the Craven Stakes, we lowered the previous course record for the mile and 110 yards by over a second. After Honeylight's Guineas success Tom Nickalls of the *Sporting Life* referred to Captain Elsey as 'standing without equal among the trainers of today', and I think no one associated with him would have disagreed. The successes at Newmarket augured well for what was to turn out to be a championship year for the Captain.

Meanwhile, I picked up some useful outside rides, notably on Angelet, a two-year-old filly of Paddy Prendergast's, on which I won at Doncaster in September. As I was claimed by the Captain to ride at Haydock I was unable to renew the partnership in the Cheveley Park Stakes, where she ran third under Rae Johnstone to the brilliant Sarcelle representing the Scobie Breasley–Noel Cannon team. I was delighted when I was asked to ride the filly in the following year's Guineas, in which she was to finish third to Rose Royal II.

Precious Heather, my mount in the 1956 Ayr Gold Cup, was a horse that I knew well. He was trained by Towser Gosden, a very shrewd man, whose son John now trains at Stanley House, Newmarket. I had won on Precious Heather twice when he was owned by Mr Gosden's wife, Peggy. Since then the horse had been sold to Alex Bird, one of the nation's most renowned punters, and in his colours we had won the Zetland Handicap over six furlongs at Doncaster in May.

In his book *The Life and Secrets of a Professional Punter*, Mr Bird recounts how he backed Precious Heather to win £10,000 in the big Ayr sprint. The race was very straightforward: Jimmy Etherington on Roman Vale was drawn next to my mount and I tracked him until inside the final furlong when we went to the front and won comfortably by a length and a half. Roman Vale was the only horse I saw throughout the race. I had now won on Precious Heather in all four races for which we had teamed up and Mr Bird was duly pleased. He revealed that he was thinking about the following year's Lincoln, although Precious Heather had not yet proved he could stay a mile.

Before that I was looking forward to the Cesarewitch at the end of that season. I had ridden in the race four times already and, since Firethorn, had improved my position, finishing seventh in 1953 on Jacmil, trained by Pat Taylor; third in 1954 on the Captain's Mixed Vermouth; and runner-up in 1955 on Jenny Lind, also trained by the Captain. Travelling back to Ludlow with Father after that race I said to him 'Third, second . . . I will win next year'. His characteristic reply was 'You'll be lucky to finish as close again'. For once his pessimism was to prove unfounded.

1956 was the first year in which I had a chance to ride for Father in the Cesarewitch. He saddled Prelone, a three-year-old and the only filly in the race. She was bred to stay, being by the Ascot Gold Cup winner Precipitation out of Loneliness, who was by the Aga Khan's Jockey Club Stakes winner Umidwar. Father had bought Prelone as a yearling at Newmarket for Mr Allen, who ran an engineering business in Wolverhampton. He had commissioned Father to spend up to £1,000 at the sales on something that took his fancy, but Father was able to secure the filly for half the price. She was a shade back at the knee which, together with the fact that she was not bred to be precocious, obviously put other bidders off. However, she had plenty of bone and Father didn't think the slight defect in conformation would prevent him from training the filly. Time was to prove his judgement right.

Prelone ran twice unplaced as a two-year-old, showing a little promise in her second run. After being soundly beaten on her first two starts at three, she started to come to hand and won her maiden at Hamilton in July, following up at Nottingham the next month. Then, at Chepstow in late September, she justified favouritism with a smooth success in the Welsh Cesarewitch. There was no doubt that she was improving fast, but on the day of the race she still started at 20–1, even with her featherweight of 7 stones. The optimistic owner had backed her at 100–1 after she had won her first race at Hamilton although, frankly, at that time 200–1 would not have been generous. I had to put up 3 lb overweight though it would have been more had I not shed some weight three days before by running four miles around the roads at home wrapped in sweaters and a mackintosh! I really suffered as a result of my efforts that day. If I'd known then what I know now I'd have done my running the night before, although these days I would probably have taken a sauna on the morning of the race. As it was, I felt thirsty from Sunday to Wednesday as a result of all the fluid I'd lost and hardly dared do more than rinse my mouth out with water in case I put the weight back on. In wasting, timing is everything, but some lessons you learn the hard way.

Although she was one of the outsiders in the 19-runner line-up Mr Allen was so confident of Prelone's success that before the race he asked Father where his daughter should stand so that she could lead her in after her victory.

It is at least one and threequarter miles from the paddock to the start of the Cesarewitch course and the jockeys usually took their time making their way over. During the previous few days it had occurred to me that this meant the horses would have the weights of their jockeys on their backs for nearly four miles in total and, more importantly, for a much longer time than in most races. The time between mounting in the paddock and passing the winning post might be as much as 20 minutes – a long time for a horse to have 7 stones plus on its back. As I pondered on this I considered how, when I was working at home, the longer I carried a bucket of water the heavier it seemed to get. But if I put it down for a short while and then picked it up again it seemed lighter. I wondered if a similar rest from her burden just before the race might work in the same way for Prelone – anyway, it was worth a try.

I left the paddock smartly and was the first one down to the start, arriving at least five minutes before the others. The usual procedure when cantering to the Cesarewitch start is to give the horses a breather by walking them three or four furlongs from the ditch over the July course to the Cesarewitch course itself. I cut Prelone's breather down to just one furlong before hacking off steadily again. Father's sister, Auntie Alex, who was watching on television was very excited when she saw us canter down on our own as she thought I was winning the race! When I arrived at the start I jumped off and led Prelone round. This is quite a common practice now but in the days of barrier starts it was rare and the handful of spectators must have wondered what was going on. Eventually the rest of the field arrived and when the starter signalled that he was ready to call the field into line I remounted Prelone.

For the first half of the race I was happy to sit towards the rear before taking closer order with about a mile to run. Just after the bushes I took up the running from Flame Royal and Kribi, and coming out of the dip we were still in front. Prelone ran on with great courage to beat Kribi under Tommy Carter by threequarters of a length. Whether my unorthodox tactics at the start had any effect on the result we'll never know, but they obviously didn't do her chances any harm.

Prelone was Father's first runner in the Cesarewitch and his first winner at Newmarket, and was certainly his greatest training triumph up to that time. My brother Tony looked after the filly at home so he was thrilled too, while I was on top of the world with both the Ayr Gold Cup and the Cesarewitch under my belt in the space of a few weeks. It really was a happy day for all of us and brought the 1956 season to a memorable close. I was again leading apprentice, was seventh in the overall jockeys' list and second to Edgar in the Northern jockeys' championship. I felt it was too early to say I'd arrived but at least I was on the road.

– 6 –

Cock of the North

AT the end of the 1956 season Alex Bird arranged a trial for Precious Heather at Lingfield Park and wanted me to ride Orthopaedic. The intention, he said, was to see whether or not Precious Heather, who was to be ridden by Joe Mercer, was likely to stay a mile. Mr Bird told me he still had the following year's Lincoln very much in mind. He came down from Manchester by 'plane and dropped in at Shrewsbury to pick me up. I had never flown in a small 'plane before and was suitably impressed. It was exciting to experience the completely different viewpoint on the English countryside that you have from a couple of thousand feet up in the air.

I had spoken a few times to Mr Bird in the paddock before riding his horses and had always found him a cheerful, genial man. I knew that he was a man who lived life in style so the 'plane was no surprise. In interviews he always maintained that he wasn't a gambler in the accepted sense of the word because gamblers took risks and chased their losses whereas he, as a professional punter, bet only on carefully calculated chances. Like Mr Bull he was extremely clever with figures. He made part of his fortune by betting on the result of the photo finish in the days when the film took five minutes to develop and there was time for a real betting market to form. He claimed the secret was to look at the winning post without moving your head as the horses came past so that in effect you were taking a 'mental photograph'. Of course, he didn't reveal this trick to the general public until the more sophisticated quick-result photo finish made this sort of betting almost obsolete.

In the trial at Lingfield Park four horses worked with Precious Heather, all ridden by senior jockeys. He worked well and there seemed every reason to suppose he would stay the mile in the Lincoln. Mr Bird and his party were well pleased and I was flown back to the small airfield outside Shrewsbury believing that, given a good draw, Precious Heather would take some beating over the Lincoln mile.

As it turned out this was not to be. As Alex Bird describes in his book, the following spring the best of the market was pinched by Chummy Gaventa, the London bookmaker. Unable to have the best odds himself Mr Bird withdrew Precious Heather from the Lincoln. However, the reason he gave to the press at the time was a little different. Clive Graham in the *Daily Express* reported that the withdrawal was due to me being unable to ride the horse as Captain Elsey was claiming me to ride Babur in the same race. What would have happened if Precious Heather had been allowed to run I can't say, but the decision may have been a lucky one for me since, in his absence, Babur and I won the 1957 Lincoln.

The remainder of 1956 was marked by two events of special significance to Northern racing. In November the owners at Highfield held a dinner in Captain Elsey's honour at the Royal Station Hotel at York 'as a mark of their esteem and appreciation and to celebrate his position as Champion Trainer'. He became the only Northern-based trainer to head the list this century and was never to repeat the feat, although he came very close on several occasions. He had sent out the winners of 83 races that season and had won £61,620 – a very large amount in those days. I was invited to attend the dinner as a guest of the owners, which was a great compliment.

At the same time Bill Nevett, who rode for the Peacocks at Middleham, announced his retirement. For many years he had been Cock of the North, as the leading Northern jockey is traditionally known. He had won 2,067 races, including the Derby three times on Owen Tudor (1941), Ocean Swell (1944) and Dante (1945). When he retired he was ninth in the all-time list. Bill rode in the same style as Gordon, sitting fairly upright and riding three or four holes longer than is the modern practice. He was very strong and could certainly make horses run. I hoped at the time that I might one day win the title of Cock of the North that had been his for so long, but I certainly didn't expect it to happen as soon as it did. Bill trained for a few seasons at Ripon and is still to be seen racing. He has kept remarkably fit and well and has hardly altered in the past few years. It is a sobering thought that he is still the last jockey to have ridden a Northern-trained Derby winner.

The 1957 season started magnificently with my victory in the Lincoln on Captain Riley Lord's Babur. In those days the Lincolnshire Handicap was run at Lincoln racecourse which closed in May 1964. It was a pleasant course, but there were few meetings there even then and it was used as a park by the general public when there was no racing. Perhaps because of this the track was not fenced all the way round; on the round course only the bends were railed and the rest of it was simply marked off with poles when a meeting was on. This wouldn't be allowed on any course now for safety reasons. Horses could and did damage their shoulders hitting such poles and jockeys could smash ankles, but the worst hazard of this system was that because there were no rails along the back straight it wasn't always obvious to the public where the racecourse actually was.

I recall one very hairy incident there at a summer meeting. There were around ten runners in the race and we were approaching a bend with about a mile to run when we were confronted by a youth riding a bicycle towards us. It is hard to believe that there wasn't a horrific pile-up, but the quick-wittedness of the jockeys averted disaster. I will never forget the look of disbelief on the lad's face as I flashed past, sandwiching him between me and the rails.

On the day of the Lincoln there were, thankfully, no such adventures. The Highfield stable had two runners in the race and, luckily for me, Edgar had chosen to ride Dionisio, who had been working the better at home. Essentially Dionisio was a seven-furlong horse, and in the sticky ground on the day he did not last out the mile. Edgar and I were drawn close to each other and, knowing he would give me a good lead, I tracked him until he started to weaken approaching the elbow and dropped back. Then with just over a furlong to run I kicked for home and, passing the two or three who were still in front of me, went on to win by a comfortable length.

A memorable day was crowned when I won the last race on Corve Valley for Father. Corve Valley was an unraced four-year-old but had recently worked well with The Maze, who was a decent handicapper, in a spin on Arthur Thomas's sand gallop. We had taken him there for a change of scenery and experience away from home. We had been quite hopeful of his success after this and it was pleasing to have our judgement proved right, particularly as we had advised the owners, who were long-standing patrons of Father's, to have a bet. Since they had had to wait until he was four to see their horse on the racecourse it was fitting that their patience should have been rewarded and it was a happy group that went home to Shropshire that night.

After this good start, the season became even better. April was a month to remember: a treble at Leicester was followed by a win in the Thirsk Classic trial on Mr Bull's game filly Orycida. Then came a four-timer at Wolverhampton; a treble at Stockton five days later, including Meldon in the Rosebery Stakes; and a double at Birmingham, one of which was Pagan Prince for Paddy Prendergast. Then it was up to Bogside and a double for Pat Taylor before returning south to Ripon and a four-timer, including a double for Bill Dutton with the good sprinter, Vigo, and the high-class stayer, Sandiacre, who set a new course record for the two miles. So, before the month was out, my fantastic run had produced 26 winners, twice as many as my nearest rivals, Doug Smith and Scobie Breasley.

The 2,000 Guineas was won by Crepello for the Murless-Piggott combination, by half a length from the Northern challenger, Quorum, ridden by Alec Russell. I rode Brioche for the Captain, but he finished seventh, finding the mile trip much too short. Later Alec completed the very rare feat of riding all six winners at Bogside, including Father's Courtlier, the 8–1 outsider in a field of three. Alec had been offered the ride on the odds-on favourite but stayed loyal to Courtlier with happy results for all concerned.

I never went through the card but twice rode five winners and a third out of six rides. The first time was at Liverpool's evening meeting in June 1961. The other was almost exactly 20 years later, at Newcastle in July 1981. It was very much a case of what might have been that day: I had won on my last two rides there on the Saturday and was beaten on the favourite in the first on Monday, before winning on the next five.

At the Guineas meeting at Newmarket I had my first ride for The Queen on Opera Score, who was trained by Captain Boyd-Rochfort. As it was the last race of the day I was pleased that Her Majesty had stayed for the race. She put me at my ease straight away by asking about the going . It had been an unusually dry spring and she wondered if things were any better in the North. I replied that it was much the same, but that Captain Elsey was still able to use his private gallops, thanks to the double layered turf. Opera Score must have been a favourite of his owner's as he was by then a six-year-old and by no means one of the stars. In true fairy-tale fashion we won by half a length from Sunstart and Peter Robinson. Although the race itself was nothing to write home about this was a great occasion for me and ranks among the happiest memories of my career. It wasn't every 20-year-old who got the chance to meet and ride a winner for his Queen. I rode two more winners for Her Majesty after that, both trained by Major Hern. I also achieved the distinction of being one of the few Flat jockeys to ride for the Queen Mother. These days she is totally committed to National Hunt racing, but at one time she had one or two Flat horses and I rode Harvest Gold for her at Kempton.

Later that season, due to Captain Boyd-Rochfort's stable having two runners, I was given the ride on another of his horses, a colt called Alcide, who was making his racecourse debut. As it turned out he was probably the best horse that I ever rode, although he gave little indication of it that afternoon when he was backward and finished in the middle. He was a bit of a character – the first time I rode him at morning exercise he dropped me straight away. 'Don't worry,' his lad consoled me, 'he's done that to everyone else who's ridden him.' Due to injury he had to miss the Derby, but he was a very easy winner of the Great Voltigeur Stakes and the St Leger. As a four-year-old he won the King George VI and Queen Elizabeth Stakes, beating Gladness with Cantelo fourth. Harry Carr, of course, rode him to all his successes.

Harry was an ideal stable jockey, very hard-working and conscientious. He made a point of starting to ride out every year on 1 February so that he would have plenty of time to get to know the horses. He also found this a help in being racing fit for the start of the new season as he suffered more than most with his weight. For my part, I admit to rarely having started before the end of the month, feeling that I had a long hard slog ahead of me through to November. When riding in a race for Captain Boyd-Rochfort Harry always tried to give his horses plenty of room. They tended to be big, long-striding types and the Captain didn't like them to be checked out of their stride in running since it takes that type of horse a longer time to recover and get back on an even keel.

One spring Harry and I rode work for Arthur Thomas on Warwick racecourse, shortly after the conclusion of a jump meeting. We had arranged to use the hurdles course and were assured that the obstacles had been removed. The head groundsman instructed us to go the opposite way round from the way they raced. After negotiating a bend, we were in full stride only to see a flight of hurdles looming up with alarming speed. We would not have been so worried if the obstacles had been facing the right way, but obviously they were sloping towards us. Never have two horses pulled up so quickly – we ended up with the horses' heads looking over the timber. Bill Wightman once said to me, 'The two most difficult things that can befall a man are trying to jump a gate leaning towards him and trying to kiss a girl leaning away from him'!

At Hurst Park in the middle of May I rode Dionisio for Phil Bull in the seven-furlong Victoria Cup. The distance was more suitable for him than the mile of the Lincoln. We won in an exciting finish by a neck from Nonchalance and Manny Mercer, with the favourite, Aberdovey, a short head away third. In the following race, I rode a nice two-year-old called Holiday Time, first time out for trainer Walter Nightingall. He ran well to be second, beaten a length by the useful Amerigo who went on to win at Royal Ascot. Holiday Time was successful in his next two starts, at Windsor and Lingfield, with Harry Carr in the saddle. I mention this only because the colt's owner was Sir Winston Churchill and it was of course an honour to ride for him. That apart, I remember the day because I went to the dogs – literally. Peter O'Sullevan gave me a lift back into London and took me to White City, where we had an enjoyable meal while watching the races.

After a four-timer at Thirsk at the end of May I was still leading the jockeys' table but the others were catching up.

Because of the hard ground, there were small fields at Royal Ascot and only four turned out for the Rous Memorial Stakes over a mile. I was riding Meldon, trained by Rufus Beasley and owned by John Cookson, on whom I had won earlier in the season. Sensualita, owned by Prince Aly Khan and ridden by Doug Smith, was expected to win, having run second in the 1,000 Guineas. Meldon could be difficult but today he was on his best behaviour. We tracked Lester on Whiraneck and soon after entering the straight were able to go easily into the lead to beat the favourite by five lengths in a new course record. It was my first Royal Ascot win. The story of how Meldon came to be bred was unusual. His owner, who was Master of the Morpeth Hounds, was riding home with his wife from hunting one day when a friend remarked on the good looks of his wife's hunter. When he learned that the mare was a thoroughbred by Papyrus (winner of the 1923 Derby, but not a great success as a sire) the friend advised him to breed from her. The resulting progeny was Meldon. There cannot be many hunters that have bred a Royal Ascot winner!

In the 1950s National Service was still compulsory, and about the only way to be exempted was to fail the medical. Many a promising racing career was ruined by military service: after two years of being fed Army food, an unfortunate apprentice was often too heavy to continue his career on the Flat. When I signed on with Father at the age of 13, the minimum apprenticeship was three years, up to a maximum age of 23. I committed myself for ten years in the hope that it would enable me to avoid the feared two years away from racing in the Army. In spite of help from Captain Elsey and one or two of his influential owners, I eventually had to go for my National Service medical. We managed a postponement or two but the dreaded day inexorably arrived. I went along with some papers from the Captain and a doctor's certificate. It was rumoured that bed-wetting was a justifiable reason for the Army to dispense with your support for Queen and country. You don't need me to tell you what was written on the certificate!

As it turned out all my precautions were unnecessary. I couldn't have been more fortunate. There were 33 of us and the other 32 were all keen to join. An intelligence test came first followed by a medical. There was a doctor from Glasgow who was interested in whether I had ridden at the nearby Hamilton races and another from Ireland who was just as keen to know if I had ridden there. I was able to tell him about riding for Charlie Weld (Dermot's father), and also of my victory in the Naas November Handicap. There were four classifications and Grades 3 and 4 were the rejects. They asked me if Grade 3 would be all right. I suggested that Grade 4 would be even better!

About this time Gordon Richards 'phoned me early one Sunday morning, and as I was still in bed it took me a while to answer. Suspecting rightly that he had woken me up Gordon rebuked me with the declaration: 'Edward, many a good man has died in bed'. I was delighted that he had called. Since I was a small boy I had admired him and dreamed of competing against him. It was partly the fact that he was a Shropshire lad like me, and partly that he was such a uniquely successful rider. Even today, with the advantage of air travel which makes it possible for jockeys to ride at two meetings in one day, no rider has been able consistently to break or even make the 200 mark season after season as Gordon did. His record had made him an idol, not just to me but to millions of small punters who backed him whenever he rode because they knew that more often than not he would deliver the goods.

One of my greatest moments was beating Gordon by a neck on a horse called Two Fifty when I was just 16. He was one of the hardest men to get the better of. He was all action when he rode: everything was going, arms, legs, the lot. He often swung his whip but rarely hit a horse – he tended to ride with a slack rein but horses used to run as straight as a die for him, probably due to his superb balance on a horse, and with his longer leathers he was able to use his legs very effectively. The present-day style of riding has made the term 'hands and heels' a misnomer. Most Flat jockeys, riding as short as they do, use strength from the thighs and urge a horse forward from there rather than kicking with their lower legs. As Phil Bull pointed out, the freer type of horse runs better for this style but there are undoubtedly a few lazy horses whose form might improve if jockeys used Gordon's or Bill Nevett's old-fashioned style. Unfortunately for them a jockey is unable to change the length at which he rides to suit the horse. Having become used to one style he can't chop and change. The length at which he rides is an essential part of his particular style.

Gordon had retired in 1954 after riding 4,870 winners and having been Champion Jockey 26 times. He had been awarded a knighthood in the Coronation year, just before he won the Derby on Pinza which was his last ride in the big race. He was still riding one top-class winner after another when a bad fall in the paddock at Sandown forced his retirement a few months earlier than planned. At the time of his call to me he was training at Ogbourne Maizey with a string of about 50 horses and had appointed Scobie Breasley as stable jockey. I had ridden my first winner for Gordon in mid-June on Palermo at Leicester. This time he was ringing to offer me the ride on Miss Dorothy Paget's Sargent in the Stewards' Cup at Goodwood and I jumped at the chance. Sargent was strongly fancied for the race and in fact started favourite, but it was not to be our day on that occasion – we were beaten two lengths by Arcancy ridden by Tommy Gosling.

I continued to get many good outside rides that season, though, and as I was doing so well Father decided it was ridiculous that I was still riding under an apprentice licence. So, although I was officially still apprenticed to him until the age of 23, he decided to apply for a full jockey's licence for me. Had he left things as they were until the end of the season my score would have counted as the best ever by an apprentice. My first winner on a full jockey's licence was for Pat Taylor on Mountain Music at York, my 90th win of the season.

Pat had also been responsible for my first outside win on Charlie B at Hamilton back in 1952, so it was an appropriate victory. He was a former National Hunt jockey who, like many others, had eventually been beaten by his weight. He trained at Beverley and worked his horses in the middle of the racecourse and on the Westwood. I often rode work for him, usually accompanied by his sister, Diane. Once, taking no chances on a green two-year-old, I was riding a bit long, and Pat shouted at me: 'Pull those effing irons up, I'd ride shorter than that round Aintree!'

I was interested to learn from Joe Mercer, years later, that he rode out nearly the full length of his leg, only shortening his leathers immediately before the start of a horse's work. By riding in this way he was able to sit on anything, no matter how much it larked around, without hanging on to its mouth. I too could never see the sense in riding very short at morning exercise. It annoyed me to see some lads riding out with their knees under their chins, thinking they were Lester Piggott. It seemed so pointless. They thought they looked so professional but the ones who suffered were the horses, who had their mouths spoiled as the lads hung on to the reins for balance.

On another occasion Diane and I were taking a couple of horses to work and she advised me to put my finger in the neckstrap, warning me 'It's saved many a good man'. No sooner had she uttered those words than the horse whipped round underneath me. Thanks to her advice, the partnership stayed intact! Some lads were scathing about using neckstraps, maintaining that it showed a lack of nerve in a rider, but to me it was far more sensible to use one than to jab a horse in the mouth. On particularly light-mouthed animals I've ridden completely on the neckstrap when cantering, leaving their mouths alone altogether. They will resist the bit but if you can get them to relax then they will accept it. Later, when starting stalls were introduced, Bruce Hobbs always used neckstraps on his two-year-olds for their first three runs. It was a sensible precaution. I learned from Frankie Durr when in the stalls to catch hold of the mane to give the horse full freedom when it jumped out. It was interesting recently to see Michael Roberts, the South African jockey, unpicking the two bottom plaits on his horse's mane so he could do the same. However, a jockey doesn't like a horse with too long a mane as it can get in the way when he pulls his whip through.

My 100th winner that year was at Doncaster on Sagebush, trained by Dougie Gunn. I had ridden against Dougie at Manchester in his days as a jockey. Manchester was always prone to fog at its final meeting and on this day there was a real pea-souper, with visibility down to a few yards. You certainly wouldn't have been able to make out much from the stands which was perhaps just as well, because it appeared to me that Dougie was trying very hard to save the dentist the job of attending to the horse's back teeth! It's possible, I suppose, that it was because he couldn't see where he was going.

When Dougie was training, his father-in-law Norman Scobie once asked me to ride a horse for him in a three-year-old maiden race at Redcar. Along with some of my weighing-room colleagues I had gained the impression that the horse was being saved for the right day. Naively I told him I would be pleased to take the mount as long as the horse was doing its best. If there was a chance that, when he saw the odds being offered, he would want the horse to be saved for a day when the price was better I felt it was only fair that he should understand that I had no intention of doing anything but my best. The betting side of the business did not interest me: all I was interested in was riding winners and I was only trying to be honest with the man in explaining the situation. With hindsight I suppose it was a tactless and stupid thing to say – it certainly didn't make me popular. A short while later Mr Scobie informed me that to save me any worry he had engaged another jockey. The horse duly won and the winning jockey received a large present with a specific instruction to tell me what he had been given. I had lost a winning ride through trying to be fair and I decided that day that if a similar situation ever arose again I would keep quiet until I was safely declared to ride.

Captain Elsey had two runners in the St Leger that year. Edgar chose to ride Tenterhooks, winner of the Goodwood Cup. This left me to ride the favourite, Brioche, who had won the Great Voltigeur Stakes at York. He ran a sound race to finish third to the great Bally-moss, who went on to become an outstanding four-year-old.

After such a good season in 1957 I found myself Champion Northern Jockey – Cock of the North – for the first time and second to Scobie Breasley in the national table. I had ridden 131 winners in all for 41 different trainers. I was living and breathing racing and would have been happy for the season to go on for ever, but I knew that even Gordon felt a winter break was necessary to recharge his batteries so I turned my attention towards the snow and the Alps of Switzerland.

– 7 –
My Fair Lady

I HAD discovered winter holidays in the break between the 1955 and 1956 seasons and had Edgar Britt to thank for introducing me to Switzerland. In fact, I had never been abroad until Edgar invited Tony and me to join him, his wife Tibby and their three youngest daughters, Joan, Anne and Marcia, on a holiday to St Moritz in the early part of 1956. I fell in love with the place and returned there several times afterwards. We always flew from Manchester to Zurich and from there took the train to the resort. The latter stages of the journey, winding up through the mountains, never ceased to take my breath away however many times I made the trip.

St Moritz stands at 6,000 feet and is one of the premier winter sports resorts in Europe. Ski-ing, bobsleighing, the Cresta Run, ice-skating, curling and horseracing on the frozen lake – there is something there for everybody. The air is wonderfully pure: Gordon Richards first visited St Moritz for that reason, having had problems with tuberculosis during his riding career. It was Gordon who pioneered this particular winter holiday for other racing folk.

I didn't ski as I was unwilling to risk breaking a limb so close to the start of the racing season. My riding career was too important to me and I felt it would have been unfair to my connections. Captain Elsey never forbade me to ski but had on more than one occasion pointedly remarked about all the plastered limbs he had seen on the decks of the cross-Channel ferries. I tried ice-skating but, after struggling round the rink, realised that the sport had no future for me and soon gave it up in favour of curling.

We played at the St Moritz Curling Club which was founded in 1880. The official rule-book suggests that the game was not meant to be taken too seriously. One of the rules is: 'Don't cry if you make a bad shot. Salt water damages the ice'. The pinnacle of my curling career was to be a member of Gordon's team that won the big competition, the Kurverein Cup.

An annual highlight, looked forward to by all, was Gordon's skittle party, which was held at the Palace Hotel where he stayed. The skittle alley in the basement was old and rustic but full of atmosphere. There was a single alley and an elderly Swiss yokel to set up the skittles and return the bowls by hand. The guests were divided into two teams and there were plenty of side bets on the outcome. After the skittles we sat down to bacon and eggs and, as the evening wore on and everyone mellowed, the conversation gave way to a good old sing-song. Gordon loved his singing, and led us in many of his favourites, usually starting with something like 'Molly Malone' and descending to 'He Hit Her on the Titty with a Hard Boiled Egg'.

I always stayed at the Steffani Hotel overlooking the square. Among the other guests in January 1958 was one of Britain's most-respected acting families, John Mills, his wife Mary Hayley Bell and their children, Juliet, Hayley and Jonathan. The family was kind enough to send a telegram to the weighing-room at Epsom the following summer to wish me luck in the Derby.

One day in St Moritz, after Hayley had had a minor accident on the ski slopes, I had gone to her room to cheer her up. She left a parti-cularly treasured message in my autograph book: 'To Edward for being such a nice person playing with me'. Unfortunately she was barely a teenager at the time!

A day at the races is a bit different in St Moritz. The two meetings are held in early February on the frozen lake. The compacted snow on the ice is about six inches deep which enables the horses to gallop on it without too much difficulty as long as they are fitted with studs in their shoes for grip. The problems with kick-back experienced on all-weather gallops pale into insignificance compared to this. My companion at the races in 1958 was a girl called Sue Brett who was staying with her cousins, Dadie Oughtred and Pat Baker (later to become Mrs Michael Stoute), at the Steffani. Sue and Pat accompanied Tony and me on the train to Zurich on our way home. The two girls went on to continue their holiday at Andermatt but I was to see Sue again sooner than I thought.

As Tony and I sat on the 'plane at Zurich awaiting take-off we opened our newspaper to see, to our horror, the headlines reporting the previous day's 'plane crash at Munich, which had tragically wiped out more than half of the Manchester United football team. I was a keen football fan – I supported Wolverhampton Wanderers – and had been thrilled to watch Busby's Babes, who had been sweeping all before them. Learning of the disaster aboard a 'plane did nothing to lessen the shock – it was not a comfortable journey.

A few months previously, I had received a letter from John Hislop with an offer to ride as first jockey to Willie Smythe, who trained for the Duke and Duchess of Norfolk at their Castle Stables at Arundel in Sussex. His other patrons included Lord Rosebery, Major General Sir Randall Feilden and Lady Irwin. 'Were I in your position, I would consider it seriously', Hislop had written. 'If you want to get right to the top as a jockey, you stand a far better chance down here.' There was a lot of sense in what he said but after such a great season, with 131 winners and second place in the jockeys' table, there was no way I could have thought of leaving the Captain.

In terms of prize-money won Captain Elsey had finished in third place in the 1957 season, but his total of 73 winners put him at the top in races won. The second-highest total of winners (59) belonged to George Boyd, who trained at Dunbar near Edinburgh, which just goes to show that the North was in a much stronger position in those days.

The Captain didn't believe in running his horses fat. He would say, 'Edward, they won't win unless they're fit, will they?' He insisted on knowing how every horse had eaten, down to the last oat, but even if the horse had left something, he seldom let it miss work. Many trainers, Father included, would ease a horse off in those circumstances. Once or twice I had suggested to Father that we were being a bit easy on his horses. One day, after working a horse for him, I made the mistake of telling him that the horse was blowing a bit. His reply was forthright as usual: 'If it wasn't bloody well blowing it would be dead, wouldn't it?'

Many of the Captain's runners wore breast girths, which were fitted to prevent a First Aid-type of accident. The gallops at Highfield are very stiff and it is difficult for a horse to get away without having a good blow. The lazy animals tend to look after themselves but it is still an effort for them to get to the top of the gallops. After pulling out, the horses used to go into the indoor school – Highfield was one of the few yards to have one at the time – where they walked and trotted for about half an hour before going to the gallops. Most trainers do their faster work two days a week, but the Captain's horses worked on three days, and on any other day that fitted in with their running commitments. The horses did a strong four-furlong uphill canter before circling round the spinney, and there the Captain and Ted King, the head lad, would decide on work plans. Very few escaped and they would be sorted out into those working a mile and a half, one mile or shorter. The usual instructions were something like 'Come a nice half speed until you get three furlongs from me, and then let them stride on. If you're going well, don't be afraid to leave the others'.

Ted stood a furlong down from the Captain. The odd lad who liked a bet tried to keep his horse back but Ted and the Captain between them missed very little. If I wanted to know about a certain horse I would ask Ted and he was seldom wrong. He was two years older than the Captain and had been with him since the beginning. He was marvellous at his job. The only time the vet came into the yard was for firing and castrating – Ted did the rest.

I felt it was my duty as a stable jockey to be as constructive as possible. Captain Elsey was quoted in an article on me as saying 'The lad knows everything that goes on in any race. If I was a betting man I could make a fortune, the things he tells me'.

The Malton trainer Bill Haigh was at Highfield for a few years and recalls being reprimanded only twice during that time. He used to look after and ride out the old favourite Crusader's Horn. After running at Beverley one Thursday and being led out on the Friday, which was normal practice, Crusader's Horn cantered again on the Saturday. Bill, feeling that the horse didn't need strenuous exercise, was steady on him. The Captain, though, was having none of it and later rebuked him, 'How do you expect the horse to be fit going at that speed?' The other ticking off was not dissimilar and concerned Bill's riding of a yearling before Christmas. The youngsters usually went sharply over three furlongs twice each morning. He was again told off for loitering, even though it was three months before the start of the Flat! No one could accuse the Captain of being soft on his horses but they seemed to thrive on the treatment.

Due to a severe spring, it was quite late before I went to Malton to have a look at the horses for the new season of 1958. For a while the Highfield horses could only trot in the school. On the odd day we were able to get a few of the early ones out in the afternoon. A few trainers took some of their horses to the beach to work and I went to Filey to gallop some for Bill Dutton, who rode Tipperary Tim to win the 1928 Grand National and trained Limber Hill to win the Cheltenham Gold Cup. Although a popular holiday resort, Filey hasn't much in common with St Moritz, but it was this day that I met up with Sue Brett for the second time. Her family lived in a house overlooking the beach and she had come down to watch the horses working. After finishing work, and recognising the interested spectator, I walked across to have a few words with her. It was a pleasant surprise to see her again but I was thwarted in my attempt to arrange another meeting as she told me she was shortly moving to London to start work there.

Soon after the end of the previous season Mr Bull wrote to me saying he wanted to change the riding arrangements for 1958. Phil Bull would be taking a first claim on me for the 25 horses that he owned and managed, while Captain Elsey would have second claim on me to ride the other horses at Highfield after Edgar.

While it was a great compliment to be retained by Mr Bull, I found the news slightly embarrassing. Through our holidays together Edgar and I had become good friends as well as colleagues. I would stay at his house occasionally and he would often give me a lift to the races.

Soon after I learned of the new riding plans, Edgar again invited me to stay for a few days at his home in Harrogate. He was his usual friendly self and it became increasingly apparent to me that he wasn't aware of the new riding arrangements. I was in a difficult position as I didn't feel it was up to me to break the news to him. On the other hand, because of our friendship, I simply couldn't leave without explaining the situation. I have never understood why Mr Bull didn't tell Edgar, as later when the same thing happened to me he wrote in good time to let me know. Fortunately, when reluctantly I at last broke the news to him, Edgar took it in good part and it did not affect our friendship.

The season started well with three winners at the opening meeting at Lincoln. We then moved on to the mixed Grand National meeting at Liverpool. For those races many racing folk stayed, and still do, I believe, at the Clifton Hotel at Southport. On Grand National day, I shared a light breakfast with jump jockey Arthur Freeman and his fiancée. Afterwards Arthur and I went to the turkish baths and later I gave them a lift to Aintree. Much to my delight, Arthur proceeded to win the big race itself on Mr What. Father's horse, Holly Bank, was seventh of the seven finishers.

Each year Lord Derby allowed Doug Smith to invite a few jockeys to watch the big race from his box. It was there two years previously that I had witnessed one of the National's saddest occasions. Only a few feet away in the adjoining box was the Queen Mother, who looked set for a famous victory as her horse Devon Loch jumped the last fence. He came clear up the long run-in with the race apparently won, only for that extraordinary collapse to happen. If his jockey, Dick Francis, had written a similar story in one of his best-sellers it would have seemed too far-fetched. The Queen Mother appeared to take the whole thing well, although she must have been distraught. It wasn't even bad luck – the horse falling at the last might have been, but not this. It was a tragedy for all concerned.

On the eve of my 21st birthday I rode a winner at Catterick and then returned to Malton to stay at The Fleece, run by the well-known former Northern lightweight jockey, Ginger Dyson, and his wife Jessie, always known to me as Mrs D. The Fleece was my second home. I stayed there whenever I was in the area and Ginger and Mrs D. were always kindness itself. Their two sons, Terry and John, with whom I played the odd game of golf, tennis or snooker, were excellent footballers. Terry played in the first team for Tottenham the year they achieved the Cup and League double. He now coaches youngsters, while John runs a successful bookmaking business in Malton.

In Ginger's riding days Father once asked Ginger to ride for him. He had bought a horse from Captain Elsey. Very few horses did much good after the Captain had finished with them and this horse proved to be no exception. After a few mediocre runs Father offered the ride to Ginger, who had ridden the horse to its only success. He was pleased to accept but soon put a dampener on hopes for another victory by revealing the inside story of the first one; there had been five runners and at the start the other jockeys suggested to Ginger that he make the running. The logic was simple – apparently none of the others were trying!

At this stage of my career I was reputed not to have a weight problem. For obvious reasons, I didn't contradict this, but keeping my weight down took a lot of self-discipline. I could still ride at 7–11 but it required a bit of an effort. The only liquid I allowed myself was three cups of tea a day. If I was thirsty I used to swill my mouth out with cold water. I ate a boiled egg for breakfast and something like cheese on toast for an evening meal. Occasionally, I treated myself to a vanilla ice cream. My evenings at The Fleece were not spent in the bar as even a glass of lemonade would have put on too much weight, but watching the television in the back room. The things you go through when you don't know any better! Once, during the winter I was about to eat an orange when I resisted the temptation, stupidly thinking I would put on half a pound. Life was more relaxing and easier once saunas became available.

My 21st birthday began with riding work for Rufus Beasley before going on to Highfield. A successful jockey in his day, Rufus rode for Jack Colling and Captain Boyd-Rochfort. He was a shrewd trainer who loved trying to get his horses ready for Royal Ascot. He was always keen to have jockeys riding work for him and, apart from myself, Edgar, Ginger Dyson, Joe Sime and Johnny Seagrave were regular work riders. A lot of his work consisted of working three or four horses together sharply over three furlongs. Recently Bob O'Ryan, his former head lad, expressed the view that although he was a good trainer he tended to be very hard on his fillies.

It was back to Catterick in the afternoon, and what an afternoon! I rode a treble and was beaten a short head and a head on my other two rides. The third winner, Basso, was trained by Pat Taylor and landed a nice touch for gambling owner Brian Nicholls. Opening at 4–1, he was backed down to 10–11 and trotted up by four lengths.

Probably the best horse ever to have run at Catterick also ran there that day, without even finishing in the first six. In the autumn of 1957, Fred Ellison, a long-standing patron of the Peacock family, wanted to interest his nephew in racing and asked Dick Peacock to buy a yearling for around £1,000 at the Doncaster Sales. At that time Tattersalls held their principal sale there and not at Newmarket. Dick took a fancy to a well-grown, brown colt which, although a bit on the leg, he particularly liked as he was by Tudor Minstrel out of a Dante mare – two of the best horses that he had seen.

The preceding lot, from the same stud and out of the famous mare Sari, made 17,000 guineas – an incredible amount 30 years ago. This caused much excitement and chatter and, Dick felt, the diversion helped to enable him to buy the colt he had picked out cheaply at only 620 guineas. It was to turn out to be one of the bargains of the century. However, Mr Ellison wasn't impressed and said he would have felt happier if Dick had spent the full £1,000 or perhaps even a few pounds more. Dick told him that it didn't matter. If he didn't want the yearling he would be happy to keep the horse for himself. A week later Mr Ellison had second thoughts and decided to take the horse in half-shares with his nephew.

On returning in mid-February from his annual winter holiday, Dick was told by his head lad, Arthur Waudly, who had ridden Dante in most of his work, that in his absence they had been doing a bit with the two-year-olds and that this particular colt had been working very well and looked something special. Tudor Melody, as the horse was named, made his debut at Catterick ridden by Ted Larkin and started favourite on the strength of his home reputation. However, he completely missed the break at the old barrier start and finished eighth of the 13 runners.

Next time out at Ripon, again ridden by Ted, Tudor Melody won easily by four lengths, beating a horse called Warrior that Peter Easterby had thought was a certainty. The colt's next appearance was at Beverley in May and, fortunately for me, Ted was claimed by his own stable at Hamilton and so I was offered the ride. Starting at 1–3 in a field of 13, he won very easily by six lengths.

The York May meeting was the next stop for Tudor Melody and a few days before, Mrs Peacock asked me to ride. However, Mr Bull planned to run one of his horses in the same race and, of course, I would be retained to ride it. Luckily for me, it didn't present a problem, Mr Bull being the man he was. He had been at Beverley and had also been very impressed. 'Teddy (he is the only person ever to call me that), if you can ride Tudor Melody, I won't run mine', he said.

This time Words of Wisdom, who had won his only previous race at Newmarket, was preferred in the betting to Tudor Melody, but it made no difference. We beat him five lengths with the third another five lengths away. As a result, he started odds-on for the Chesham Stakes at Royal Ascot, and again the result was another comfortable five-length victory. It was after this race that his owners were made an offer they couldn't refuse and Tudor Melody was sold to a Mrs Abercrombie to race in America. His British swansong came in the Prince of Wales Stakes at the York August Meeting where he wasn't impressive in beating his sole opponent Grey Marsh two lengths. I had to push him out and at that stage he was probably feeling the effects of his past efforts. He was allotted top weight in the Free

Handicap with 9 stones 7 lb and was therefore the official champion two-year-old.

Tudor Melody later ran in the States where he raced for two seasons, but he won only two races. He was a clean-winded horse who required little work. Sam Armstrong, father of trainers Robert Armstrong and Susan Piggott and a leading trainer himself, reported after a trip to the States that the horse looked like a hat-rack. It sounded very much as though he was being over-trained. He had certainly proved something of a bargain for his once doubtful owners. He won ten times his purchase price on the racecourse and was sold for 33 times the initial outlay. It is the chance of acquiring such a bargain that encourages many owners in racing. Tudor Melody eventually returned to Ireland to stand as a stallion. From there he moved to the National Stud at Newmarket where he proved an outstanding success, siring the Guineas winner Kashmir II as well as Welsh Pageant, Tudor Music and many other top-class horses.

My first winner at Goodwood was Be Careful, owned by William Hill and trained as usual by Captain Elsey. Be Careful, by My Babu, a lean, light-framed, whippety type, had made her debut at Doncaster earlier in the month when we thought she would be good enough to win. The same owner also had another good two-year-old in the yard in Cantelo, who had already won her first three races. Be Careful was the faster filly at home and yet she could manage only third at Doncaster. I was disappointed, feeling that she obviously wasn't as good as we first thought.

The Goodwood race, over five furlongs, was full of incidents at the start. One horse bolted, unseated its rider and was withdrawn, while the Queen's filly, Partick Thistle, unseated Lester and, after kicking him on the thigh, also got loose. However, she was reunited with her jockey and they got off to a flying start while Be Careful dwelt. At halfway, Partick Thistle looked unbeatable; but what Be Careful lacked in stature she more than made up for in courage – she had a heart as big as herself – and gradually we made up the ground. Lester's filly was stopping and close home we got up to win by a comfortable two lengths.

Be Careful was one of two runners from Highfield in the Gimcrack Stakes at York; the other was Billum, ridden by Edgar, who had won his previous two races, including the Somerville Tattersalls Stakes at Newmarket. Billum had put his head in the air in the closing stages on that occasion but in spite of this some punters, who clearly had more courage than the horse, made him 9–4 favourite. Be Careful was 10–1. Jimmy Lindley led on the much-fancied Firestreak, but Be Careful was always in close touch, and taking up the running with two to run, we won easily by three lengths. On the morning of the race, William Hill made one of his rare appearances at the stables.

On leaving, he beckoned Sandy Tierney, head lad on the farm side, and asked his opinion on his filly's chances against Billum. Sandy had always been a great fan of Be Careful and told Mr Hill to start preparing his Gimcrack speech! He was the first bookmaker to win the race.

Be Careful was next seen in the Champagne Stakes at Doncaster and got home by a neck from her only serious challenger, Carnoustie, who received the full Lester treatment. Be Careful had one more run, in the Cheveley Park Stakes at Newmarket, but was not the same filly that had won at York and Doncaster and could finish only sixth behind Lindsay and Rosalba. The first two home were ridden by brothers Manny and Joe Mercer who were in surprisingly good form considering they had been celebrating Joe's engagement to Harry Carr's daughter, Anne, the previous night at the Bedford Lodge. As a three-year-old Be Careful ran once, confirming the fear that she hadn't trained on, and was then retired to her owner's stud.

By a stroke of good fortune, Sue Brett was at Royal Ascot representing her cousin, whose horse King's Coup was running in the Royal Hunt Cup. By this time she was working in London and, after meeting her in the jockeys' stand, I invited her out on the Friday. *My Fair Lady* had just opened in London and was already a great success, and getting tickets, particularly during Ascot week, was on a par with winning the pools. Sometimes in life, though, it isn't what you know but who you know that counts, and seeking help in the weighing-room Harry Carr put me in touch with Harry Claff, box office manager at the London Palladium. He worked the oracle and came up with two tickets for that evening's performance. Taking Sue to see *My Fair Lady* was a hard act to follow, but after winning on Cantelo on the Saturday at the Ascot Heath meeting, we were back in the West End that night to see Harry Secombe topping the bill at the Palladium.

I barely had time for a drink after the show before grabbing a taxi to Heathrow in time to catch my flight to Copenhagen for the Danish Derby. We touched down at 2 a.m., with Harry Secombe's voice still ringing in my ears. I was met by Oslo trainer 'Raggen' Johansen, who took me by taxi to my hotel. I was hardly into a sound sleep before he was back again knocking on my door. We had a quick breakfast before going to the racecourse at Klampenborg to see Flying Friendship, my mount for the Derby. The Norwegian-owned and trained horse had already won the Swedish Derby for Lester Piggott. In an exciting finish, we got home by a neck from Buster Parnell's mount. There was a celebratory dinner afterwards and when I eventually got to bed I didn't need any rocking. The following morning, I flew back to London. Fortunately, my booked mounts for that day were at the evening meeting at Birmingham. After all that, I arrived home at Ludlow just short of midnight. The days of the jet-set jockey were just taking off.

Later that summer, Bill Rickaby, Jackie Egan and I caught the early morning flight to Oslo. We were riding in the Norwegian Derby at Ovrevoll, on the outskirts of the city. The racecourse is cigar-shaped with a sharp turn at either end. On fast ground, scrambling round the bend into the straight could be a bit hairy. I used to tell myself that I was an idiot riding there but kept going back. On this day, it never stopped raining which suited Flying Friendship, and he completed the Derby treble.

Normally trips abroad are one big rush, but this time I was able to enjoy a tour of Oslo with the owner's wife. I found the Kon Tiki raft incredible. It was difficult to imagine that Thor Heyerdahl and his six-man crew had drifted across the 4,300 miles of the Pacific on such a flimsy, balsawood craft. From there I was taken to the top of the ski-jump which, even in the summer without snow, gave me butterflies in my stomach. Each to his own, I suppose – perhaps the fearless ski-jumpers would have their reservations about race-riding.

In early August I was reunited with Babur, on whom I had won the previous year's Lincoln. He had completed the double this year with Edgar up. Babur was a better horse with some give underfoot, and it was clear that if he was to have a good chance of winning the Redcar 5,000, rain would need to fall. My equivalent of a rain dance was to wash the car. It often seemed to rain after I had done that and so I tried it that Saturday morning. Sure enough, around midday, it began to drizzle. The rain grew so heavy that by the time of the race the going had been officially changed from the good to firm of the previous day to yielding. It was enough for Babur to win. He beat King's Coup, owned by Sue's cousin Dadie, who would have preferred the going to have remained firm.

My second successive century was completed at Ayr in September on a horse trained at Malton by Ernie Davey. The last of my winners that year was provided by the enigmatic Billum, who won the Dewhurst Stakes at Newmarket with the subsequent Derby winner Parthia back in third. Once again, Captain Elsey sent out the highest number of winners, 72, and finished runner-up to another Captain, Cecil Boyd-Rochfort, in terms of stakes won.

The season was rounded off with the annual Northern Jockeys' dinner and dance, held that year at Wilsic Hall near Doncaster. I never had any fears about riding in the Derby but the thought of escorting Sue and introducing her to the weighing-room crowd filled me with apprehension, not to mention the worry of having to make a speech, a duty that falls to the leading jockey. We left from Sue's cousin's home but not before Dadie, having recognised my nervous state, had prescribed a valium.

It was a foggy night and the nearer we got to Doncaster, the worse it became. Several of us had arranged to meet up with Joe Sime at the Danum hotel in Doncaster, as he knew the way to the venue. Liverpool-born Joe, who was seldom seen without his pipe, lived within a mile of the racecourse and rode for years for Sam Hall. He never won a classic but was successful in most of the big handicaps including three Ebors and Wokinghams, two Manchester November Handicaps and Ayr Gold Cups and a Cesarewitch. He was well-respected and liked. A convoy followed Joe's car, with visibility down to a few yards. We had been travelling for some time before Sue and I realised that something wasn't quite right. We were travelling the wrong way up a dual carriageway! Fortunately for our peace of mind we were towards the back of the queue. Miraculously, we all arrived unscathed! After that experience making a speech seemed no cause for nerves and I sailed through it. All in all, it was a memorable evening with which to round off the season.

– 8 –
Cantelo

IN the spring of 1959 we were thrilled to hear that after his long and distinguished career the Captain had been invited to lunch with the Queen. I was unable to repeat the previous year's birthday feat since that day was a Sunday, but I did the next best thing and rode a four-timer the preceding day at Catterick. One of these winners provided Pat Rohan with his first as a trainer, exactly a week after he married Bill Dutton's daughter, Mary. And the horse's name? Dutton! This was pure coincidence as the horse had been trained in its earlier days by Harry Wragg for the Begum Aga Khan and had not joined Pat until just after the previous Christmas.

Meanwhile my brother took the headlines at the end of May when he won the Thirsk Hunt Cup on King's Coup – I was pleased that he had been given the chance to ride this good winner. The following month I had a great winning streak. In one week's racing I rode trebles at Doncaster, Liverpool and on both days of the weekend Haydock meeting. With a couple of singles thrown in for good measure these 14 winners put me only two behind Doug Smith in the jockeys' table. I was doing a great deal of travelling by now, and after winning on an outside ride for Noel Murless at Nottingham I managed to get home to Ludlow for the first time in five weeks.

At Stockton in the middle of August Edgar told me that he would be retiring at the end of the season and returning to Australia. I had mixed feelings about this news. On one hand, I would be sorry to be losing such a good friend. Edgar was a tough competitor but that hadn't stopped him from being really helpful towards me. On the other hand I knew that his departure would give me further opportunities at Highfield. That day at Stockton, both Edgar and I rode a winner for the Captain. Edgar's mount was Silent Waters, whom Bill Elsey always irreverently referred to as 'Pee in the Bath'.

Looking at the form notebook reminds me that my win, on Diamantine, was not without incident. The stirrup leather buckle broke early on in the race, and I was lucky to stay in the saddle. I had long forgotten the incident, but I well remember a more recent occurrence at Ayr, when I was short of room between Steve Cauthen and the rails. My left stirrup iron shattered and the support for that leg disappeared in an instant. I was lucky not to come off, but was immediately faced with the problem that the whole of my body weight had been transferred to the other side. Solving this difficulty isn't easy, especially when travelling at 35 miles an hour on a galloping horse. The solution is to free the other leg, but that is easier said than done. All ended well, however, thanks to the co-operation of my mount.

One of the finest feats of horsemanship I ever saw was when the late Tim Brookshaw rode Wyndburgh into second place in the Grand National, in spite of the buckle breaking on one of his leathers at Becher's second time round, obliging him to ride over the rest of those fearsome fences without stirrups. He was only beaten a length and a half by Michael Scudamore on Oxo. His only comment when questioned about this amazing feat was 'I expect I will be a bit stiff when I do the milking in the morning'!

Towards the end of August I renewed my partnership with Flying Friendship in the Stockholm Cup, run, as are most big races in Europe, on a Sunday. When Sunday racing eventually comes to this country, these forays abroad will become a thing of the past. This time the schedule was really tight. I had three hours in Sweden, and half of that time was spent in a taxi travelling from and back to the airport. Had there been the slightest hitch in the travelling arrangements all would have been in vain. Once again luck was with me. I arrived on time and won the race by half a length on the sharp dirt track in use then. Flying Friendship had lived up to his name.

Things did not always go so smoothly. On another occasion, Bruce Raymond and I were sitting in a 'plane at Heathrow awaiting take-off. Due to a technical problem, there was a delay, although we were assured that it would only be a matter of minutes. The minutes soon stretched into an hour and a half and it became obvious that we were not going to make it to the races in time. There was little point in staying on board and we explained this to the steward. Normally we carried our saddles with us but that day they had insisted on storing them in the hold. We were allowed to disembark provided we went into the hold to identify and retrieve them – fortunately we were able to spot our saddle bags.

I had an even more nerve-racking experience that year when I had to fly from Scotland to Copenhagen, again to ride Flying Friendship in a big race on a Sunday. I was in mid-air en route from Glasgow to London when I realised I had left my passport in my hotel at Ayr. It was too late to do anything about it, so I had to talk my way on to the Copenhagen flight and – more difficult – through passport control at the other end. Eventually they let me in after I deposited my driving licence with them but warned me I would have considerable trouble re-entering Britain without a passport. After the race, in which Flying Friendship ran only moderately, I managed to contact the Scottish hotel-owner, who luckily was also a friend. He drove to meet me at Prestwick with my passport and was able to convince the officials that I was not an illegal immigrant!

In 1959, at the age of 22, I realised an ambition many jockeys wait a lifetime to achieve when I won the St Leger. My mount, Cantelo, was owned by William Hill and trained by the Captain and was the first Yorkshire-trained horse for 85 years to take the classic. She was a well-grown, bay filly with an attractive broad head and large honest ears, more workmanlike than impressive and rather angular, but she showed power in every movement and was a most resolute galloper.

Bred by her owner, she was by the French stayer Chanteur II out of Rustic Bridge, who was by Bois Roussel. Cantelo won all of her five starts as a two-year-old: her first race was at Haydock, and after this nice introduction she was sent south to Ascot for the Fenwolf Stakes on the Saturday following the Royal Meeting. She had to be ridden out to narrowly justify favouritism by half a length. Her victories were easier at Stockton and Thirsk in her next two outings, and then she went on to the Royal Lodge Stakes, run over the round mile at Ascot. By then Cantelo had started to give a few problems at home, mainly by refusing to go back down the gallops after her first canter unless somebody led her. At Ascot everything went well until she was asked to face the gate as we came under starter's orders. She resolutely refused to do this and it looked as though she wasn't going to take part. We were eight minutes late off and it was only thanks to the help of the assistant starter and the patience shown by the Jockey Club's chief starter, Alec Marsh, that she eventually began the race on reasonable terms, losing only a length or two as the tapes went up.

Cantelo settled close to the leaders and, although we were a little squeezed for room on the turn into the straight, we soon found a run. In the end we won a shade comfortably by two lengths. In winning this race she had shown herself to be a very useful filly but not yet top-class. I wanted to thank Alec Marsh for his patience at the start, and left it until Christmas when I sent him a present, with thanks from Cantelo. Mr Marsh wrote thanking me but pointed out that I shouldn't have done this as he didn't want to be put in a compromising position. He also mentioned that he had told the authorities. Mind you, he didn't return the drink!

Cantelo did well through the winter and made her reappearance in the Cheshire Oaks in early May. She started joint favourite with Seascape, a useful filly owned by Mr Jim Joel. Because of her antics at Ascot, Bill Elsey came down to the start and held her, but she jumped off without any problems. We raced in second place behind Seascape, went to the front on the bridle five furlongs out and came home the very impressive winner by six lengths. It was a performance which resulted in her starting a short-priced favourite for the Oaks. The going was firm at Epsom which wouldn't have worried Cantelo too much, but I would have preferred it slow, to test the stamina of the 1,000 Guineas winner, Petite Etoile, trained of course by Noel Murless and ridden by Lester. Doug Smith had actually been the successful jockey at Newmarket, Lester having chosen to ride Collyria. We were several lengths clear early in the straight at Epsom, but Lester was able to close the gap comfortably and easily pass us to win hard held by three lengths. The third, Rose of Medina, also trained by Noel Murless, was ridden by Eph Smith, and finished five lengths behind us. There is little doubt that Cantelo was a better racemare than my future Oaks winner Pia – it was unfortunate that she was born in the same year as such an outstanding filly as Petite Etoile.

Just under a fortnight later, Cantelo gained some compensation with a game win in the Ribblesdale Stakes at Royal Ascot and returned there in mid-July for the King George VI and Queen Elizabeth Stakes. She again ran a good, sound race, but she was not up to overcoming Alcide and Gladness and was beaten six lengths into fourth place. Cantelo was then put away until the autumn. Before the Doncaster St Leger meeting it was announced that she would run in the Park Hill Stakes and, if none the worse for that race, would be saddled again for the St Leger.

The Park Hill, run over the St Leger course and distance, is often known as the fillies' Leger. It was a race that her owner, as a big breeder, was keen to win. Cantelo started at 9–4 on and took up the running with three furlongs to go in what had been a slow-run race. With those around me apparently beaten and the St Leger at the back of my mind I was keeping her going but at the same time did not want to be unnecessarily hard on her. Unfortunately, Collyria came past with a wet sail and went on to win by a length and a half. This represented a turnaround in the Oaks form – in that race Collyria had finished seven lengths behind us in fourth. Cantelo came out of the race well. As the gallops had been hard at Malton she was a better and fitter filly for the St Leger than she had been for the Park Hill. Most experts had written off her chances in the big race.

Eleven runners went to the post for the final classic of the season and the odds-on favourite was the Derby winner, Parthia, despite the fact that he hadn't been out since Epsom due to a bout of coughing. Kalydon, an improving colt who had won his last five races in style, and Epsom Derby runner-up and Irish Derby winner Fidalgo were both preferred in the betting to Cantelo.

She was a very different filly from the one that had given so many problems at Ascot a year before and she was really cool and calm down at the start. We didn't go the first time and had to turn round and come in again, but she behaved perfectly and settled nicely in third place as Prime Value and Geoff Littlewood set a strong gallop that soon had the field well strung out. When the pacemaker weakened shortly after entering the straight, I took up the running and sent Cantelo on with about three and a half furlongs to run. Having learned from the previous race, I let Cantelo make full use of her stride, at the same time remembering that at Doncaster it was still a long way to the winning post. Good filly that she was, I was able to keep just a touch in reserve for when the challenge came. Parthia made a short-lived effort, but with just over a furlong to go Fidalgo and Joe Mercer started a run which promised to carry them to victory. Had there been any weakness in Cantelo's stamina Joe would have been buying the champagne in the weighing-room instead of me. As it was we stayed on too resolutely for Fidalgo and beat him by one and a half lengths. Parthia weakened to finish fourth.

It was great to have won my first classic, especially on a horse trained by the Captain. He had done so much for me and, with the possible exception of the Derby, the St Leger was the one race that he had always wanted to win. As Cecil Gurdley, who looked after the filly and travelling head lad Gerry Blum, who now trains near Newmarket, led me back to the winners' enclosure, I was sorry to hear some dissent among the crowd. I have always felt that had Cantelo not been owned by William Hill, then the country's leading bookmaker, the jeering would never have been heard. There wasn't a straighter man in racing: every horse he ran was out to do its utmost and he never bothered me for information. During his early days he amassed a large proportion of his fortune by having the courage to lay horses in the Derby which he felt, on breeding, were non-stayers. More often than not his judgement proved correct.

Captain Elsey, who was walking with the aid of two sticks at this time, made a brave attempt to laugh off the crowd's reactions, joking to Tom Nickalls of the *Sporting Life*, 'I trained my first winner at Beverley in 1903 and I've trained a few since, but this is the first time that I have ever been booed'. Nickalls himself wrote later: 'It was perhaps the greatest of all of Captain Elsey's innumerable training triumphs, yet an ignorant minority of the crowd through fit to boo this splendid filly and her straight-as-a-die jockey, Edward Hide'.

My horoscope in the *Daily Express* that morning said that I would have a disappointing day but, apart from those few disgruntled punters, it was the greatest day of my racing career so far. If I look at my horoscope and don't like what I read, I have only to think back to the St Leger of 1959.

But the controversy over Cantelo's apparent turnaround in form carried on for some time afterwards. Gimcrack in the *Daily Sketch* described the race as 'the Turf's most embarrassing big race result for many years', and claimed that the Doncaster stewards had blundered for failing to hold an inquiry, but admitted that the ugly scenes were due to people not understanding Cantelo's case. Most of the racing journalists agreed with the last statement and defended both Cantelo and my riding of her in the Park Hill. One correspondent wrote: 'With the St Leger in view Edward Hide was understandably concerned with giving Cantelo as easy a race as possible. But when a long-distance event has been so slowly run in the early stages, as this race had been, there is always the possibility of something coming out of the blue with a devastating burst of speed'.

I was especially pleased to have Gordon Richards' support in print. He said that had he been riding Cantelo in the Park Hill he would not have won either. 'Hide brought out Cantelo at the right moment to win her race but she was run out of it', was his opinion.

Looking back from 30 years on, if I had really sent Cantelo about her business after turning into the straight there is little doubt that we would have won the Park Hill. In trying both to win and to have a horse left for the classic I fell between two stools. I don't suppose I am the only person to look back on something and say 'If only . . .'

Disappointingly, Cantelo wasn't a great success at stud, proving very difficult to get in foal. To my knowledge Cambridge, who raced in the colours of David Robinson and was useful, was the only offspring that she had. Cantelo certainly did me plenty of favours – she was my first classic winner and my 100th winner of the season. William Hill was very generous: he had a standing order with Weatherby's to give his jockey £50 or ten per cent, whichever was the greater. This was much appreciated as there were many races worth only £207 to the winner in those days.

The 1959 racing year was marred for everybody by Manny Mercer's fatal accident at Ascot on 26 September. Manny's mount, Priddy Fair, stumbled when parading in front of the stands and dropped him close to the running rail. He never recovered consciousness and he was pronounced dead on arrival at the first aid room. I rode the unplaced favourite in the race but none of us were aware of the tragic outcome until we got back to the weighing-room. Joe Mercer and I shared the same valet in Fred Dyer, and one look at Joe's stricken face told me all I needed to know. The whole of the weighing-room was shattered and the last race was abandoned. Even though it was so long ago, recalling that fateful afternoon and particularly Joe's agony moves me to tears. My brother and I drove back home to Ludlow that evening in stunned silence.

Manny was a natural and would have remained at the top for many years. Joe was famous for his immaculate style but his elder brother was equally proficient. Manny was a lover of fast cars, although his driving did settle down as he got older. Once when travelling to York, I was stuck in a queue of traffic at Wentbridge on an uphill stretch of road with a blind, right-handed turn ahead. Manny, obviously in a hurry to get to the races, pulled out from behind, and accelerated past the stationary traffic on the wrong side of the road, disappearing from sight round the bend. Considering the risks he took on the road, it seems ironic that he should have lost his life in such a simple accident.

At Hamilton the following week, for the first and only time in my career I rode the same horse in two races on the same day. The horse was Blondantese, and the first race was a six-furlong handicap in which she looked sure to win approaching the last furlong but shirked her task when asked to go on and win and was beaten a neck. Her trainer, Pat Taylor, probably felt that he would teach the filly a lesson. Had she tried harder at her first attempt it would have saved her from further exertions in the one-mile three-furlong maiden race later on. Once again she faltered when asked for her effort but stayed on to finish second, beaten a length and a half. In the opinion of the *Raceform* race-reader, she was possibly capable of winning a race over a long distance. This must have given Blondantese something to think about on her return journey to Beverley, for only four days later she ran again in a seven-furlong handicap at Catterick and this time made all the running to win by two lengths, giving the runner-up 29 lb.

In the Newmarket Oaks, run at the end of October, with the aid of Water Wings, I took my revenge on Collyria, who had beaten Cantelo in the Park Hill. Although Collyria had the full benefit of L. Piggott's encouragement we held on by a head for a sweet success.

At the end of the season, Captain Elsey gave a farewell dinner to Edgar and his family and presented him with a silver salver. The Britt family sailed for Australia in mid-December and I travelled down to Tilbury docks to say farewell and to express my appreciation for all Edgar's help. We have kept in touch and he later told me that he had been tempted to return by a terrific offer from the McGraths in Ireland. In fact, he said he could have written his own cheque but was put off by the travelling to Ireland plus the trips over to the United Kingdom. Instead, he decided to continue his role as a journalist for the Australian *Sunday Telegraph* reporting on Saturday racing. This kept him involved in the sport while giving him the chance to enjoy his retirement. My lasting memory of Edgar is that of a real gentleman with strong views on the subject of race-riding. We discussed his ideas many times and some of them influenced me for the rest of my riding career.

Jockeys are often criticised for looking round. In Edgar's opinion if a jockey couldn't look round without unbalancing his horse then he had no right to call himself a jockey. 'Jockeys don't have the benefit of a rear view mirror', he would say. 'They need to know what is going on behind them.' I agree with Edgar – for two reasons. The first is that, for the sake of your horse's future handicap, it is stupid to win by an exaggerated distance; and second, because of this, you need to be aware of what is going on behind to avoid being caught on the line by a fast finisher.

It was Edgar who advised me to always take a hold two or three inches shorter than usual on the reins on a sharp or tight track. This makes the horse race more freely – things tend to happen more quickly on a sharper track, and the horse is more likely to be able to take a split-second opening. Of course, there is always the danger that a horse will run itself into the ground if it runs too freely. Jockeys have to ride each horse and race on its relative merits, which is why it is foolish to tie good jockeys down with instructions and why in racing good jockeys last a long time – they keep learning.

The evening that Edgar left I went across to the BBC Television studios in Shepherds Bush for the Sports Review of the Year. I used to get invited to events of that sort in those days and enjoyed them tremendously. They gave me the chance to meet up with the likes of Denis Compton, John Surtees, Judy Grinham and Mary Bignall, along with the Yorkshire cricket team and their captain, Vic Wilson. Vic lives just down the road from me now and recently supplied us with some straw!

The Southern Jockeys' dinner was held at the Savoy that year and a few of us based in the North attended, including Joe Sime, Ted Larkin and Johnny Greenaway. From there we went on to the Astor Club where the star attraction was a striptease act by a young lady who had a truly remarkable talent. After she had shed her clothes she was left with a tassle on each boob and buttock and was able by dextrous movement of the relevant portions to rotate these tassles in contrary directions. I was still a naive young lad unused to such 'sophisticated' entertainment, and the evening was a real eye-opener for me – I didn't know such skills existed!

The following day, still in a state of shock after the night before, I attended a lunchtime reception at Claridges, which was memorable for the fact that a grand piano which had been brought in especially for the occasion went missing. Some men in overalls walked in and removed it, right under everyone's noses. Nobody stopped them to query their actions and the piano was apparently never seen again. After two days of witnessing such strange goings-on in the capital I was relieved to be returning to the sanity of Shropshire.

– 9 –
Stable Jockey at Highfield

THE sensation you get when a galloping horse collapses underneath you at over 35 miles per hour is not easy to describe, nor is it one you would ever wish to experience again. It happened to me in the Champion Sprint at Redcar in 1960. The horse was called Compere and had a history of breaking blood vessels. Even so, I did not immediately realise what was happening when he suddenly fell back from his handy position, lost all his impetus and swerved towards the rails. By the time I registered what was wrong it was too late. All control of the horse had gone and seconds later he crashed heavily to the ground, coming to rest under the far rails and pinning my legs beneath him.

Quick-thinking racegoers helped lift the horse off me and I was fortunately unscathed. But it was obvious to everyone that poor Compere was beyond help. A post-mortem showed that he had broken a blood vessel in his lungs and had literally drowned in his own blood. At first I didn't appreciate how lucky I had been to escape serious injury or worse, but when the course doctor examined me he pointed out a deep dent in my skull cap. 'That hat probably saved your life,' he informed me, 'although I think you're probably made of teak anyway'. The running rails had been knocked right out of alignment and three men had to hold them in position for the next race. However, I didn't give myself time to dwell on my brush with death – an hour after the accident I rode Mr Bull's Anne of Hollins to victory.

'Breaking a blood vessel' has become an all-too-common occurrence on the racecourse these days. What actually happens is that under the stress of fast work, when the horse's blood pressure rises and the pressure within the chest fluctuates due to the muscular movements involved in galloping, bleeding occurs in certain vulnerable areas of the lung. Recent research has shown, surprisingly, that the vast majority of horses have some bleeding in their lungs after a race, but in a few horses the bleeding is much heavier than normal. It is fortunately very rarely severe enough to kill them as it did Compere, although it did happen again six years later to a horse I was riding, Gallegos, also at Redcar. On that occasion I managed to all but stop the horse before he collapsed and came over backwards and I was able to bale out safely.

What happens more often is that the blood forces its way up the windpipe and makes the horse choke and gurgle as he swallows the blood. The jockey has to pull him up as he realises the horse is in distress. Whatever the outcome, it is a very dangerous weakness.

In Hong Kong, bleeding is quite common, perhaps because of the climate, or perhaps because the horses live permanently indoors in air-conditioned stables. They take the condition very seriously indeed there. Any horse that bleeds from the nostrils, whether it is during training or in a race, is always examined with an endoscope by a vet, and if the cause is a ruptured vessel in the lungs it is compulsorily retired for three months. If it happens again it is banned for life. Perhaps they care more for the safety of the jockeys over there.

Admittedly, such a system would be impossible to police in Britain where trainers find it much easier than they do in Hong Kong to keep quiet about 'bleeders' during home gallops. I was told of one well-known trainer who put a jockey up on a horse which he knew had bled at home without giving him any warning at all. Apparently, his words to the owner beforehand were, 'Let the bugger run. If it goes wrong we'll collect the insurance'. In fact the horse did collapse and die in the race and for all I know the insurance money was collected, but what neither the owner nor the trainer had thought of was the poor jockey, who was badly injured in the resulting accident.

In America, horses that are known to bleed are usually treated before a race with the drug Lasix, which lowers the blood pressure and reduces the chances of a blood vessel breaking. I suppose such a system does reduce the risk to jockeys, but it also gives the horses on the drug an unnatural advantage and is probably not good for the thoroughbred breed in the long run: if 'bleeders' can win top races people will go on and breed from them and if, as some people believe, the weakness is at least partly hereditary the percentage of bleeders in the population is likely to increase.

The tragic irony in my accident on Compere was that only the previous September Manny Mercer had ridden the horse at Ascot. He had accepted the mount knowing that it was prone to breaking blood vessels even then. It had bled in its previous race and was to do so again when it next ran. But in Manny's race it showed no sign of its weakness and ran well to win. Two days later, on a 'safe' horse, going no faster than a trot on his way to the start, Manny was thrown and killed. Life does indeed play some strange and cruel tricks.

That 1960 season, when that fall at Redcar occurred, was my first and, as it turned out, only season as first jockey to Captain Elsey following the retirement of Edgar. Sadly, the Captain himself was to be forced by ill-health to retire in the October of that year. He had severe problems with his leg throughout the season and was in much pain from a blood clot which was restricting the circulation in the leg. He had a spell in the Belvedere nursing home in Scarborough for treatment and it wasn't until the York May meeting that he went racing for the first time. Consequently his son Bill took over more and more of his responsibilities during the year.

For me it was a season in which I seemed prone to accidents. The Compere incident was just one in a sequence of falls. The run had started in the first week of racing at Liverpool, when a horse called Luminalis had dropped me on the way out of the paddock. In putting out my hand to save myself I hurt my wrist. The pain was severe although the injury was diagnosed as 'only a sprain'. After two days off and a visit to an osteopath who reassured me it was nothing serious I was back in the saddle, with five rides lined up for the following Monday. But it was months before the discomfort went, and it was years before I was able to play tennis without feeling a jarring pain in my wrist each time I hit a ball, although for some strange reason it didn't affect my golf. Years later after a fall in Stockholm I had the wrist X-rayed and an old fracture showed up on the picture. I couldn't remember ever having fractured my wrist until I thought back to the fall from Luminalis. Some sprain!

My most bizarre accident of the year happened at the Epsom spring meeting and was partly my own fault. Between the finish and the paddock a public road crossed the track. Now they have built an underpass for it but in 1960 they simply used to cover it over with coconut matting when racing was on and stop the traffic during the running of the race. The method of stopping the traffic was to tie a bit of rope to a pillar box on one side of the road and get someone to hold it up on the other!

I had just ridden Torullo to finish second to Sir Winston Churchill's Vienna in the Blue Riband trial. Bill Elsey and I had travelled down by rail and were short of time to catch the five o'clock Pullman back to Yorkshire, so instead of trotting back to the unsaddling enclosure I sent Torullo into a hack canter to try to save a minute or two. As we crossed the road something startled Torullo and he shied sideways, slipping on the coconut matting. His feet went from under him and he fell, pinning me underneath. When he tried to get up he found he couldn't because his head had somehow ended up under a milk float laden with bottles which was parked waiting to cross the road! When trapped some horses panic and struggle. Others just lie and wait for help to arrive. Fortunately both for me and for the milkman's customers Torullo came into the latter category. He lay motionless while the police and his lad extricated me from underneath him and then dragged him out from under the milk float. Amazingly, neither of us were much the worse for the experience, although I did miss the train!

Friday 13th seems to feature strongly in my life as I have recounted, and it was on that date in May, my brother Tony's birthday, that I rode two horses for the Captain at Haydock. Both gave me unforgettable rides. The first, Infatuator, had always given trouble despite his undoubted ability. He had been a difficult yearling, and in his first race at Manchester had hung so badly that he had been disqualified from third place after almost putting another runner over the rails. Because of this tendency I decided to get over to the stands rails at Haydock as quickly as possible so that at least we would not endanger any other horses this time. This I managed to do, but despite the guidance of the rails Infatuator continued to hang right. We were leading the field as we approached the stands but I felt if I pushed him any more I was in serious danger of going over the rails and joining the bookmakers. Somehow I managed to keep him in front and won by a length, but my troubles were only just beginning.

Soon after the finish at Haydock and just on the bend there is a chute which is used for the one-and-a-half mile start and here the running rail comes to an end. There was never any chance of Infatuator making the bend. With no rail to guide him he simply careered straight into the hedge lining the course, somersaulted through it as he hit the wire strung in the middle and disappeared across country, leaving me to extricate myself from the hedge.

Bill joined me in giving chase after him over the Lancashire countryside. Nowadays in exceptional circumstances, provided the stewards are satisfied that the proper weight has been carried throughout the race, they are allowed to use their discretion and let the result stand, but then, if you didn't weigh in within a certain time, 20 minutes I believe, you were disqualified. Fortunately we caught Infatuator in the nick of time and I just managed to pass the scales and change for my next ride. Perhaps it would have been better if I had been too late.

My second mount was a horse called Prins Eugen. He, too, was what is euphemistically known as a 'character'. He had a great liking for the comforts of home and hated to leave his stable. Before his previous race he had refused to go down to the start until I dismounted and led him. Maybe he had a warped sense of humour and saw the funny side of making me do the running for a change. I didn't know what to expect at Haydock but he appeared to be on his best behaviour. We got to the start with no trouble and after the off he raced willingly for four furlongs until we came to the paddock turn.

Of course, as Prins Eugen knew very well, even though it was his first visit to Haydock, just beyond the paddock there was a nice comfortable stable waiting for him, and while the rest of the field bore left he pulled himself up and made a beeline for his box. Prins Eugen was without doubt a very intelligent horse but great intelligence is not necessarily a very desirable quality in a racehorse. The result is often a constant battle of wits between horse and jockey. In this case it was the horse that won!

Both horses at Haydock had emerged unharmed from their escapades. There's an old saying in racing that only the good horses injure themselves. A horse that emerges from a nasty experience unscathed is usually written off as being no good. Zarco, another member of the Highfield stable, proved that there are exceptions to this particular rule. On one occasion Zarco's saddle slipped right back and unseated his rider. With the girths bringing about the same reaction as a bucking bronco strap, the two-year-old careered off the gallops in a panic. He charged across a busy road, jumped into and out of a paddock, across the tarmaced stableyard and crashed into the riding school. That particular building had a five-foot breeze-block base with an asbestos covering above it which his head had smashed straight through. He ended up surveying the interior of the riding school. Amazingly, not only did he get away scot free, but within a few days he had won his first race at York. He later won the Somerville Tattersall Stakes by an easy six lengths at Newmarket, and was then sold to America for 25,000 guineas – a considerable amount in those days.

Neither Infatuator nor Prins Eugen were of that calibre, but fortunately my mishaps that day were not serious. Oddly enough, both horses were owned by Mr Jim Joel, who was the most considerate and gentlemanly of owners. Shortly afterwards I received a letter from him apologising for the unpleasant experiences his horses had given me at Haydock that day. He added that he was sending both of them to the July Sales so I wouldn't have to endure further uncomfortable rides. It was typical of the man to put the safety of his jockey first.

Fortunately none of my spills that season put me out of action for long and once again I was able to accept a ride in the Derby, although this time my mount, Oakridge, was not of the calibre of some of Highfield's previous contenders. In some ways, I feel that Oakridge was a victim of the stable's success. Because Highfield had been regularly producing a runner in the classic I think the Captain and Bill felt there was some pressure on them to find a runner every year. Unfortunately Oakridge, although almost certainly the best in the stable of his year, was really not classic material and with hindsight I'm sure he would have been better off not running at Epsom. We finished seventh to St Paddy and Lester. Oakridge had already been beaten in both the Guineas and the Dante and later finished third and fourth in the Great Voltigeur and the St Leger respectively.

He ran good races on each occasion but he was a typical example of a horse that eventually lost interest in racing because of having been continually pitted against horses that were just that bit too good for him. By the time he eventually ran in an event in which he had a good chance, the Liverpool St Leger, he showed he was tired of the game by running a really sour race. The ground was slow that day, and that nearly always finds out a horse with doubtful courage as it takes more effort to persevere. There is no doubt in my mind that all Oakridge's courage had been used up in hopeless battles earlier in the season.

While it is a perfectly valid argument that there is no chance of winning a classic unless you actually participate, it is equally true to my mind that Oakridge could have won a fistful of races had he been aimed at the second division rather than the first. And there are probably many more like him in racing's history.

Towards the end of the season the stable went down with the cough and didn't have a winner for three weeks. No one spoke of the 'virus' in those days. When a horse coughed and was off-colour it simply had 'the cough'. The remedy was to keep it off work until it stopped coughing and appeared better which didn't usually take more than a week or two. Since the advent of the 'virus' life has become much more complicated. The blanket term 'virus' is used today to explain a multitude of symptoms and sometimes simply as an excuse when a horse runs badly. It is a handy scapegoat for a trainer when the alternative is to blame the horse, the jockey or himself.

The virus is therefore probably not quite as prevalent as reports in the press would have us believe. Even so, the sort of epidemic which affects a whole stable and then lingers on, sometimes for a season or more, is much more common now than it ever was. A variety of reasons have been suggested to explain this. Personally, I believe it is more than mere chance that the increase in the virus has coincided with the increase in the use of chemicals in farming. These days youngstock on studs in arable farming areas are very lucky if they avoid contact with the chemicals applied to neighbouring crops. The Ramblers Association claim that one billion gallons of pesticide are sprayed annually on the British countryside and this can drift over large areas as a vapour. In addition, both the hay and straw used in racing stables may have been sprayed with herbicides or pesticides before harvest. Of course chemicals cannot 'cause' a virus but I'm sure that inhaling these substances into the lungs doesn't do the lung tissue any good and might make the animal vulnerable to infection. Agro-chemicals certainly are not all harmless as many farm workers have found out to their cost.

The other factor which has I think played its part in the way the virus now lingers on is the introduction of compulsory vaccination. The trouble with the anti-viral vaccinations is that they are not like our smallpox vaccinations which offer complete protection. All they do in many cases is reduce the severity of the symptoms so that sometimes the horse can have the virus without the trainer being aware of it. The result is that he often carries on working the horse, sometimes doing more damage than if the horse had caught a really bad bout and had to be laid up in his box for three weeks. Often now the first sign that a horse has the virus is if it fades unexpectedly in a race, and by the time that happens the damage is done. It can take months rather than weeks for it to completely recover if it has been made to exert itself when it was sick. In many ways in the good old days before all these jabs were introduced life was a lot simpler.

I was talking once along these lines to trainer Frank Carr who started his career working for the Captain. I asked him if they had ever had the virus at Highfield while he was there. 'The Captain's horses get the virus?' he exclaimed. 'They were on the move too much for the virus to catch them!'

In spite of the cough Captain Elsey was again leading trainer in terms of number of winners. In the last seven seasons in which he trained he averaged 73 winners with 78 horses, figures which today's top trainers with around 200 horses in their yards must envy. He was approaching his 80th birthday when he announced his retirement in October. Bill, who as assistant trainer had been in charge of much of the day-to-day running of the yard since his father's spell in hospital, was now to take over the reins completely. At the final meeting of the year at Manchester I rode the Captain's last winner, Pink Foot, in the very appropriately named Farewell Handicap. It was sad to think this would be the last time I would ride for the great man.

In December 50 representatives of the press from all over the country held a presentation and lunch in Captain Elsey's honour at the Mayfair Hotel in London. It was the first time that such a retirement lunch had been given to any trainer, and it was an eloquent tribute to a man so respected by all sections of the racing community.

The winter of 1960–61 was rather a special one for me as it was during this time that Sue and I were married, having announced our engagement shortly after Royal Ascot. One member of the popular press, when he learned that we had first met in St Moritz, asked 'Did she ski down the mountainside into your arms?' 'Of course not', I replied, 'Don't be so bloody silly'. The next day his report on our engagement appeared stating that Sue had 'skied down the mountainside into jockey Edward Hide's arms'!

I have always been both superstitious and a bit of a believer in destiny, and this belief was strengthened many years ago when Sue's mother brought out an old, yellowed newspaper cutting. Sue's uncle, Sydney Baker, father of Pat Stoute and Dadie Oughtred, had died in September 1951 and her mother had kept the account of the funeral service from the *Hull Daily Mail*. The article named the many mourners who included Sue Brett, as she then was. Nobody had looked closely at the reverse side before but on turning it over I couldn't believe my eyes. On the other side of the single-column cutting were some racing results, and the race that headed the list was The Gwent Selling Handicap Plate at Chepstow where the first place went to Ritornello ridden by E. Hide – my first ever win!

We were married in the off-season in January from Sue's home in Filey. It was chancing it somewhat to have a wedding at that time of the year on the east coast of Yorkshire, but it was a brilliantly sunny day and we followed the sunshine by boarding the RMS Caronia to Jamaica for our honeymoon. The service on board the ship seemed superb to us two innocents: two waiters attended our every need; the menu was endless but if there was anything we wanted that was not there we only had to ask for it. Sam and Mrs Armstrong were on board and he would stride up and down the deck keeping his eyes open for potential owners. He was very helpful in keeping me straight about shipboard etiquette.

We had travelled very little up to then and the contrasts and atmosphere we encountered in Jamaica were markedly different from anything we had met before. After living through 23 English winters, arriving in the heat of Jamaica was like emerging into a turkish bath from an icy shower, and we were relieved to be met by the two Jamaican owners who had horses in training with Captain Elsey. We were soon ensconced in their air-conditioned car for the colourful journey to Ocho Rios, where they had put an apartment at our disposal. We hired a car and explored the island. One day we were swimming in the sea at Doctor's Cave when I thought I recognised a familiar face floating by, so tanned that I was not sure whether I was right or whether it was one of the natives, but yes, it was Charlie Smirke. He invited us round to his apartment where he lived in grand style, even having his meat flown in from Miami.

I have many amusing memories of Charlie during his riding days in England. He had also been in Fred Dyer's corner of the weighing-room. There was a hairbrush and comb for our use but we all avoided using it after Charlie because it was always thick with the Brylcreem he applied lavishly to his hair. It is one of the duties of the Clerk of the Scales to check that the colours the jockey is wearing match those on the racecard. One day, the elderly official peered over the top of his half-rimmed glasses and inquired of Smirkie, 'What are your colours?' The reply was something like 'If you put those effing glasses further up your effing nose you would be able to see for yourself what the effing colours are!' Needless to say, this observation resulted in an appearance before the stewards.

Another time, at Bogside, Charlie, who had always had a weight problem, is reputed to have passed the scales without a saddle, with only the number-cloth draped over his arm. It was typical of his devil-may-care attitude to life. Who else but Charlie, on a 100–8-on shot owned by the Aga Khan, would have won a two-horse race by a hard held head? And this before the days of the photo finish when the decision could so easily have gone against him!

While we were at his flat Charlie 'phoned William Hill, who also had a holiday home in Jamaica. 'Hi, Bill,' he said, 'I've got your jockey here.' Even though Mr Hill was one of my main owners I would never have dreamed of speaking to him with such familiarity. It was more 'Yes sir, No sir, three bags full, sir'. Nevertheless, he invited us to his lovely home up on a hill above Montego Bay. It was like a dream world for us in those days. His white-coated manservant, Cooper-Thwaite, greeted us. At lunch we ate outdoors from a large glass table with fresh flowers arranged underneath so that it seemed as though we were eating off a tablecloth of flowers. Local dogs hung around and I was interested to see that none was allowed to go away hungry, which revealed a softer side of the big businessman I had not seen before.

The honeymoon over, we flew home via New York. The spacious stone-built house we were to live in at the start of our married life was in a quiet road on the outskirts of Malton. We named the house Myron after my first winner for the Captain, although our neighbour Dr Hughes, who was clearly possessed of a fertile imagination, suspected that Sue had named it My-Ron after a previous boyfriend!

Ernie Davey, who trained nearby in Norton, was a contemporary of Grandpa Edwards and he invited Sue and me to his bungalow on one occasion for supper and an evening of reminiscences. I remember one story he told that night which concerned a National Hunt jockey, Arthur Thompson I believe, who, riding in a novice chase at a small North Country course, was being seriously hampered by an ignorant amateur rider. According to Ernie they were out in the country when, after being pushed into yet another fence wing, Arthur reached across and managed, at full gallop, to remove the bridle from the head of his adversary's horse. He then handed it to him, saying 'Now let's see how clever you are'. Ernie chuckled appreciatively as he recounted this tale. I imagine that it was a feat he would sometimes have liked to have performed himself in his riding days. He was a great old character but was never one to suffer fools gladly. As a result, he was not over-popular with some of his stable-lads who, he felt, fitted into that category.

Towards the end of his career Ernie was incapable of walking unaided and got about mainly with the help of an old car which he drove either in first or in fourth gear. Around lunch-time one day the faithful car succumbed to this insensitive treatment and broke down at the far end of his gallops a mile from home. Ernie instructed the stable-boy who was with him to call at the garage on his way home to lunch to ask them to send a mechanic to rescue him. The boy obviously felt he had a score or two to settle with his boss, and while he did eventually deliver the message he delayed doing so until his return for evening stables. The mechanic turned up to find a fuming Ernie still at the wheel having been imprisoned in his car at the end of the gallops all afternoon.

I was soon back riding at Highfield. Bill had been assistant trainer to his father since 1951, so he was well-versed in the Highfield routine and there were no dramatic changes when he took over. He had served in the RAF during the war and still harboured a deep passion for 'planes and flying – in fact it was a standing joke among the staff that if the string were working on Highfield gallops and a 'plane passed overhead the horses were instantly forgotten as his eyes looked longingly skywards. However, he never forgot the horses for long, and under his supervision Highfield continued to produce a string of good winners. He had 80 horses for his first season and life carried on much as before. The first winner I rode for Bill was Black King in the Rosebery Stakes over a mile at Stockton, a race the Captain had won seven times in the past 12 runnings. Regrettably, the course closed in 1966, although it opened again for a short time under the name of Teesside Park only to be closed again permanently in August 1971. From a professional point of view it was an excellent track, and the Rosebery was regarded as a classic trial. Black King went on to win the Queen's Vase at Royal Ascot thus giving his trainer the distinction of saddling a winner with his first runner at the Royal Meeting.

At the end of April 1961 I had a nice win on Apostle in the Jockey Club Cup at Newmarket which between 1959 and 1962 was run over a mile and a half. (It subsequently became a two mile race.) I had won the Old Newton Cup on him the previous season and the ride was offered to me by his trainer, Staff Ingham, because his connections felt that Scobie Breasley didn't get on with him. Before the race Mr Ingham warned me that once I was on board the horse I should in no circumstances get off, even if there was a delay at the start, as if I did Apostle was liable to try to eat me for lunch. Apparently, he was quite a savage. I didn't need warning twice. Fortunately there was no need for me to dismount until we were safely in the winners' enclosure.

These days you very rarely come across a really savage horse although there are plenty of tales of 'man-eaters' from days gone by.

The only other I ever encountered, and that years later, was a horse called Ubedizzy trained by Steve Nesbitt. I rode him only once, in a conditional sprint at Newmarket. No one had warned me of his reputation and I had no problems at the start or during the race. My first inkling that something was wrong came when I unsaddled the horse afterwards. As I undid the girth I let it fall and it just touched his off-fore leg. The effect was electrifying. Instantly, Ubedizzy sank down on his knees and started biting everything in sight. He had his lad on the floor and was ripping the coat off his back and trying to kneel on him. The lad was screaming, and people were trying to drag him away. I don't mind admitting that I got well out of his way. I heard later that on another occasion he had bitten off someone's finger – after his display of rage in the unsaddling enclosure that day I wasn't at all surprised. Whenever he ran after that he had to wear a muzzle. Why he should have become that way I don't know, it must almost certainly have been through some bad experience early in his life.

In 1961 Highfield housed a horse of exceptional promise in Phil Bull's Sostenuto. Because he had split a pastern in May his debut was delayed until the autumn, when he won the Gainsborough Stakes at Hurst Park without being extended and went by the winning post on the bridle, ears pricked, six lengths ahead of his nearest rival. After the race Clive Graham in the *Express* reported that the son of Never Say Die had galloped smoothly into the position of probable winter favourite for the Derby. Sostenuto didn't win the Derby – he didn't even run in the race. A week before the 2,000 Guineas he split another pastern, which put him out for most of the season. He must have had brittle bones. After the great hopes held for him the disappointment felt by all connected with him was tremendous. There must be many horses over the years who, for one reason or another, have been unable to fulfil their early promise. He was able to run again eventually that season but managed to win only a couple of small races at Stockton and Liverpool

Sostenuto stayed in training as a four-year-old but gave some indifferent performances and didn't seem to put any heart into his races. However, he came good at York when he won the Ebor Handicap by eight lengths when ridden by Don Morris. Bill had three runners in the race: I rode Black King and Johnny Greenaway rode Oakville. Two days later, again at York, I rode Oakville and we flashed past the post locked in battle with the Irish-trained hot favourite, March Wind. On pulling up neither of us was sure which had won. Sometimes on such occasions, to lessen the disappointment if the verdict goes the other way, the jockeys agree to 'save' on the result, which means that whoever wins gives whoever loses some of his winnings. The race was worth over £2,000 to the winner – a lot of money in those days – so I suggested a saver of £25. This met with a short and sharp retort from March Wind's jockey. We ended by sharing the percentage after a dead-heat was announced.

In the 1961 Derby, I was offered the ride on Harry Wragg's Psidium but had to turn it down as I was retained to ride Oakville for my stable. Harry had two runners in the race that year and Aussie George Moore was flown over to take the ride on the other, Sovrango. Psidium had run with promise when third in the Kempton Guineas trial but had beaten only four in the 22-runner Guineas itself. He started at 66–1 and was ridden by French jockey Roger Poincelet, the seventh jockey to ride the colt. Psidium was last turning into the straight at Epsom. It was very unusual to win from so far back, but win he did. Had I ridden Psidium, I would probably have tried to put him in a more prominent position and he might not have finished so well.

Sostenuto was the first foal of Arietta on whom I had finished third in the 1956 1,000 Guineas. How time flew – I was now winning on horses whose dams I had also ridden to victory! Arietta's second foal was Romulus, again bred by Phil Bull, who was sold privately as a foal to the American Charles Engelhard. On King George day at Ascot in 1961 I was given the ride on Romulus, trained by Fulke Johnson Houghton, in the Virginia Water Stakes. He won by a very impressive four lengths.

Charles Engelhard was just starting his very successful spell as an owner in Britain. He had great regard for the stock of the brilliant Italian champion, Ribot, and apart from Romulus, other Ribots that did him proud included the Irish Derby and St Leger winners Ribocco and Ribero. The champion miler of 1969, Habitat, also carried Mr Engelhard's colours, but his greatest triumphs were of course with Nijinsky, who won the triple crown in 1970.

In September 1961 I received a letter from David McCall, Mr Engelhard's racing manager, offering me a retainer. Mr McCall realised that I had connections with the Elseys but was prepared to offer me a second retainer if I could be available for the big races, such as the classics. Unfortunately, I was unable to work things out. Bill, as I mentioned, had 80 horses and was very likely to have runners in both the Guineas and Derby.

I rode High Noon for Bill in the 1962 Derby. A respectable fifth at Newmarket, he didn't do so well at Epsom in the year in which the race featured more casualties than a novice steeplechase. Near the six-furlong post I was upsides Wally Swinburn on Romulus. We were both a bit short of room and I had just called 'You all right?' No sooner had he shouted that he was than down he went. Six more horses fell and Geoff Lewis's mount, King Canute II, had to be destroyed after breaking a leg. Romulus himself emerged from the mêlée bleeding from several cuts and lame behind. Wally was admitted to hospital with neck injuries and was detained with other jockeys including Stan

Smith, who had concussion and an injury to his shoulder; Tommy Gosling and Harry Carr, who both had serious concussion; and Geoff Lewis, who was lucky to escape with only a slight injury to his arm. It was a miracle that no jockey sustained permanent injuries from the horrific pile-up. That was the year that Larkspur won, ridden by Australian Neville Sellwood. Ironically he was shortly to be killed himself in a racing accident.

– 10 –
May Double

I HAVE a lot to thank Vestal Girl for. She was only a one-paced stayer in her racing days but was the dam of both Henry the Seventh and Henry's Choice, two horses that served me well. Henry the Seventh, who raced in Mr Joel's famous colours and was trained by Bill Elsey, started his three-year-old career in controversial fashion at Thirsk. Entering the final furlong Sweet Solera, who had won the 1,000 Guineas trial at Kempton on her previous race, hung in and veered sharply across causing me to snatch up. We stayed on but were beaten threequarters of a length. It was against Mr Joel's principles to object, the stewards didn't hold an inquiry and the result stood, even after the bookies had offered Sweet Solera at 2–1 against keeping the race.

After such a rough race 'Henry' seemed to lose confidence and I am sure that it affected his outlook on racing. In his next race he beat only three of the 22 runners home in the 2,000 Guineas. Worse was to follow. After a three-month rest he next ran in the Magnet Cup at York with Cliff Parkes riding, but under only 7–7 was tailed off entering the straight. Six weeks later I was back on him. Dropped in class and fitted with a pair of blinkers he won his maiden by a fast-diminishing neck over 11 furlongs at Doncaster. He went on to win a maiden at closing at Thirsk and a similar race at Newmarket, both of which acted as further confidence-boosters, showing the horse that racing could be quite fun and was not always akin to a rugby match. With a 6 lb penalty he took his chance in the Cambridgeshire. Leading inside the final furlong, Henry the Seventh couldn't quite sustain his effort and dead-heated with Violetta III, ridden by Cliff Parkes and trained by Harry Wragg.

He must have had pleasant dreams through the long winter nights for he put up a decidedly smart performance the following spring at Redcar in the Zetland Gold Cup when giving 21 lb and a two-lengths beating to Better Honey, who went on to win the Bessborough Stakes at Royal Ascot. At the Ascot meeting, Henry the Seventh himself won the Rous Memorial from Royal Avenue, and that booked him a ticket to take his chance in the Eclipse Stakes at Sandown.

He was a very lazy horse at home and took nothing out of himself, so he had to be worked in blinkers and was also taken to Thirsk racecourse to work after racing in the hope that the atmosphere would get his adrenalin running. Before the big race, it looked touch and go whether I would be able to renew my successful partnership with 'Henry' as I had sustained a severely bruised hip in being thrown at Haydock the previous day. Two hot baths relieved the stiffness and I decided that I felt fit enough to ride in my first Eclipse. It wasn't a good race that year but Henry the Seventh, the 11–8 on favourite, won by three lengths to give me my first win at the track. A wheelbarrow of lead would hardly have been sufficient to represent Henry the Seventh's improvement since his run in the Magnet Cup. It felt more like tons than pounds or stones.

In August, it was announced that 'Henry' would be syndicated for £3,500 per share. He ran once more in the Lyons Maid Stakes at Sandown but was no match for Vienna, and following that defeat Mr Joel took the unusual step of reducing his share price to only £2,500.

Henry's Choice didn't have quite the same ability as his brother but he contributed to my five wins in one day at Liverpool in 1961 and won three more times that season, including the November Handicap at Manchester. He was trained for Mr Bill Harrison by Rufus Beasley at Malton. Rufus, apart from being a trainer, was a keen hunting man, a fact which brought us together on one memorable occasion. I had hunted periodically at home but had never had a proper hunting coat. As I had started hunting more regularly, I ventured into York one day to be kitted out. Of course, I might have known I wouldn't find anything off the peg to fit me. A familiar Irish drawl greeted me as Sue and I walked empty-handed back to the car. It was Rufus. I explained why we were in York and he said, 'Come back to my place, I'm sure I have a couple of coats tucked away in the attic'.

Rufus had been a jockey years before and in his riding days must have been my sort of build. We called round in the evening and he produced two top-quality coats, one of which could have been made for me. He invited us to join him and his friend Dr Jock Parker in a glass of wine and we sat in his old-fashioned study, talking and reminiscing by a warm fire, getting more and more mellow and relaxed as the wine slipped down. It was not until it was time to leave that I realised I was not in too good a state to drive. 'I'm fine', said Sue. 'Give me the keys and I'll drive home.' Rufus had a drive round a circle of lawn at the front of his house. Sue started off, waved goodbye to our host – and drove straight across the centre of the lawn. Staying in second gear all the way we crawled home. We learned later that Rufus was notorious for his champagne cocktails, and that we were only two of many who had been 'entertained' almost to the point of oblivion. Later that evening George Morley, who was supplying our mounts for the following day's hunting, 'phoned. Sue was incapable of answering. He mentioned the next day that I sounded very strange: it is a wonder I was able to speak at all!

I enjoyed my hunting, at first with the Derwent where George kept his horses, and later, after we bought a farm and had our own horses, with the Middleton. Sue went to Leicester Sales and bought a wonderful hunter, a thoroughbred by Border Legend called Border Lord, although at home he was known as Fred. He was recommended to us by Major David Swannell, the senior handicapper. Later I bought an Irish hunter from Pat Rohan. He was called Killenaule but, because he had short, fat, hairy legs we named him Ernie. 'Handsome is wot handsome does' and he was a brilliant hunter. I have to confess that on slow days I could think of better ways of filling in my time, but on good days there was nothing to beat being out with hounds. Hunting is a great schooling ground for horses and riders and many a jaded racehorse has been freshened up by a few days' hunting. One day that always produced good sport was the day after the Gimcrack Dinner at York, when the late Lord Halifax and the Middleton Hunt would invite the dinner guests to the meet the following day at his home at Garrowby.

For the 1963 season, the horses owned and managed by Phil Bull were to be ridden by Don Morris, who was also attached to Highfield. Don had ridden Sostenuto to win the Ebor for Mr Bull the previous season. I wondered whether Mr Bull had lost confidence in me but he stressed that that wasn't the case. He simply wanted a jockey of his own upon whom he could call to ride anywhere. It was exactly the same reason that he had given when signing me to replace Edgar for the 1958 season – the wheel had turned full circle. Sadly, less than four years later, in December 1966, Don and his girlfriend were killed in a head-on collision just outside Malton. It was on a clear, wide road late at night, but as there were no survivors, nobody really knows what happened.

A memorable victory for me in the spring of 1963 was on the nine-year-old gelding Scottish Memories, who gained his 24th success, and his first on the Flat, over two miles at Haydock. It crowned a remarkable five weeks during which he also won over fences and hurdles. The week before the gelding had won a chase at Punchestown when piloted by Terry Biddlecombe and then carried Bobbie Beasley to victory in a Taunton hurdle race. Scottish Memories was lodged at Arthur Thomas's for the Haydock race but returned to Paddy Sleator in Ireland afterwards.

For Father, back at Lawton, all the events of 1963 were over-

Battling it out with the leaders during a race in Oslo in 1957.

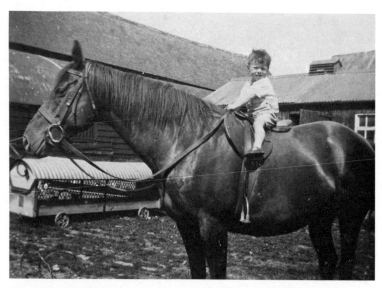

At two I found walking hard work — so I took a ride instead! The horse's name was Marigold.

Riding is very much in the blood. Here Grandpa Edwards poses for the camera with his children, Trixie, Olive, Connie (my mother), Enid, Grace and Ken.

1950, the year of my first race. Sixpence, my first pony, is now partnered by my sister Jill under the guiding hand of brother Tony.

'Thanks very much, that was very nice but now I've got to go and sweat it all orf.' My weight wasn't such a problem in those days.

Two special horses: Ritornello (ABOVE) was a part of the family even before she gave me my first winner; while Remember Me (BELOW), held by Father, won three times for me in 1952, ensuring that he will never be forgotten.

Aged nine I told Gordon Richards' brother that I meant to 'become a jockey and beat Gordon'. In 1953 I did just that on Two Fifty – a dream fulfilled.

Discussing the 1958 Derby on Epsom Downs with Captain Charles Elsey, who was one of the biggest influences on my career.

Two winners: Flying Friendship and I (TOP) are congratulated by owner Ludwig Braathen after winning the 1958 Derby – the *Norwegian* version. In the 1959 Oaks (BELOW), with Water Wings' help, I gain my revenge over Collyria, ridden by Lester, for that shock defeat in the Park Hill Stakes.

R. Anscomb, Newmarket.

Cantelo, trained by Captain Elsey, gave us both our first St Leger win.

The Daily Mail.

William Hill (RIGHT), Cantelo's owner, with his racing manager, Phil Bull, and me.

With my colleagues: Sir Gordon Richards (TOP), my boyhood hero, compares trophies with me on the curling rink at St Moritz. Greville Starkey, Ginger Dyson and I (BELOW) watch the camera warily.

shadowed by a disaster which happened at the end of the year. Three days before Christmas, as he was preparing to go to bed, he looked out of the window and saw flames leaping from the stables. He alerted the rest of the family and they managed to get three horses out of the inferno before they were driven back by the heat and smoke. They let 20 horses out of the stables in the adjacent block in case the fire spread and they galloped off into the dark countryside. Seven horses were killed that night in a fire believed to have been started by an electrical fault. Incredibly, the next day all the loose horses were rounded up unscathed. They had stayed in the company of the stable's old grey hack and his placid influence had saved them from harm.

Sue and I arrived the next day and helped to clear away the remains. It was a gruesome task but Father was too overcome and too closely connected with the stable's inmates to tackle it himself. One of the yearlings lost in the fire had been looked after by Jimmy White, who had first started my superstition about the green and red bands. Jimmy was a good and lucky lad – the horses he looked after always looked a picture and were invariably successful. When Father was asked to take in a poor, small black colt which had only cost 100 guineas he suggested that Jimmy looked after him until something better came along to replace the yearling that had been killed. Jimmy 'did' the horse throughout his career and he went on to win 11 races including the Lincoln. The horse, Ben Novus, proved to be yet another bargain buy.

In October 1966, I won a small conditions race at Stockton on Ben Novus who, at that time, was a four-year-old. It was the first time the horse had tackled a mile and, with his future handicap mark in mind, I won the race cleverly by half a length. Afterwards, I told Father that I thought Ben Novus could be an ideal type for the Lincoln. When the weights were published, however, I was pleased for the horse's sake but disappointed for mine to see that he was allotted 7 stones 10 lb. For a long time, owner and trainer contemplated allowing me to ride the horse at overweight – I could do 7 stones 13 lb at the time – but in the end Peter Robinson was given the ride. Ben Novus preferred give in the ground but, unusually, the going was hard at Doncaster. The horse also needed to be produced late and Peter rode him perfectly to win by half a length. Had I allowed him to win by as far as he could at Stockton, he may well have had sufficient weight for me to ride him in the big race, but with the extra weight the handicapper would have given him he would almost certainly have been beaten. However, in his next race, also at Doncaster, I was able to ride Ben Novus to victory in the valuable Zetland Handicap.

Over the previous few years there had been mounting pressure in the press to follow the American example and use starting stalls. Mr

Bull also came out strongly in favour of using the stalls in his Gim-crack speech. As a consequence, the Jockey Club starter went on a nationwide tour to introduce the mechanism, turning up at Malton in February 1964 at the Talbot Hotel, where a film was shown. After-wards, we went on to Pat Rohan's where a demonstration had been arranged. Two horses took part: one went in, the other refused. The experiment was a 50 per cent success or a 50 per cent failure depend-ing on which way you looked at it! At first I wasn't looking foward to the starting stalls, because I felt that at the barrier start I had an advantage over many jockeys, particularly apprentices and less-experienced riders. With starting stalls, everyone has a much better chance of getting off on level terms.

Nowadays it is of little importance to a jockey who is responsible for pressing the starting button, but when the barrier start was in operation it was often essential to know the starter's idiosyncrasies. There was one starter I used to be wary of. He was a familiar face at the Northern meetings and used to shout and bawl at the jockeys as though they were in the army. He had not always behaved like that but his attitude was probably the result of Johnny Greenaway, the Northern lightweight jockey, having once criticised him for not taking charge at the start. 'You have to have control of them', Johnny had said. 'You must exert your authority', and from then on that was what he tried to do. The trouble was he didn't always seem sure himself of just what it was he wanted us to do and he would sometimes change his mind halfway through giving us one of his orders. As a result I always took it with a pinch of salt when he wasn't happy with a line and said 'No, no, jockeys, we can't go like that'. I always made sure the other jockeys turned before I did because on numerous occasions, after the horses had all started to turn and were in a heap, he would change his mind, shout 'Come on, then!' and press the lever! Another lesson I learned was that you should never tell him when you were on a difficult horse. It paid to tell some of the other starters as they would try to keep an eye on you, but this starter seemed to take less notice since he had a ready-made excuse for the trainer if the horse got away badly.

This brings to mind the oft-repeated story of Gordon Richards at the old barrier start. Gordon was brilliant at the gate and his aptitude often led to jealousy and claims that the starter favoured the champion. One day the runners were coming in for about the fourth time when the starter called out, 'Are you all right, Gordon?' Harry Wragg, quick as a flash, shouted 'Yes, sir' and, already on the move, got a flyer.

The first race in Britain for which starting stalls were used was the Chesterfield Stakes at Newmarket on 9 July 1965. Leading trainer Jack Jarvis was completely against them. 'I hate them', he said. 'It is not in the best interests of racing to have starting stalls. I fail to see why owners in this country are forced to submit their horses to this experiment simply because of a few moans from stay-at-home punters after one of their horses has suffered at the start.' As with many things in life, it is fear of the unknown that makes people wary. However, it didn't take us long to appreciate the benefits of the new starting stalls. From a jockey's point of view the chance of being baulked by a badly-behaved horse at the start was virtually eliminated.

Space King gave Father his most valuable success thus far when taking the Magnet Cup at York that year. He was a horse that anybody would have been proud to own, a really honest individual with ability. As usual, the Magnet Cup was a very competitive race – the fourth horse, Tarqogan, had occupied the same place in the previous year's Derby. Father had fallen in love with Space King on seeing him as a foal at Newmarket and had bought him for 1,100 guineas. He won 12 of his 35 races and was placed in another dozen, later making a name for himself as a sire of numerous jumping winners, including Brown Chamberlin.

For the September meeting at Ayr I stayed at the Craiglea Hotel at Troon, as usual. When I was at the racecourse that morning to ride a horse of Bill Elsey's a canter, Peter Robinson told me that he wanted to work his Ayr Gold Cup mount, Compensation, and asked me to ride the lead horse, Black Jack, who was a decent handicapper. We worked three furlongs and Peter's instructions were to jump off and to go as fast as I could. After half a furlong I looked to see that he had given me about 12 lengths start, but it wasn't long before he cruised up to me on the bridle. This was a very impressive piece of work, and had I been a betting man I could have made a killing as on the soft ground he needed the horse went on to win the big race the following day by an easy three lengths at 10–1.

At the same racecourse in May 1965 I won the Glenburn Selling Handicap Plate on Three Six, trained by Russ Hobson. It was my 1,000th winner on home soil, and to mark the occasion the course executive presented me with a whip.

In mid-1965 Phil Bull sent a letter to Bill Elsey confirming that he would be moving his 18 horses away from Highfield, including the six he managed for William Hill, thus ending a highly-successful association that had lasted 15 years. Although it didn't concern me directly, because Don Morris was riding the horses owned and managed by Mr Bull, it was a big blow to the yard. For each of the five years that Bill had been training he had sent out more winners than anybody else in the country. The 1965 season, which yielded only 48 wins, turned out to be the first relatively poor year for Highfield, largely because of one of the worst coughing epidemics known.

Meanwhile, a small farm close to where we lived came on to the market and I took a friend, Alan Lambert, who farmed in a big way in Holderness and Ireland, to look it over for us. His report was favourable. The situation was right – it was only three miles from Malton – and as it was only 45 acres it was big enough to be useful but small enough to be easily manageable and not to interfere with my racing. We went along to the auction and were able to buy the property, Low Farm at Huttons Ambo, for £11,000. To acquire it we had to pay about £3 an acre more than the average price of land at that time and Jimmy Etherington told me later that people were saying 'What's happened to Edward Hide, he must have more money than sense'!

Of course the next decision to be made was what to do with the place. A variety of advisers from the 'Min of Ag' descended on us to reveal the pros and cons of dairy farming, pig-keeping and egg production, but we decided that as what I knew most about was horses we would start a small stud, though we did farm some of the land and keep pigs as well. We continued to live in Malton and Eric and Betty Petch moved into the cottage on the farm. Eric was maintenance and terrier man for the Middleton Hunt. He was a splendid, big, strong man, always cheerful and helpful, and did the work of ten men. In his spare time he and I put up post and rail fences and, with the help of Jack Ronald, a retired MMB inspector who lived in the village, we converted a milking parlour and carthorse stalls to loose boxes and slowly improved the place. I derived great satisfaction from doing things myself.

I went off to the December Sales at Newmarket to try to buy a mare and bought four! Sue was left behind to get the boxes ready. After quite a long wait she was expecting our first child in May and complained that she was in no condition to be carting bales of straw around. 'Nonsense', I said, 'Boyd-Rochfort's stable-girls ride out when they're six months pregnant', a remark which didn't go down too well.

We had marked off two horses in the catalogue, a chestnut Nearula mare called Rosecroft Honey in foal to King's Bench, and a two-year-old filly by Darius called Susiana. The latter was beautifully bred, out of Mrs McCalmont's great mare Lorelei, also the dam of Honeymore, Xerxes, State Pension and other good animals. Susiana was being sold out of Geoffrey Brooke's yard as she obviously didn't have the necessary racing ability. I was able to buy her for 850 guineas and Rosecroft Honey for 1,000 guineas. Going round the outside ring, I noticed a three-year-old that I had ridden on more than one occasion. She was a Sound Track filly called Sing High who had won and been placed in the Northern Free Handicap. I was able to buy her for 450 guineas and was offered an immediate profit. I decided to keep her as she was the type of animal I was looking for, a scopy sort with some form. Finally, I bought a beautifully-made but small Doutelle filly named Nautical Tune for 560 guineas. The latter subsequently bred small animals and we sold her. Rosecroft Honey bred two foals, both winners, before going down with lymphangitis and having to be put down. Susiana and Sing High stayed with us until into their late teens when the former had to be put down and the latter ruptured her uterus foaling. They became part of the family and also did very well for us.

Susiana bred six individual winners and Sing High seven individual winners of 22 races. In fact, all four horses I bought at Newmarket bred winners for us. As I was a jockey neither my wife nor myself were allowed to own a racehorse but I wrote to Weatherby's to ask if it were permissible to lease one to someone else on a free lease. I was told it was not, under any circumstances. Only a day or two later I was discussing this with Tony Murray, who told me he had had the same problem, but that it *was* possible to lease under the name of the stud. I wrote back to Weatherby's explaining that I sold under the name of the Huttons Ambo Stud and wished to lease under the same name and, sure enough, the reply was that that was different and would be quite in order.

I leased a colt called Rhine King who was born with enormous curbs and whom no one wanted to buy. Sue's cousin Dadie took him off our hands and put him in training with her brother-in-law, Michael Stoute, to help get him started in his training career. I rode my 100th winner of the season in 1972 on him at Warwick. The same year Michael bought an I Say colt out of Sing High called Top Speed from us and won three races with him as a three-year-old. The first winner I bred was May Double, bought by Tommy Shedden. She was so named because our daughter Elizabeth was born four days before Rosecroft Honey had her filly in May 1966.

When May Double was a foal we sent her to Lord Allendale's stud in Northumberland after she was weaned as he had a filly foal needing company. The following summer I was riding at Newcastle and was invited to stay by Lord and Lady Allendale at their lovely home at Bywell. We were taken up to our rooms and, unaccustomed as we were to the ways of the aristocracy, were somewhat taken aback to be put in adjoining rooms, Sue in the main bedroom with the double bed and me in the single-bedded dressing-room. Mother had long held a theory that tying a sock around your neck was a remedy for a sore throat, an affliction with which in my younger days I suffered a lot, and I carried an old grey sock around in my case. It was convenient for keeping all my medications together so imagine my embarrassment when I went into my room and found that the butler had not only unpacked my case – including my sock – but had laid the sock on the dressing-table with all the contents lined up in a neat row: aspirins, vick, cough sweets, 'pee pills', laxatives, the lot!

Another useful horse I bred was Thief Lane, who Denys Smith

trained for 'Topper' Robson. He took a big chance when he passed him on to the owner announcing 'You needn't pay me until he wins'! He won five races as a two-year-old, two of those victories coming on consecutive days at Catterick. He was a lazy horse and as he was not very intelligent stood a lot of hard races. Altogether we have bred the winners of over 50 races although we usually keep only a couple of mares. They give us tremendous pleasure, we look after them ourselves, the mares foal at home and we prepare the offspring for the sales.

A few years after we started the stud, when I won the Derby on Morston, Mr Budgett gave me a nomination to the horse and we sent Susiana to him. Unfortunately she didn't get in foal but he let me try again the following year. Deciding not to take the same risk again, I went to Newmarket and bought a young Reform mare called Fountain to use the nomination. She was trained by Major Dick Hern and had been a winner as a two-year-old. Beautifully bred, she is a half-sister to the champion French sprinter King of Macedon and numerous other good horses. She hasn't the best of front legs and her progeny to Morston was similar. Later, however, she bred Royal Fountain which Luca Cumani trained to win the Wood Ditton and Heathorn Stakes at Newmarket. In the Benson and Hedges Gold Cup at York he led to the distance before finishing close up behind the winner, Master Willie. I have won on many of the horses we've bred including Pepperita, Rhine King, Top Speed, Mandlestone, Indian Call and Singing High. Winning is always nice but it is an even better feeling when it is on a home-bred horse.

When Sing High had her filly foal by Julio Mariner it was obvious that all was not well. The vet was called in and although it was thought at the time that she would be all right she deteriorated and five days later had to be destroyed. Then began several traumatic days. We couldn't get the foal to suck from a bottle but she lapped the milk from a bowl like a dog. The first foster mother we found was not successful but then we heard of an Irish draught mare near Retford who had lost her foal. Sue wrapped our foal in a sleeping bag and she was taken on the back seat of our car to Retford. There wasn't even time to put the dead foal's skin over our foal – the mare was overjoyed at having a baby again, anyone's baby! A week later the foster mother and foal came back to Huttons Ambo and the foal thrived.

When she was two I leased the Julio Mariner filly to Northumbria Leisure to be trained by Jimmy Fitzgerald. She was subsequently named Singing High and I won two races on her, including the Long John Whisky Handicap at Ayr, and we were beaten a head in the Ripon Rowels. We now have her at home and her first foal is a colt by Tower Walk which we have named Top Scale. We sold a half-share to our friends Alan and Rosie Black and hope to have a bit of fun with him.

It was rather inconvenient living in Malton. Whenever I went to the farm Sue had to stay behind in case the 'phone rang for rides. We kept pigs in the orchard and she complained they had the best site on the farm with wonderful views facing south. Sue designed a house and took the plans round to several builders for quotes. I realised then that I would have to give in and sell the house in Malton and build one at the farm. The quotes were all too high and then one day, as luck would have it, I was attending the Vaux Dinner at Redcar and found myself sitting next to Alderman Bob Cattle, ex-Lord Mayor of York and a building contractor. We got on to the subject of house-building and he told me not to do anything until he had quoted a price. Fortunately his price was acceptable, so the pigs moved out of the orchard and we moved into our new house in April 1968.

In February 1966 the *Sporting Life*'s Aubrey Renwick telephoned with the sad news that Captain Elsey had died. He was 85. His health had taken a turn for the worse the previous September when his leg had been amputated. I owe more than words can say to the Captain for giving me the opportunity to ride good horses and for all his help and advice over the years. He was like a second father to me; if ever I had a problem with regard to racing, I could always go to him for advice. I admired him and greatly respected his opinions: he had tremendous knowledge of horses and racing and it is a great honour to have been so closely associated with him. Phil Bull said of the Captain: 'He was much more than just a skilful trainer. Everyone who knew him regarded him not merely with respect, but with real affection'.

So a number of factors contributed to the atmosphere of sadness that infected Highfield Stables as I arrived to start riding work a month before the start of the 1966 season. Things brightened up in May when Sue gave birth to a daughter who we named Elizabeth. I was too tied up with my job to be able to spend much time with her but we took her racing a lot, and she loved all the attention the other racegoers gave her. As far as my riding was concerned, it wasn't to be a vintage year – I ended up with 59 winners. Lester enjoyed a tremendous season and was only nine short of his double century, but no other jockey managed to reach three figures.

Of significance, though, was a double I rode at Newcastle in August for Sir Gordon Richards when stable jockey Scobie Breasley was side-lined. It turned out to be a taste of things to come. The following spring Father was told by Gordon's close friend, Bill Kelly, that I was in the running for the job as stable jockey, although I heard nothing further that year. Sandy Barclay, an 18-year-old Scottish apprentice based with Harry Whiteman, deposed me as Cock of the North in

1966. His tally of 71 was only four short of my 1956 post-war record for an apprentice. As a result of his success, Sandy was given the job as second jockey to George Moore for Noel Murless at Warren Place.

The Murless-Piggott partnership had ended when Lester had decided not to ride the stable's filly Varinia in the Oaks, preferring the hot favourite, Valoris, trained by Vincent O'Brien. Lester's success owed as much to his judgement off a horse as his brilliance on one and he was rarely wrong. Valoris won and Varinia was only third. Lester's decision showed his single-minded determination to be on the right horse on the right day. But it was a selfish decision as well as a courageous one, and in 1967 it looked like backfiring on the Long Fellow. That year, the Murless stable carried all before it with successes in the 1,000 Guineas, 2,000 Guineas, Derby, Eclipse and King George, courtesy of Fleet, Royal Palace and Busted. However, it could have been worse for Lester. Although he and Ribocco finished only second to Royal Palace at Epsom, the partnership went on to success in the Irish Derby and the Doncaster St Leger, on both occasions beating a Murless runner into second place. Thereafter, starting with Sir Ivor in 1968, Lester and Vincent O'Brien went on to dominate the European racing scene for the next decade.

It was my custom to visit Highfield just before Christmas to give the staff their presents and to look over the horses to see how they were wintering. It was sad to see the horses stabled in only the main yard – the farm side was now empty. Bill told me that the business was running at a loss, and we agreed to cut the retainer by half. Highfield had started the 1965 season with 83 horses; it had only half that number with which to go to war in 1967. The loss of around 20 horses owned and managed by Mr Bull left a big gap, and one or two other owners who had dropped out hadn't been replaced. When winners dry up, horses are sold or sent to stud and potential owners look elsewhere. The decline becomes a vicious circle.

Fortunately, one of Bill's horses, Pia, turned out to be the year's Oaks winner. She had failed to reach her reserve of 600 guineas as a yearling and Stephanie von Schilcher, stud manager to the filly's owner, Countess Batthyany, approached Bill at the sales to have a look at Pia and the other two they were selling on behalf of the Ballykeane Stud in Ireland. Bill thought they were quite ordinary but he jokingly said, 'If you can't sell them, you'd better send them to me'. They couldn't, and the Countess took Bill up on his offer. They agreed to put Pia in training on the condition that the other two were leased out.

Described by her trainer as a plain filly, Pia had a cosmopolitan background; she was by the Guineas winner Darius out of the German-bred mare Peseta II, who raced in France. What we couldn't see was the one thing she did possess – a big heart. Pia ran six times as a two-year-old winning three of her starts and running second twice. She followed her debut second at Haydock with an easy all-the-way win at Newcastle against modest opposition. Those tactics were repeated in the Cherry Hinton Stakes at Newmarket, where for the first time she met St Pauli Girl, who was to become a regular rival, and beat her half-a-length.

The Seaton Delavel Stakes at Newcastle was ruined as an effective race when we, and several others, were unable to jump off on terms after a horse unseated its rider immediately in front of us. 'Starts' like this reinforced the case for starting stalls to be universally adopted. Pia was one of the outsiders for the Lowther Stakes, possibly because many hadn't appreciated how badly she had been affected by the Newcastle 'schmozzle' of a start. She battled on to win this one, which was then run over five furlongs, by a head from Meander. Although she extended that margin to three-quarters of a length in the Cheveley Park, she was herself out-pointed on that occasion by the Murless filly, Fleet.

Pia took a long time to come to herself in the spring and actually made her debut in the 1,000 Guineas where, considering her form, she seemed almost ignored in the market at 33–1. She led into the Dip and fought on with great courage to finish fourth to Fleet, beaten just over half a length. Fleet was a lady of moods and had planted and refused to race at the start of her intended reappearance in the Thirsk Classic Trial. Come Epsom, Pia had a choice of engagements, between the Oaks and the Ebbisham Stakes which was for three-year-old fillies over one mile 110 yards. Had the decision been left to me, I would probably have chosen the easier race, but fortunately Bill decided to go for the Oaks, reasoning that it would be better for her stud career if she could be placed in the big one rather than win the Ebbisham.

There were 12 runners and Fleet, who hadn't run since the Guineas, was favourite. Pia had disappointed previously in the Musidora, which had been run on heavy going, but on the day at Epsom she travelled comfortably and led over a furlong out to hold on well, reversing Guineas placings with both St Pauli Girl and Fleet, who were second and fourth respectively. Had I been more confident of success, I probably wouldn't have made plans to ride at Haydock that evening. However, the stable was running a two-year-old, Captivated, with an excellent chance and so I had to miss the opportunity of being presented to the Queen.

After the races I returned to Southport and 'phoned home, expecting Sue to still be excited about Pia's victory. She sounded very quiet and I realised something was amiss. She explained that only half an hour earlier her father, who was staying with us at Malton, had collapsed and died. It was totally unexpected as he had been a very fit man, although he had become very agitated when Sue, who was expecting our second child that December, was jumping up and down and shouting me home while watching the Oaks on television that afternoon.

Pia finished a disappointing last of six on unsuitable ground in the Yorkshire Oaks before going on to dead-heat with Pink Gem, ridden by George Moore, in the Park Hill Stakes. George's mount didn't help my cause by leaning all over me in the final furlong, preventing me from using my stick. Had there been a patrol film, there is little doubt that I would have been awarded the race outright. Pia's old adversary St Pauli Girl, incidentally, was two lengths back in third place. Having won this relative stamina test over an extended one and three-quarter miles, Pia could perhaps have been forgiven her disappointing run in the Sun Chariot next at Newmarket over one and a quarter miles. However, her last appearance was in the Champion Stakes, over the identical course and distance to the Sun Chariot, and she ran an excellent race to finish fourth to Reform, Taj Dewan and Royal Palace. By the time she retired Pia had won £34,713 in total. She remains the last Northern-trained filly to win the Oaks; perhaps she is the last there will ever be now that the South dominates racing. If that proves to be the case, then I suppose it was a pretty special honour to have ridden her to this notable victory.

- 11 -

Working with a Legend

SIR Gordon Richards telephoned me one sunny summer evening not long after we had moved into the new house at Huttons Ambo. Gordon had been training for the previous four years at Whitsbury. For 13 years his stable jockey had been Scobie Breasley, but I knew that Scobie was about to retire and that Gordon would therefore be looking for a replacement. My intuition proved to be well-founded. Gordon asked if I would be interested in riding as his stable jockey the following season. Interested? He had to be joking! I thought back to those years when I had ridden little Sixpence around the fields pretending to *be* Gordon, and now here he was asking me to be his stable jockey. The prospect filled me with excitement.

Ten days later, I met Gordon and Lady Richards for a general discussion over a picnic lunch. I wasn't expected to give him an immediate answer but obviously he needed to know before too long. The main advantage for me, apart from the fulfilment of a youthful dream, was the prospect of riding better-class horses. Gordon had attracted some influential and successful patrons since he had started training, among them Michael Sobell and his son-in-law, Arnold Weinstock, both of whom were to be knighted in the early 1970s.

Michael Sobell had taken up racing as a relaxation from business. In 1960, following the death of Miss Dorothy Paget, he had purchased her Ballymacoll stud and 120 of her horses. He had already bred many winners including the good miler Reform, who had been trained by Gordon and had recently retired to stud, having won 11 of his 14 races. Another of Gordon's main owners was Lady Beaverbrook, who was a determined bidder at the yearlings' sales. Once she had taken a fancy to a horse she was seldom thwarted; she was rumoured to have sometimes named a horse before it had even entered the sale ring!

For me, Gordon's offer was very timely. It was becoming increasingly obvious that Highfield was no longer the force it had been in terms either of quality or of the quantity of horses in the yard. It was around this time that the North-South divide really started to hit the Northern trainers, and Highfield seemed to be bearing the brunt of it. The reasons for this widening chasm were diverse, but the better roads that were being built were certainly a contributory factor. Up to this time most of the big owner-breeders had kept a couple of horses in training in the North. In general these would be their second-string horses, animals that were unlikely to win top-class races in the South but would pick up less competitive races in the North quite easily. This type of horse was very welcome and often made an important contribution to a stable's tally of winners. But the advent of motorways and bypasses, together with improvements in horsebox design, took much of the stress out of transporting horses by road. Now the owners could just as easily have all their animals trained in the South, and send them on raids up to the North, often travelling up and back in the same day.

The 1968 season was to be my most disappointing in terms of winners for 13 years. My supply of good rides was drying up. The chance to ride for a man of Gordon's calibre was a tremendous morale-booster at such a time. In all walks of life success breeds success, and in racing it's a true saying that good horses make good jockeys – no jockey yet born has been able to go without the horse, not even Gordon and Lester rolled into one.

Nevertheless, the decision wasn't clear cut. It would be a big wrench to move away from Highfield after 17 successful years during which I had been Cock of the North six times. I would be a relative new boy in the South, and would have to establish myself over again. Out of politeness, I told Lord Allendale, one of the major owners at Highfield, about Gordon's offer. This served only to make the decision tougher, for he personally offered to up the retainer by a substantial amount for the following two years.

Another disadvantage would be having to leave the farm and the new house and finding someone to look after the mares and young-stock, something we had always done ourselves. Thinking about it now, I suppose some people wouldn't have made the same decision. After all, I had a comfortable place to live with my family and a secure job, and if I had been less ambitious I could have been quite happy going along in the North. At the end of the day did it really matter? Clearly it did. I did not want to settle for being an also-ran. After a good deal of thought, I came to what had to be the inevitable decision career-wise and accepted Gordon's offer.

Towards the end of the 1968 season I was given a taste of things to come when I teamed up with one of Gordon's two-year-olds to win at Doncaster. The horse, Test of Friendship, was not in this case an appropriately-named horse as I can't recall a serious cross word with

Gordon during the following couple of years. Since Wally Swinburn was riding in France, we were able to rent his house at Burghclere for the first year. Both Hampshire trainer Bill Wightman and Lambourn trainer Major Peter Nelson approached me with offers of second retainers. Much as I would like to have accepted Bill Wightman's offer, I plumped for the Major's as he had the more powerful string, but I did ride for Mr Wightman on numerous occasions.

In taking over from Scobie Breasley I was following in illustrious footsteps. Scobie had ridden for Gordon almost from the start of Gordon's training career – something that speaks volumes for both men. It's always a good sign when two people can work together for such a long time. Right from his early days in Australia, Scobie had had an obsession with riding on the inside. He told me later that this had got him into trouble with the authorities over there as it often caused other jockeys problems. I saw a good example of this one day at Royal Ascot in a one-and-a-half mile race. As I was drawn alongside Scobie, I was able to observe his determination to get on to the inner rail. Although surrounded by horses, he took a shorter hold on the right rein to turn his mount's head inwards, and if anybody happened to be in the way, tough!

Obviously, there were times when Scobie's preference for the inner cost him a race or two, but on the other hand it certainly won him many. I usually preferred to ride a race in which I had more flexibility to manoeuvre. If I wasn't sure which of the two horses in front of me was going the better I tried to keep my options open by positioning my horse to track both. This didn't always go down too well with my fellow jockeys. Scobie's argument for his particular tactic was that there was only one side to worry about. My recollection of Gordon Richards as a jockey was that he seemed to prefer to be up with the leaders, although he could ride a waiting race when required. When I rode for him Gordon usually liked his horses to be settled off the pace and given plenty of time, and I've always felt that Scobie's influence had a hand there.

Whitsbury, where Gordon trained in two yards rented from William Hill, was an hour's drive south-west of Newbury. The gallops were some of the best in the country, nicely on the incline without being as stiff as those at Highfield. David Elsworth now operates from there very successfully under both rules. Every trainer has his own system of preparing horses: that is one reason why riding work for various people is so interesting. Captain Elsey used different methods from Father, and Gordon in his turn differed from the Elseys. I appreciated Gordon's meticulous attention to detail; he would never risk damaging a gallop by crossing it in his Land Rover but would always go the long way round, even to reach a spot only a few yards away.

He was always very concerned that the horses shouldn't become bored. Most trainers with a number of horses to work in a morning would keep the string circling at the bottom of the gallop, waiting for the jockeys to come back from working the previous batch. The horses that ended up working last would have a long time to think about it. Gordon always did his best to avoid this and would send the horses off on a long circular walk while they were waiting their turn to gallop so that they were always relaxed when it finally came.

Gordon's work riders, Brian Procter and Tony Kimberley, will also recall that he preferred to work his horses in threes and fours. Each piece of work was organised as if it were a military operation. The horses would set off in single file. About three furlongs out the last horse would move up to the one in front; then the two would move up to the second, and then all three would catch up with the leader. They would all stride on for the last two furlongs, past the boss at the top of the gallops. Woe betide the rider of the leading horse if he went before the other horses had the chance to draw upsides! Although they didn't hang about early on, Gordon hated it if his horses were struggling as they passed him; he liked them to finish with some zip and to have enjoyed their work. He was renowned for his long sight and hearing and there was very little he missed on the gallops.

While he watched all this, Gordon would often be active, too. One hand would be beckoning, calling a horse on; the other raised to slow another down. When on the odd occasion he took off his hat, threw it on the ground and jumped on it, you knew that things hadn't gone as smoothly as he had intended. But he wasn't a man to harbour a grudge and grievances were soon forgotten. He was very good at public relations and was well-respected by his lads. Tony Kimberley described him as a terrific employer.

Morgan Scannell was head lad and had full authority in the yard. However, if someone had a grievance and threatened to leave, Gordon would say to the lad, 'Call into the office and have a word before you go'. He possessed a silver tongue – he could have sold sand to the Arabs. Often the lad would emerge shaking his head, believing that it was he, after all, who had been in the wrong.

Gordon had a twinkle in his eye which betrayed a dry sense of humour. One day a lad who had annoyed his colleagues was put in a sack and buried in the muck heap, just his head protruding, to teach him a lesson. No sooner had the job been done than the lads heard Gordon's car approaching and dived for cover. Gordon, seeing the head sticking out, stopped the car. 'Now then, son, what are you doing in there?' they heard him ask. 'I think I must have annoyed somebody, sir', was the reply. Having experienced such pranks himself in the past Gordon, of course, realised what was going on. 'It'll do you good,' he commented, 'you needed to lose a bit of weight, anyway', and he promptly got back into his car and drove off.

It has been said that Gordon wasn't as good a trainer as he was a jockey, but after a riding career like his that was expecting the impossible. After all, he didn't start training until he was over 50 – an age at which he could easily have gone into graceful retirement. While he may never have made it to the very top as a trainer he was definitely in the first league; he never overrated his horses, placed them well and gained notable success with such horses as Pipe of Peace, Court Harwell, London Cry, Induna, Greengage and Reform.

If I had a criticism of Gordon's training it was only from a purely selfish point of view: by the time I joined the stable he was content to take a more leisurely, less ambitious approach than my own. He trained a number of horses for Mrs Anne Biddle, who owned the Pollardstown Stud in Ireland. One day he said, 'Edward, two or three of her two-year-olds are only capable of winning at somewhere like Folkestone. I'm going to send them back to Ireland to let her have a bit of fun with them over there'. I would have been happy to have gone to Timbuctoo, never mind Folkestone, for a winner, but I wasn't in a position to argue. Gordon was never one to rush his horses – he usually gave a horse a few days off after running and a minimum of two weeks between races – so it wasn't until 1 April that I was asked to ride work for him.

Tuesdays and Fridays were work days and I would usually arrive at about 7.30 a.m., in time to join him for breakfast. As soon as the meal was over, Gordon was out of the dining-room in a flash, heading for his Land Rover, which would be parked by the front door. I had to be quick or I was in danger of being left behind. While we were eating our breakfast, the first lot would have been on their way to the gallops. By the time we arrived, the horses were ready to canter. Gordon believed in a steady canter; Captain Elsey's horses had gone a bit faster and these days, Henry Cecil's go faster still. They all produce winners so who is to say which method is right?

As part of his policy of avoiding boredom in his horses Gordon was a great believer in giving them a change of scenery. He made good use of Salisbury racecourse and would take them there on the odd morning or on a race-day to gallop after racing. On the first day I rode work at Salisbury, I left Newbury at 6 a.m. I rode three separate lots there, dashed back to the stables to work two more, and after breakfast worked another two before changing on the gallops and leaving at midday to ride at Ascot. This may sound hectic but it was what I enjoyed – being involved. The spring is the most exciting time of a racing year; hopes are high because all the unexposed horses are good until proved otherwise.

As I had expected, we were a bit slow off the mark and it wasn't until May that I rode my first winner for Gordon: Beauty, at Salisbury. In the meantime, I had made a good start with Peter Nelson, riding four winners for him. Among those was Fortissimo, who was successful at Ascot. He had previously beaten Crozier a short head in the John Porter Stakes at Newbury, but the placings were reversed in the Stewards' Room after an objection from the rider of the runner-up, Duncan Keith. Whatever the stewards had decided that day it would have been controversial. The chief steward at Newbury, Lord Sefton, had sold his Kingsdown Stables to Fortissimo's trainer Peter Nelson, but was also said to have no great affection for the horse's owner Major Victor McCalmont. He was in a no-win situation – someone would have accused him of bias whatever the outcome of the inquiry! My brother Tony was also working at Kingsdown that year as a 'supervisor', Father having retired at the end of the 1968 season.

Lady Beaverbrook's Miracle, who went on to win the Solario Stakes, had been showing promise at home and I thought he would go well in his first race at the Newmarket Guineas meeting. Halfway through the five-furlong race I was tucked in behind the leaders and, unsure of a clear run, I had switched him to the outside. We made progress and were in with a chance at the Dip but weakened to finish a close sixth. Later that afternoon, Gordon took me to one side. 'Edward,' he said, 'as long as you ride for me, never do that again. Stay where you are. Nine times out of ten the opening will come and if it doesn't, don't worry, there'll always be another day.' He couldn't have given my confidence a bigger boost. That's what any jockey would like to hear, and coming from Gordon I knew he meant it.

Whenever you are not sure of getting a clear run at the back of your mind you wonder if the trainer or owner will be able to take it if you don't find a way through. That worry sometimes makes you over-anxious, and so you pull your horse out for a run on the outside even though you are thus running the risk of unbalancing it, and of course it will have further to run. Now I knew that I didn't have to worry about this any more when I was riding for Gordon, and implicit in his words was the reassurance that he would always back me up with the owners if the need arose.

After that, whenever he said to me in the paddock before a race, 'Drop it in, give it a chance and come the nearest way', I had the patience to wait for the openings which, strangely, nearly always came. It was positive thinking, I suppose. When you have confidence in yourself and in your trainer, things usually go right.

I once mentioned Gordon's words to another trainer. 'I'm exactly the same, Edward', he agreed, but I knew that he didn't mean it. If a horse of his was beaten I could imagine him saying to his owner, 'What the hell is Hide up to?' and if the owner had wanted a change of jockey next time he would have been happy to go along with him. Few trainers were as loyal to their jockeys as Gordon. Another trainer would avoid speaking to me as I unsaddled, if his horse had only been placed when he thought it should have won. Instead he would go to the horse's offside and mutter, just loud enough for me to hear, 'Hard luck horse. It wasn't your fault' as he patted its neck comfortingly. That sort of thing did wonders for your ego!

When I first went South Duncan Keith appeared to have a grudge against me. I could never fathom out why, but it was suggested that he was jealous, feeling that he should have been offered the job with Gordon. I couldn't quite work this out because he had as good a job, if not a better one, with Peter Walwyn.

In the 1,000 Guineas he was riding the second favourite, Lucyrowe, for his own stable, and I was riding Knighton House for Gordon. We were drawn together, and in the early stages of the race I was tracking a fancied horse and Duncan wanted my position. There was a bit of argy-bargy – nothing serious – I told him to eff off and held my place. In any race, let alone a classic, you don't give an inch until you know your chance has gone. That is virtually all that happened. Lucyrowe was beaten ten lengths behind the fourth horse and I finished just behind her. I didn't find out until much later that Duncan had blamed me for costing him the Guineas. That was absolute rubbish – what I found hardest to believe, though, was that Peter Walwyn took him seriously. Up to that point, I had ridden a few winners for Peter, but he never asked me to ride for him again. After Morston won the 1973 Derby, he was overheard expressing the opinion that Morston must have been a bloody good horse to win with me riding him! Lucyrowe later proved herself a top-class filly, beating Knighton House into second place in the Coronation Stakes at Royal Ascot and adding the Ebbisham and Sun Chariot Stakes to her tally. So the Walwyn stable's high hopes of her in the 1,000 Guineas were justified, but it certainly wasn't me that sabotaged her chance.

Duncan's hostility reached a peak of absurdity after a large field of maidens had run at Newbury one day. A few heated voices were raised when the jockeys returned to the weighing-room. There had been one or two problems during the race and Duncan laid the blame squarely at my feet. I let this go on for a while before I enlightened him: I hadn't even been riding in the race but had been a spectator in the stands. He didn't quite know what to say to that! I felt a certain amount of sympathy for Duncan because he had a serious weight problem which was obviously worrying him. In 1972 he was forced to quit because of his losing battle with the scales; 'it's either that or risk a nervous breakdown', he said. Later on we got on well enough together. When you're riding against each other day in, day out it is pointless and dangerous to harbour grudges.

At the end of July, Gordon told me that there had been a break-down in the relationship between himself and William Hill over the second yard and that he would therefore have to leave the stables.

He had never liked the smaller yard because the horses had to come out on to a dangerous road. He was now on the look-out for another place to train. Apparently, at one stage Lady Beaverbrook offered to set Gordon up at Freemason Lodge at Newmarket, but he was adamant that he would never go to Headquarters to train. He preferred the downs and enjoyed the privacy of his own gallops. Until the end of September I was on tenterhooks, my hopes see-sawing. One day Gordon would be full of confidence that he had found a suitable place, and the next hopes were dashed. At the end of the month came the good news that Gordon would continue to train at Whitsbury and wanted me to carry on riding for him. The bad news was that he was keeping only the top yard, with 34 boxes and only Messrs Sobell and Weinstock and Lady Beaverbrook as patrons. Back in the summer Peter Nelson had informed me that Major McCalmont wanted me to ride as first jockey for his stable. However, we eventually agreed to continue with the previous arrangement whereby he had second claim on me.

One of the biggest disappointments when I arrived at Whitsbury was the news that the potential stable star, Hymn, had suffered a hairline fracture of the pelvis and would be side-lined for some time. He had been so impressive in winning his only start towards the back-end at Newmarket that Scobie had told Gordon he could be retiring a year too soon. It was September before Hymn made his reappearance, winning a conditions race at Salisbury in effortless fashion. It was then decided to aim him for the Irish St Leger.

The evening before the race Gordon and I flew to Dublin. In the morning he had me up well before 6 a.m., and together we went to the Curragh where, after a preliminary canter, Hymn worked a sharp four furlongs. Gordon loved his walking – he would often take off in the afternoon after curling in St Moritz for a hike through the woods – and even then, at 65, he had me tagging along as we covered every yard of the one-and-three-quarter-mile St Leger course. I had worked up a healthy appetite by the time we got back to the Shelbourne Hotel. Disappointingly, though favourite, Hymn finished only third to Reindeer and Deep Run.

These days it is common to see jockeys coming over to the stands side at Goodwood when the ground is soft. I feel that I pioneered this particular tactic. On the first day of the September meeting in 1969 I noticed that the officials' cars going down the stands side to the various starts had made the going firmer. The following morning I discussed this with Gordon over breakfast, and he was in full agreement with my unorthodox plan to race on the ground consolidated by the cars. This method resulted in four winners, including two for our stable. Although cars no longer go down the track today the stands side is still favoured in wet weather.

One of Gordon's winners that day, incidentally, was the two-year-old debutant, Rock Roi. This horse, transferred to Peter Walwyn when Gordon retired, became notorious for passing the post first in both the 1971 and 1972 Ascot Gold Cups, only to have the races taken away from him after failing the dope test on the first occasion and hampering the runner-up on the second.

Before the start of the 1970 season, Sue and I bought a house on the outskirts of Newbury. Gordon and Major Nelson's strings were backward and it wasn't until Good Friday that I first rode out for Gordon. Nonetheless, we had our first winner at Newmarket in April with Richboy, who went on to land the Britannia at Royal Ascot. I rode a double at Alexandra Park in May – my first winners on the track we called the 'frying pan'. This venue, unpopular with jockeys, was a sharp, right-handed track. The 'handle' was the five-furlong course, the start of which was out of sight of the stands. The one mile and one mile five furlong starts were in front of the stands, and the horses ran down the straight, completed one or two circuits of the round course and came back up the straight to the finish: round the frying pan and up the handle! No jockey was sorry when the course closed at the end of that season; with the camber against you, it could resemble a skating rink after a shower of rain.

Folkestone was another course I was happy to avoid after my experience there that summer. I rode the favourite for John Dunlop in a mile-and-a-half race, and although I was beaten, I was relieved to complete the course in one piece. Two horses fell and another stumbled so badly that it failed to recover and was tailed off. The last two races were abandoned. This was another course where, when it had rained on firm ground, the jockeys wished they were riding elsewhere. After riding a winner there later in the season for Bill Wightman, it wouldn't have bothered me if I'd never set eyes on the place again! My brother Tony was also thankful that I came away in one piece on that occasion, because I was to be best man at his wedding the following day at Newmarket. We managed to fit in nine holes of golf in the morning, to calm the nerves. Tony married Susie Liddell, whose mother is from an old-established racing family of Newmarket. The reception was held at the racecourse.

As Gordon's lease at Whitsbury was due to expire in the autumn of 1970 there was again an element of doubt about the future. At one time, Gordon had hoped to move to Manton, where he had always wanted to train, and Whatcombe, where Arthur Budgett trained, was another possibility. Finally, Jakie Astor sold West Ilsley Stables to the Sobell-Weinstock partnership on the specific condition that Dick Hern remained as trainer and Joe Mercer as jockey. Gordon's new role was to be racing manager to the Sobells and Lady Beaverbrook, and I was out of a job.

The main reason for coming South in the first place was the chance to work with Gordon. Having ridden 139 winners in my two years with him, I felt that the move had been a success and would have been prepared to stay in the South had a decent job come up. Travelling back from Brighton races one day, Peter Nelson and I came to an agreement that I would ride as first jockey for him the following season. Before he left for a trip to France in August he called in at my house and dropped off a draft contract for me to peruse while he was away. Upon his return a fortnight later, I turned up to ride work at Kingsdown only to discover that Major Nelson's offer was more or less withdrawn – it appeared that they would not now be taking on as many young horses as they had first thought. Clearly he had changed his mind while he had been away.

Shortly afterwards I was offered a job with Geoff Barling, who trained a string of 40 horses at Newmarket and who had recently enjoyed international success with Tower Walk. Within a week of making the offer he wrote to me, saying that as he hadn't heard anything, the owners had instructed him to look elsewhere. I hadn't been aware of any urgency for my decision. After one or two other possibilities had been explored I accepted an offer from Bill Elsey to return to the old firm. I had kept on the farm, so it was back home.

At Yarmouth in September I won an ordinary nursery on Pouve The Gri, trained by Tommy Gosling. It completed a personal milestone for me: I had ridden a winner on every course in Great Britain. Nine of these – Alexandra Park, Birmingham, Bogside, Hurst Park, Lanark, Lincoln, Manchester, Stockton and Worcester – are no longer in use. At Newbury in late October, I rode Gordon's last runner, Desert Singer, who finished sixth of 30. Before we went back to Yorkshire Sue and I threw a party for some of our friends in the South. We had enjoyed a fuller social life there than at home; most Saturday evenings we used to meet up for a meal with several of the jockeys and their wives. Joe and Anne Mercer and Jimmy and Pat Lindley were particularly kind to us during our time in the South.

In retrospect I feel that the two years spent with Gordon were the happiest of my racing career, and I regret that our association was such a short one. I was flattered to read Gordon's tribute to me in an article by Tim Richards. He said: 'Edward rides with his head, never knocks horses about unnecessarily and is always thinking about his mount's future'. Coming from him this meant a tremendous amount to me. Many people have been instrumental in the success I've enjoyed but Father, Captain Elsey and Gordon are the three I would single out as having had the most influence on my career.

– 12 –
Waterloo

AFTER two years away from Highfield I returned in fairytale fashion when I won the 1971 Lincoln on the stable's Double Cream. Originally, Bill Elsey had fancied Pabella for the race, and for a while it looked as though she would be my mount at Doncaster. However, Double Cream began to improve as the race drew nearer, and when Pabella worked disappointingly and then coughed she was withdrawn and I switched mounts. Because Double Cream was a free-going horse, in his last piece of work Bill sent him up on his own over seven furlongs. Most horses look good passing trees, but he gave me a great feel and really impressed me so I was optimistic for the big race. Nonetheless, he started at 33–1.

Not over-endowed with courage, he was happiest when up with the leaders and out of trouble. He had the early pace to dispute the lead and I sent him on at the three-furlong marker. He stayed on well to beat Tandy by half-a-length. After the race a delighted Bill Elsey was quoted as saying: 'We intend to go on as we have begun'. Unfortunately, as far as Highfield was concerned, the Lincoln was one of the few things that went right that year. At the end of May the stable once against went down with the virus. Bill believed it to be the same strain as the one that had affected the Hern stable in the late 1960s. Sam Hall's yard was also affected. The horses looked well, ate well and worked well, but when the chips were down they found nothing at the end of their races. Bill sent out only 15 winners and in the middle of August he told me that for purely financial reasons he would be unable to offer me a retainer for the following season. One small consolation was that one of the 15, Pepperita, which Sue and I had sold as a yearling, was the first horse from our stud that I rode to victory. Obviously, I derived great enjoyment from the previous ten winners we had bred, but this one was particularly satisfying. As stable jockey I had been involved with her at Highfield so had been connected with her from start to finish.

On hearing of my return Northwards Bill Watts, who trained at Richmond in Yorkshire, had approached me to ride for him when not required by Highfield. We also agreed that whenever possible I would ride work for him twice a week. Bill, the son of Jack Watts, comes from one of racing's most famous families. Bill's father, who died in 1988, trained the St Leger winner, Indiana, in 1964 and also enjoyed successes with Ovaltine and Sing Sing from Machell Place, where my brother Tony had been based for some years.

One of Bill's early ambitions was to become a jockey but he soon grew too heavy, and on leaving school in 1959 he became assistant trainer to his father before becoming a race-reader for *Raceform*. Bill always said that he learned a lot from that three-year spell, particularly as regards the way certain trainers placed their horses. He went back for another period as assistant to his father before branching out on his own in 1967 at the Pegasus Stables in Newmarket. At the end of 1970 Bill took over Hurgill Lodge at Richmond from Walter Wharton.

I had ridden Bill's first winner on the Flat, Rasping, at Catterick in 1968. His first-ever winner, Prospect Pleases, had scored over hurdles at Leicester only a few minutes earlier. He started the 1971 season with 31 horses which, due to his success, he has more than doubled now. The death of Charles Engelhard in March was a big blow to the stable, but his nine horses stayed on to race in Mrs Engelhard's name. I have always regarded Bill very highly as a trainer. He gives much thought to the entering and placing of his horses and to the work arrangements on the home gallops. He has a choice of two gallops; the low moor and the high moor. The low moor is the old Richmond racecourse and the remains of the stand are still there. The sharp, right-handed bend at the bottom has caused me to miss a few heart-beats. The yard is approached by a steep climb out of the town, and the gallops are further up the hill on high, exposed ground. They call it a lazy wind up there – it doesn't go round you, it goes straight through.

Bill had achieved his greatest success up to then in the Royal Hunt Cup the previous season with Calpurnius, who gave me my first winner for the stable that year. At the start of the season you are always full of hopes although there seldom prove to be many swans among the geese. After riding work that spring, however, Bill and I realised that we had a couple of exciting prospects in Winter King and Waterloo. Winter King made his debut at York ridden by Brian Taylor – I was claimed by Bill Elsey to ride one of his – and beat Philip of Spain in a close finish. Three weeks later, I rode him to win the Cock of the North at Haydock, which he won without coming off the bit. Regrettably he split a pastern shortly afterwards and was unable to race again, in spite of a nine-hour operation at the Newmarket Research Station. It was a blow to me but must have been an enormous disappointment to Bill, as a young trainer just establishing himself. He rated Winter King every bit as good as Waterloo – he might well have been my best chance of winning the 2,000 Guineas, the only classic I missed out on.

Waterloo was a strong, lengthy, attractive filly by Bold Lad out of the Hyperion mare, Lakewoods, who had been unable to win a race for Jack Watts. She too made her winning debut at York, the day before Winter King. She beat the odds-on Pert Lassie, a filly of Henry Cecil's who had won her previous start at Newmarket. Her starting price was 14–1, although that would undoubtedly have been much shorter had she run the day after Winter King. Waterloo went to Royal Ascot next for the Queen Mary Stakes, where the going was completely different – it was now so heavy that there was a course inspection in the morning. Bill and the filly's owner, Mrs Susan Stanley, one of Bill's long-standing patrons, deliberated at length the day before over withdrawing Waterloo. As it turned out, they need not have worried; she was very impressive and won as she liked, coming home alone six lengths clear of her nearest rival.

After that performance it was disappointing when, next time out, we were only fifth to Sun Prince in the Prix Robert Papin at Maisons-Laffitte. She then suffered another reversal at the hands of Rose Dubarry in the Lowther Stakes at York. Although Waterloo had made all the running in winning the Queen Mary, Bill decided to have her held up on her next start at Ayr in the Harry Rosebery Trophy, in which she comfortably landed the odds. Her next race was the prestigious Cheveley Park Stakes at Newmarket, in which she was again held up before coming through smoothly to confirm what a top-class filly she was by beating the French-trained filly Marisela by a length and a half. After this, she was sent to her owner's stud for her winter holiday before returning to Bill to be prepared for a tilt at the 1,000 Guineas.

The spring of 1972 was very cold and wet in Yorkshire and, as the filly's classic loomed, I worried that Waterloo wouldn't have time to come to herself. When she ran in the Thirsk Classic trial in the middle of April she was beaten seven lengths into third place by High Top, who made all the running and was to go on to win the 2,000 Guineas. We were not surprised to be beaten but, with the big race only 12 days away, I was despondent because of the short space of time she had in which to show the necessary improvement. However, six days after Thirsk we galloped Waterloo, receiving 3 lb from the four-year-old Loudoun Gale, who was to win the William Hill Gold Cup at Redcar later that season, and giving 21 lb to Lyrello, another four-year-old and a useful Northern handicapper. It was a stiff task indeed for her at that stage of the season, but Waterloo answered our prayers by beating them in the gallop by four lengths. This was an impressive piece of work, and enabled us to go to Newmarket with renewed hope. For me, Bill's handling of Waterloo between Thirsk and New-market was his greatest training achievement while I was with him. Bill had realised that extra work was necessary but hadn't overdone it, and Waterloo arrived on the day ready to run for her life.

Even though Waterloo had not hit the front until approaching the Dip in the Cheveley Park, I felt I had gone too soon as she had idled once there. I was therefore determined to delay my challenge until as late as possible. Bill's advice in the paddock was, 'When you're ready to go, count to three before doing so'. Waterloo was drawn towards the outside and, after we jumped off smartly, I tucked her in behind the leaders and then looked for a suitable filly to track. Tony Murray was going well on the favourite, Rose Dubarry, the filly that had beaten us in the Lowther, and so I dropped in behind them. Rose Dubarry squeezed through a gap to take up the running approaching the last quarter of a mile, and I followed her through and produced Waterloo to lead on meeting the rising ground with less than a furlong to run. We came clear to win by two lengths, with Marisela again taking second place just ahead of Rose Dubarry. Waterloo's win was the first Northern 1,000 Guineas success since Honeylight in 1956 and the first classic win for the North since Pia in 1967. She had been sent up to Richmond with the idea of trying to win a small maiden race and had certainly exceeded those modest hopes.

Many great racemares have something masculine in their make-up and it is interesting that Bill always claimed Waterloo was more like a colt than a filly to train. She seldom came in season while she was in training, which made planning her work much easier. Perhaps this masculinity helps to explain why many top racemares are difficult to breed from. Cantelo proved almost impossible to get in foal and Petite Etoile had only two live foals in her first eight years at stud. Park Top also had a poor breeding record. Waterloo, however, was something of an exception to the rule and did go on to produce winners, the best to date being the high-class two-year-old Water Cay.

It is a physical fact, so I have read, that the female of most species is handicapped in competing against the male by having a smaller heart and lungs, less blood in her system and therefore fewer blood cells to carry oxygen to the muscles. In human sport as well as horse-racing it is self-evident that the 'masculine' female participant has an advantage over her more feminine opponent. But perhaps we should not then be surprised when some of these 'tomboys' do not later take kindly to traditional feminine activities like motherhood! On the subject of the battle of the sexes, 1972 was the year the Jockey Club sanctioned the running of a limited number of races restricted to women riders. This caused a lot of controversy at the time – few people then envisaged that by the 1980s there would be professional women jockeys competing against the men.

I had no objections to allowing women to ride: I thought it was only fair that if boys were given the chance then so should girls. However, I always felt they were fighting an uphill battle. Even if some girls might be physically strong enough to compete on equal terms with men, and this I doubt, the prejudice of owners and trainers against female jockeys means that most would be extremely lucky ever to have enough experience of race-riding to be much good at it. It costs owners the same to put up a girl apprentice as it does to employ the best jockey in the country, so it's hardly surprising that they don't give them many chances. It is very expensive to keep a horse in training; most owners, not unnaturally, want their horse to have the best poss-ible chance every time it runs, which of course means having the best possible rider. The few women who have achieved success in this country have usually managed it through having relatives loyal enough to give them the rides they needed to gain experience and develop their skill. If owners are prepared to give women rides on their horses they often prefer to do it in 'amateur' races, in which most of the other riders are women.

Waterloo's classic win was an added bonus in my first year as a freelance rider. This was the first time in 19 years that I hadn't been retained by a stable, and it was a totally new ball game for me. It turned out to be the most successful period of my whole career; from 1972 to 1977 I averaged over a century of winners per season. The only time I failed to top the ton was in 1975, when I was side-lined for two and a half months recovering from a broken leg.

The advantages of being retained by a leading stable are obvious: one has the security of a firm base and is guaranteed good horses to ride. A retained jockey has many decisions made for him – when there is more than one meeting in a day, for example, it is more often than not the claiming stable rather than his preference that determines where he goes. One of the advantages a freelance jockey has is that if he is offered a particularly good ride well in advance he is in a position to accept it, whereas a retained jockey has to wait until his own stable's plans are finalised before he is able to commit himself. Today the final declaration time is ten o'clock on the day before the horse is due to run, and often it is not until after that that the retained jockey is able to make final plans regarding outside rides.

One of the ways in which a freelance jockey can be reasonably sure of acquiring rides is riding work for those trainers who don't retain a jockey and who are willing to offer him rides. I was fortunate in that in the North Bill Watts, Mick Easterby, Rufus Beasley and Dick Peacock were all pleased to have me ride work for them, as were Michael Stoute, Bruce Hobbs and Bill Wightman in the South. I hoped that from that group of trainers a nucleus of good rides would materi-alise. I soon realised that early in the season it was important to see as many trainers as possible to establish whether they had any early sorts in their yards that would enable me to ride early winners. Later on, the form book was often the best guide. It is winners that count. Something Captain Elsey told me years ago has always remained firmly imprinted on my mind: 'Edward, if you don't train winners you soon cease to be a trainer'. The same rule applies equally to jockeys.

A successful jockey is a good jockey, but the reverse of that statement is not necessarily true. To get to the top of the tree takes more than riding skill. For a freelance, certainly before the days of agents, one of the most important factors was a thorough acquaintance with the form book so that on the occasions you had a choice of rides in a race you knew which one to choose. Linked with this, you also needed the diplomacy to keep connections happy when you had to turn them down, so that they would come back again another day. Few trainers appreciated the skill needed for this balancing act better than Mick Easterby, who told me on more than one occasion that I should have been a politician. I also had to learn to push myself forward. Early on in my career there were times, as I was watching a race from the stands, when a trainer would say to me, 'If I'd known that you hadn't a ride in this race you could have ridden mine'. Talk is cheap, but I made a mental note that in future I would make sure they knew when I was available.

In becoming more positive in chasing rides I took my lead from those who were already successful. One day in the weighing-room at Birmingham Doug Smith, who certainly wasn't one to sit and wait for rides to drop in his lap and who was then Champion Jockey, commented that he wouldn't like my 'phone bill. 'I don't like it either, Doug', I replied, 'but I'd sooner have mine than yours.' Lester, great jockey that he was, fully appreciated that to win it was necessary to obtain the ride on what he considered had the best chance of winning. It was rumoured that if Lester thought there was a better chance of getting the ride through the owner then he would by-pass the trainer. He in turn probably learned this tactic from his predecessor, Gordon Richards, who was one of the shrewdest ever when it came to ending up on the right horse. Sometimes, if he had the chance to ride a few fancied horses in one race, he was able, through talking to the trainers, to rearrange their horses' programmes so that he could ride the 'dangers' in other races instead.

Chasing rides was frowned upon by less successful people, but being a jockey is a tough and very competitive business. You can ask politely for rides until you're blue in the face, but unless you deliver the goods no one will give them to you. There are many ways in which trainers turn you down — one of the most popular get-outs is 'I'll speak to the owner and get back to you'. That is often the last the jockey hears from him. Another is: 'I haven't decided yet whether it runs or not'. It often did, but with someone else riding! There were plenty of races in which I knew I would be lucky to ride and I was therefore happy to accept the first that came my way. But when I had the choice of riding several in a race and had perhaps been offered what I considered the second or third best available I would try to keep my options open for as long as possible, checking with my first choice to see if I had a chance of riding it before coming to a decision.

Knowing the characteristics and quirks of trainers was very much part of being a freelance jockey. I soon learned to take some of their statements with a pinch of salt. If, for example, one of them rang up and asked me to ride something that they said was in with a great chance I knew this meant 'With a lot of luck in running, it might be in the first four'. On the other hand, there were those who said 'I think you should try to ride this for me', which I knew meant they considered it had a very good winning chance. You developed a mental form book for the way different people made their approaches. I always went where I thought I had the best chance of riding a winner; distance was never the main concern, one outstanding mount at a far-off meeting was preferable to two or three place chances at a local course.

My first year as a freelance couldn't have started better than with Sovereign Bill's success in the 1972 Lincoln. Sovereign Bill, who started joint favourite and landed a gamble, had already split a pastern three times and, as it was his first race for a year, it really was an outstanding piece of training by Newmarket-based Peter Robinson. The horse had joined Peter the previous May, wrapped in bandages. It was a happy postscript to the race five years earlier, when Peter had ridden Father's Ben Novus to victory. Sadly, in 1978 Peter was to die of a heart attack while returning from Salisbury racecourse.

In 1972 I rode a few winners for first-season trainer Michael Stoute. I had first met Michael in May 1966 when he was working for Pat Rohan. Pat seemed to have an endless stream of visiting cousins from Ireland, and initially Sue took Michael for one of them. Michael had only recently arrived from his native Barbados where his father was Commissioner of Police. He had turned up on Pat Rohan's doorstep with £25 in his pocket. He started to take out Sue's cousin, Pat Baker, and we saw a lot of him after that. From a very early stage it became apparent to me that all Michael needed was a bit of luck to reach the top in his chosen profession. He was always asking questions and expected full answers; he was keen and very self-confident. Sue used to tease him that he was all 'yap' and told him that was 75 per cent of what was needed to be a successful trainer.

Michael had been interested in horses from an early age, which was not surprising considering that the family home was right next to the Garrison Savannah racecourse in Barbados. His mentor was

Freddie Thirkell, an Englishman who had been apprenticed to Matt Peacock at Middleham and had gone out to the West Indies to ride before turning his hand to training. As a little boy, Michael followed Freddie everywhere, wanting to know about everything connected with the horses. One day when he asked 'Will I be a jockey?' Freddie replied, 'When you tell me which came first, the chicken or the egg, I'll tell you'. Michael went home and plagued his parents all evening for the answer!

One of his assets is that he is a good organiser. He spends a lot of time with his horses. Despite all his success as a trainer, Michael often threatens to come back in his next life as a jockey, to which I reply, 'Just because you have the ability to train a few horses what makes you think you'll be any good as a jockey?' He had no racing background as such but was willing to learn from all who could help him. Michael thought very highly of Bobby O'Ryan (father of jockey turned racing journalist, Tom), Pat Rohan's head lad. He used to pick my brains, too, for my views on certain aspects of racing. More recently I have been interested to hear his opinions in return.

From Pat Rohan Michael moved to Headquarters, where he furthered his knowledge with Doug Smith and 'Tom' Jones. Michael married Pat at Filey in June 1969. He spent the previous night at our home at Huttons Ambo and was very nearly late for his wedding as a result of having had a bet on one of my rides at Bath that afternoon and hanging on for the result. He needn't have bothered, because it wasn't in the first three. He started training at the small Cadlands yard before he and Pat purchased Beech Hurst at the top of the Bury Road in Newmarket. One trainer remarked that it was a foolish buy as it was an unlucky yard, and that it would be difficult to get staff because it was too far out of town for anyone to walk there. How wrong he was! I don't know of anyone who has achieved so much in such a short time. One sign of this success is that most of the staff drive up in their own cars! Diamond Sutra, who won at Catterick in mid-May, was the first of 94 winners I rode for Michael.

I am used to meeting nervous fillies in the paddock, but Rowena Sutton qualified as the most nervous owner I have ever ridden for when her filly Mayday Melody made her debut at Newcastle in August 1972. Rowena was literally shaking like a leaf. Later, she told me the story of Mayday Melody. With her very limited funds, she had wanted to purchase a horse to show jump or event but was persuaded by her mother to have a go at racing with a filly, already named Mayday Melody, which was known to be still for sale having failed to reach her reserve at Doncaster the previous autumn. Rowena admits that most of her mother's enthusiasm stemmed from the fact that Mayday Melody was from the second crop of her own stallion, Highland Melody, and that she was trying to muster as many two-year-olds to go into training as possible. Her mother also said, tongue in cheek, that she knew 'Mayday' was a good sort as her owner, a local farmer's daughter, had shown her in the hunter class at Derby County Show, where she'd come fourth!

After much consideration and discussion, Rowena decided to put her filly in training and, even after learning of her far-from-impressive pedigree and discovering how little she had cost, Bill Watts agreed to train her. He still had a bit of a shock when he first saw her, and diplomatically pronounced her to be 'strong'. Later, he confessed to Rowena that when she had requested, soon after 'Mayday's' arrival, that she should not be run in sellers, he had had to bite his tongue. 'What the hell have I taken on here?' he had said to his wife, Pat. 'This silly cow sends me a donkey-bred, plain-looking animal with the biggest head and biggest feet you've ever seen, and then says don't run the bugger in a seller!'

Bill saw no reason to change his opinion until the first time he asked the filly to go three-parts speed, working with three winners. Bill told the lad that when she tired he was just to sit still and not to push her. Far from tiring, when the four of them passed him near the end of the gallop, Mayday Melody was the only one on the bridle. It was pretty obvious that running her in a seller might not do her full justice, although it would undoubtedly have been a hell of a bet. The first time she ran it was apparent that the world and his wife thought she would take all the beating.

Years later, Rowena wrote to me reminiscing about that first race. 'Mother and I drove to Newcastle with the Watts. During the journey Bill tried to hint gently that he thought the filly might go well and wouldn't be surprised if she even won, but knowing that I wasn't interested in betting, and seeing through the driving mirror that I had turned a funny shade of green, he just left it at that. When, just before the off, I realised that she was quite a warm favourite I almost collapsed on the spot and nearly missed the whole thing. Somehow, having my own horse running in my own colours was almost too much for me. I shook like a leaf for most of the day and when I wasn't feeling extremely ill felt totally numb. Pat Watts was very kind to me and told me after they had passed the post that Mayday Melody had won, as at this stage I was still trying to focus my binoculars. Pat sat beside me on the stand for a few minutes as I felt rather faint and then helped me to find the winners' enclosure!'

Mayday Melody turned out to be good enough to compete in the first division and went on to win five races and to finish in the frame in the Vernon's Sprint Cup and the Prix de Meautry. She was also very successful as a broodmare, producing Chapel Cottage on whom I was to win the Cherry Hinton Stakes in 1983.

Gordon Richards, now managing Lady Beaverbrook's horses, rang me in October to tell me that Lady B. wanted me to ride the horses she had in training with Scobie Breasley. As much as I appreciated the request, I had too much going for me in the North to give up to ride a handful of horses in the South, so I had to decline. My first year as a freelance had gone well in terms of overall winners, especially with the successes of Waterloo. At the end of that season I was voted Flat Race Jockey of the Year at the annual Derby awards of the Horserace Writers' Association. When I received the award, a replica of Hyperion's hoof, I took the opportunity of thanking the press for all the co-operation and help they had given me throughout my career. I have always appreciated their helping hand and have never doubted that their good publicity aided my success. We all have jobs to do and it is to our mutual benefit to help each other. There was the odd reporter I did my best to avoid, but I am happy to say that over the years I came to regard most of the members of the racing press as my friends.

People are always complaining about reporters who misquote them or get facts wrong, but the only time I felt I had real grounds for criticising the press was on the day of the 1960 Derby, when the *Daily Sketch* provided their readers with a list of the jockeys' personal details. How the readers felt it was going to aid their selections to know the zodiac signs, colour of eyes and marital status of the riders I can't imagine, but I suppose it helped to fill up the page. Certainly these statistics were compiled without the hindrance of much research. Joe Mercer had been married to Anne for only 18 months and yet they were credited with three children! They did even better for me, describing me as single with two children. They knew more than I did.

That year I was also guest of honour at the Stable Lads' Northern Boxing Championship Dinner in Manchester. I was pleased to be invited but didn't look forward to the prospect of making a speech in front of some 600 people. I have always found public speaking an ordeal. Perhaps at the root of this is my early experience at the Shuttle-cock Dinner at St Moritz when, in front of 150 people, I was called upon by Lord Lucan, no less, to make a short speech. As a last-minute guest this task had been furthest from my mind, but I managed to blurt out a few words. I long ago decided that if having to 'say a few words' was the only penalty for being successful then I was prepared to pay it!

– 13 –
Morston

THE Derby has long been regarded as the greatest horserace in the world. Even to be given a ride in the big race is an achievement, and it is every jockey's dream to win the Blue Riband of the turf. Obviously few realise this ambition. Lester Piggott had a fantastic record in the race but it has eluded many other greats of the turf including former Champion Jockey Joe Mercer and five-times Champion Doug Smith. Indeed, it was only on his 26th and final attempt that Gordon Richards won it. When in 1973 Morston passed the post first at Epsom he fulfilled my own lifelong ambition. Furthermore, a particularly unusual sequence of circumstances led to our victory in the race.

Morston was bred, owned and trained by Arthur Budgett, for whom I had ridden the odd winner over many years. I have always wondered what might have happened had Gordon succeeded in buying the Whatcombe stables from Arthur Budgett when he was looking for a suitable set-up to prolong his training career. Mr Budgett may well have retired, but what would have happened to Morston? Would he have been left with Gordon or would he have been sent elsewhere? As it was, Morston made his debut in a maiden-at-closing at Lingfield where, in the hands of Frankie Durr, he beat the previous winner, Kinglet, from the Dick Hern stable. Frank obviously had first option on Morston for the Derby, which was chosen as the next race for this chestnut son of Ragusa even though Arthur Budgett thought it too soon for him. He believed Morston would benefit from being given as much time as possible in which to develop. However, as he felt there wasn't an outstanding horse in that year's race, he decided to let him take his chance. Frank had ridden Mon Fils to win the 2,000 Guineas that year for Richard Hannon and therefore had a choice of rides. Between Lingfield and the Derby Frank rang Richard Hannon and, expressing doubts about Mon Fils staying the trip, said he thought he should ride Morston, which Richard understood. Fortunately for me, Frank had second thoughts and subsequently changed his mind.

Meanwhile, I had been offered the ride on the outsider Flintstone, but had turned it down – as he had no chance I thought I would be better off riding at Ripon that afternoon, where I would have two or three winning chances. Twelve days before the big race, I was summoned from the weighing-room at Haydock to take a 'phone call from trainer Bernard Van Cutsem, who asked me to stand by to ride his Derby favourite, Ksar, as it was doubtful that stable jockey Willie Carson would be available, having been kicked on the ankle at Warwick the previous day. Willie, who never let on that he had actually cracked a bone in his ankle, was working hard to get himself fit, and after the accident travelled daily to London for treatment. As the race drew nearer, it appeared that Willie was indeed winning his fitness battle, but Mr Van Cutsem didn't want to take any chances and asked me to come to Newmarket on the Friday before the race to acquaint myself with Ksar. Willie actually took part in the same gallop to keep an eye on how his horse worked. The colt's owner, Lord Rotherwick, was also present along with Julian Wilson and the BBC cameras.

I stayed overnight at the Stoutes', and at breakfast that morning I received a 'phone call from Arthur Budgett asking me to ride Morston. I explained to Mr Budgett that I was standing by for Willie but that I expected him to be on Ksar at Epsom, and Mr Budgett agreed to give me until Sunday to confirm that I could ride for him. The form of Morston's win at Lingfield certainly didn't look up to Derby-winning standard, but on the plus side he was out of Windmill Girl, the dam of Blakeney, who had won the race for Mr Budgett only four years previously. I was still pondering on whether to ride at Ripon instead on Derby day, but Pat Stoute reasoned with me that there was, after all, only one Derby. I suppose there was never really any doubt that I would take the opportunity to ride an unbeaten half-brother to a Derby winner. From breakfast that morning, then, the die was cast. On Sunday morning, I explained the situation to Mr Van Cutsem and he agreed that it was unfair to keep me in reserve any longer, and I confirmed my acceptance of Mr Budgett's ride.

As I was riding at Newcastle on Monday and at Redcar on Tuesday, I had no chance to go down to Whatcombe to sit on Morston and so, come Derby day, I still hadn't even set eyes on the horse. I travelled to Epsom by train from York. Carrying a large holdall containing my saddle, helmet, whip and boots I boarded the bus from the station up to the racecourse. It would have been quicker to have walked as there was already a huge crowd assembling: the eventual total of 250,000 was the largest attendance since Coronation year in 1953. I saw Morston for the first time as I walked into the paddock. He was a fine, big chestnut colt who was taking everything very calmly and didn't look in the least bit perturbed. I couldn't have had more under-standing instructions from Mr Budgett, who dissipated the pressure on me by explaining that he thought Morston was a great horse in the making and, much as he would like to win the Derby a second time, whatever happened I was not to hurt the colt. 'He's an inexperi-enced horse', he added. 'Give him time to find his stride. Win if you can, but I do not want him knocked about.'

The first and second favourites, Ksar and Mon Fils, were in front of us as we paraded in front of the stands. They were receiving plenty of attention from the crowd at the rails but Morston, in only his second race ever, wasn't bothered in the least. In fact, his phlegmatic approach to the day must have been an important factor in his event-ual success. In the race Morston, my 13th ride in the Derby and number 13 on the racecard, settled nicely towards the rear. As in the Guineas, Mon Fils attempted to run the field into the ground and set a very fast pace. The turning-point of the race for me was when Willie Carson and Ksar came past as we were going down Tattenham Hill. I knew how well Ksar had gone when I had ridden him the previous week and, knowing he would give me a good lead, I moved out and tracked him from then on. Rounding the corner we were in the middle of the field, no more than seven lengths off the leader which was still Mon Fils. Straightening up for home, I remember thinking, we're still going well, we've got a chance! Obtaining a clear run Willie and Ksar hit the front with about two furlongs to go with me on their tail, and then, as they approached the final furlong, we quickened past them, resisting a late challenge from Lester and Cavo Doro, who was hang-ing in on me a little. Lester, with his stick in his right hand, was unable to give his mount the Roberto treatment. Had he done so, it would have been very close, but as it was we held on well to win by half a length. Morston, remarkably for a horse of such little racing experi-ence, had run home as straight as a gun barrel on Epsom's tricky camber. Bois Roussel in 1938 had been the last horse to win the Derby on only his second appearance on the racecourse.

Considering that he had just failed to win the Derby on a horse he had bred himself, Lester was prompt with his congratulations. 'Well done', he said as we were pulling up. I felt myself beginning to be overcome by the knowledge of what had just taken place. In order to return to the unsaddling enclosure before the tears of joy ran down my face, I did my best to think of anything but the fact that my ultimate dream had just come true. It is difficult to put into words the elation I felt at that time – it was, of course, simply the pinnacle of my career.

It is the custom after winning the Derby to buy champagne for all the lads in the weighing-room and Fred, my valet, organised this for me. I have kept the day's racecard bearing the signatures of all the jockeys who rode in the race. Still riding now are Philip Waldron (now in Hong Kong), Pat Eddery, Paul Cook, Sandy Barclay, Willie Carson, Geoff Baxter, Ernie Johnson, Greville Starkey, Taffy Thomas and Freddie Head. Now retired are Yves Saint-Martin, Lester, Joe Mercer (now racing manager to Sheikh Maktoum Al Maktoum), John Gorton (training in Australia); Frankie Durr, Geoff Lewis and Eric Eldin, all now training here; Buster Parnell, George Moore (who has retired after training in Hong Kong); Tony Murray (now a presenter with Racecall and S.I.S.); J. Cruguet, T. Murphy, the late Brian Taylor and the late Bill Williamson. After the race, for the second time in my life I had the honour of meeting the Queen, who offered her congratulations. Later I travelled back to Yorkshire and shared a champagne meal on the train with Malton trainer Frank Carr, his wife, Rose and Cliff Parks, the well-known Northern lightweight. We arrived back at York station just in time to re-live the race all over again via the television at the Station Hotel. There was a great welcome waiting for me when I finally arrived home. Elizabeth and William, then aged seven and five, had, with Sue's help, put up flags, and between two telegraph poles a banner bearing the legend 'Welcome home, Dad'.

It was back to reality the next day at Carlisle, but the sporting Northern racing public applauded me from the weighing-room to the entrance to the paddock for my first ride. We had a small family dinner to celebrate after racing on Saturday. Over the next few days I received many telegrams, telephone calls and letters of congratulation, but perhaps the one that touched me most was a letter from Captain, later Sir, Cecil Boyd-Rochfort. Previously the Queen's trainer, the 86-year-old Captain was by then living in retirement in Ireland and was very much the elder statesman of the turf. His hand-written letter was addressed simply to E. Hide Esq., Jockey, Malton, Yorks. 'I must send you this line of my greatest congratulations on your magnificent win in the Derby', he wrote. 'How pleased you must be. Alas, I see little racing these days, but luckily can watch it on television, and we get very good pictures over here. I have known you for many years and am glad to say you rode a few winners for me. I have always had the greatest regard for you as a jockey and a man and I was so delighted to hear on television your name at the finish. I had no idea he had any chance – in fact his name was strange to me. It was also nice to see an English owner, and bred and trained by him and ridden by you.' I was very moved that at his great age Sir Cecil had taken the trouble to write.

Morston came out of the Derby well and Mr Budgett decided to train him for the St Leger, with the Great Voltigeur Stakes at York as his stepping-stone for the final classic. In mid-August he was taken to Newbury to gallop after racing and so impressed the head lad, Tom Dowdeswell, that of the four Derby winners he had been associated with he rated Morston better than both Blakeney and Tulyar and a close second to the 1934 Derby winner, Windsor Lad. Ominously, there was a trace of heat in Morston's near-fore, and the following day the tendon blew up. Sadly, he was immediately retired. The second and last time I sat on Morston was during Royal Ascot week when I visited Whatcombe to have photographs taken.

Unfortunately, unlike his half-brother, Blakeney, Morston wasn't an outstanding success as a stallion and he has ended up at Norton Grove Stud at Malton, just down the road from me. His best winners were Morcon, Mr Fluorocarbon, Whitstead and More Light. My last link with the Windmill Girl family came the following year when I rode Cley, an Exbury half-sister to Morston, to win at Newmarket. Having achieved my lifetime's ambition it seems churlish to have any regrets, but if there is one thing I am a little rueful about it is that I was not involved with Morston in the build-up to the race and his last bits of work. It would have given me more personal satisfaction than I had just sitting on him for that short time.

For old time's sake, I recently called in to see the old boy and gave him a thank-you pat and some tit-bits, but I wouldn't pretend that he remembered me.

– 14 –
Mick, Lochnager and Mrs McArdy

AS a freelance in the mid 1970s I was fortunate to have the support of Barry Hills and Michael Stoute in the South and Mick Easterby in the North. Between them they trained around 200 horses. To start a season with such strong backing would appear to place me in an enviable position, but there were understandable problems when they had runners at different meetings on the same day and I had to choose which to ride. Because of my quest to ride winners I tended to find that I pleased one stable at the expense of upsetting the other two, but there was no way round it: it was very obvious that if you get winners you are offered more rides. When the winners drop off, so do your opportunities and you soon find that 'your' horses are being offered to other jockeys. It's all too easy to be sucked into that downward spiral. So, first and foremost, I had to look after my own interests in picking my mounts. On the occasions when I did ride a horse just to please someone, no one was happy when it finished among the also-rans.

These days single stables may house 200 horses, and life must be simpler for a jockey attached to one of these than it was for me as I tried to keep three different trainers happy. On the whole though, in spite of occasional differences, the arrangement worked out fairly well for me and I was very fortunate to have the chance to ride for three such trainers. In the 1974 season, winners came with such regularity that I reached a century as early as 30 August, when I rode Vice Squad for Jeremy Tree at Chester. In comparison, my previous fastest 100 had been achieved at the Doncaster St Leger meeting. I was snapping at the heels of Pat and Lester in the jockeys' table and was so keen for winners that I was unwilling to let anything stand in my way.

I stayed with the Stoutes at Newmarket for the July meeting, and on the morning of the concluding day I noticed a few spots on my skin. I didn't think much of it, and after riding that afternoon travelled to Doncaster for the evening meeting where I had three rides before returning home to Malton. It was straight into the sauna on the Friday morning in a bid to clear the rash. At York that day, I had five rides and two winners. My weighing-room colleagues would have been justifiably angry had they known the truth – I had chicken pox! Until that day at York, I hadn't felt too poorly but that night, the spots on my face and head really irritated me and I awoke on Saturday morning feeling bloody awful and looking worse. Ryan Jarvis had booked me to ride Long Row in the big handicap at Ayr that afternoon. I certainly wasn't in a fit state to drive up there on my own, but luckily Brian Connorton agreed to drive my car. Long Row duly won, making the 460-mile round trip all worthwhile. Ryan told me later that having heard of my ailment he had the colours fumigated when he got them home! I was not well enough to ride at Ayr on the Monday and our family doctor advised staying at home the following day but, not for the first time, I disobeyed orders and was back on Tuesday. I suppose I was being rather selfish, but fortunately, as far as I know, nobody caught the dreaded infection from me.

At the end of the season I was third to Pat Eddery – only 11 winners behind him – with Lester dividing us. It was the closest I was ever to get to winning the Jockeys' Championship; my total of 137 would have been sufficient to win two years previously. My memorable victories that season included the Nunthorpe Stakes (soon to become the William Hill Sprint Championship) at York on Blue Cashmere for Michael Stoute. Joe Mercer had been engaged but had been hurt by a fall from Auction Ring in the paddock before the Gimcrack. I was delighted to be given the ride, but having ridden winners for Michael since he started, it was disappointing that it came my way only as a result of Joe's misfortune.

Now and again old geldings come on to the scene and capture the public's imagination. The first horse of this type I was associated with was Crusaders Horn, many years ago. Other public favourites that spring to mind were Le Garcon D'or, Boldboy, Bedtime, Chaplain's Club, Glencroft and O I Oyston. In 1974 I had the pleasure of riding Arthur Budgett's grand old horse Petty Officer to win the Timeform Gold Trophy at Redcar, giving 31 lb to Guy Reed's Dakota, which I had ridden to victory in the King George V Handicap at Royal Ascot. Petty Officer joined Mr Budgett's yard as an unwanted yearling. Ron Smythe had bought him but returned him because he discovered he was a crib-biter. After he arrived it appeared that he was touched in his wind as well. Col Wright decided he had better cut his losses and offered to sell him for £500. Luckily, Mr Budgett persuaded another of his owners to take a chance with the horse, and he went on to win 12 races and £45,000, at that time the biggest total of money ever won by a gelding. I won on him on three occasions, including his 12th and final success in the Jockey Club Cup at Newmarket.

The following spring Bill Williamson, who was then racing manager to Ravi Tikkoo, the Indian-born oil tanker tycoon, asked me to ride Mr Tikkoo's Dermot Weld-trained Steel Heart in the 2,000 Guineas. With the request came the offer of riding as first jockey for Mr Tikkoo. He had 70 horses in training, based mainly with Scobie Breasley and Ben Hanbury. But I was enjoying my success as a freelance too much to accept the retainer and Frankie Durr got the job. Steel Heart didn't stay and was well beaten behind Bolkonski in the Guineas, but the meeting will be remembered for the stable lads' strike.

On the first day about 200 stable lads, who were on strike for better pay, sat down across the track at the two-furlong marker before the first race. Even after they had been cleared from the course by the police no one was really sure that they wouldn't dash out in front of us at some stage of the race. Fortunately no such incident occurred, but the lads re-assembled to disrupt the runners going to the post for the second race and some ugly scenes followed, notably when Willie Carson was dragged from his mount and hit across the thigh with his own whip. Willie managed to remount and cantered back to the stand where he appealed to racegoers to help sort out the situation. A crowd of spectators responded to his request and, led by trainers Atty Corbett and Ryan Price, they headed down the course and confronted the strikers. For a while the scene looked more like a football stadium during a riot than the setting for two of the world's classic horse-races. Eventually the police once more intervened and racing was able to continue without further interruption.

Although I had some sympathy with the stable lads' cause I felt the way they chose to publicise it was irresponsible and counter-productive. By the end of their demonstration you'd have been hard pushed to find anyone watching racing that day who had a good word to say for them. It was true that there were some very good lads working in stables who were worth far more than the minimum wage, but in my opinion the overall standard of labour was, unfortunately, not what it had once been. Frankly, some of the lads would have been unemployable were it not that they were of use in getting horses to and from the gallops, whereas without others some stables would have ground to a halt. Guy Harwood and I were staying at the Stoutes' and, glad as I was to have him as a bodyguard when penetrating the picket-line on the way to the races, I wasn't so keen on his company when I had to share a twin-bedded room with him as he was driving the pigs home so loudly I had to retreat to the bathroom and sleep there for the rest of the night!

Come June, things were still going very well and I was level with Pat Eddery in the jockeys' table. From 26 May to 13 June, I clocked up 4,000 miles in the car (fortunately I was friendly with *Timeform*'s Colin Russell, and we often shared transport); took eight flights and sweated off 14 lb in the sauna, for 82 rides and 18 winners. The moral of this is that you have to capitalise on the opportunities that come your way because you never know what's around the corner: for the next three months I was to be out of action after breaking my leg in a fall at York on, of all dates, Friday 13 June.

At the Knavesmire, I was riding in the first race of the day for two-year-old fillies on Bewerley for Mick Easterby. She was dropping out after failing to hold her position when she caught the heels of the runner in front, stumbled, pitched on her head and catapulted me over the top. I turned a complete somersault before landing awkwardly. I didn't need a medical opinion to tell me that my leg was broken.

Our poor son William, then aged eight, had joined us at the races that day. Never very keen on horses, he had somehow been persuaded to don his best bib and tucker and come with us. He was with Sue in the stands when she saw me fall. She instructed him, as if speaking to one of the dogs, 'Stay there and don't move until I get back', and dashed off to see me. It was some considerable time before she was able to rescue him. I think that was the final straw for Will as far as racing was concerned.

I was taken to hospital by ambulance and an X-ray diagnosed that the top of my left shin bone had been broken off. Mr Haw, the surgeon, explained that he would have to insert a screw to join the bones together again. Sue and Will arrived in time to see me being wheeled into the operating theatre, saying to the surgeon: 'I don't mean to be rude, but you do know what you're doing don't you? I want the best because I can't afford to be off for long.' Sue was mortified but Mr Haw took it in good part, assuring me he was perfectly capable!

I had been due to ride the German five-year-old Star Appeal in Italy the following Sunday. Star Appeal, trained by Theo Grieper, was a stable-mate of Lord Udo, whom I had already partnered to win the Henckel-Rennen, the German 2,000 Guineas, the previous season. Lord Udo was owned by Mr and Mrs Mehl-Mulhens who were famous for their 4711 Eau de Cologne. Most trainers in Germany train at the courses but they had a very big, private training establishment, featuring two gallops and an immaculately-kept racecourse, situated in a walled park to the east of Cologne. Star Appeal's owner, Waldemar Zeitelhack, had planned to send his private plane to Teesside for me. Greville Starkey took over and won the Gran Premio di Milano. Naturally enough, he kept the ride for the rest of the season, winning the Eclipse Stakes the following month and then the Prix de l'Arc de Triomphe itself, at the massive odds of 125–1. I watched the Arc at home. Greville rode a brilliant race, taking all the right openings, but I believe I am still entitled to think that my accident cost me a winning ride in Europe's most prestigious all-aged race. But in racing it's all swings and roundabouts, and I can't help feeling that Greville himself was unlucky not to ride another Arc winner 11 years later on Dancing Brave.

Much has been written about Greville and Dancing Brave's fast-finishing second to Shahrastani in the 1986 Derby. It seemed to me that circumstances conspired against Greville on the day. Until Epsom the furthest distance that Dancing Brave had run was a mile. In both the Craven and the 2,000 Guineas the horse was held up before coming through to win well. Over a mile and a half in the Derby Greville had no option but to follow a winning formula and again settle Dancing Brave in the early stages of the race. The horse wasn't suited by the track but the biggest problem was the unusually slow pace for the first half of the race. Because of this, the other runners were able to quicken at the same time as Greville was trying to take closer order on the descent to Tattenham Corner. It wasn't until well into the straight that Dancing Brave was balanced and able to use his stride. For Greville, the winning post came a few yards too soon. Walter Swinburn on Shahrastani, about whose stamina there was no doubt, had ridden the perfect race, having been in fourth place before leading two furlongs out and staying on strongly to win by half a length. As is so often the case, there was one runner too many. Had Shahrastani not run, Dancing Brave would have been a comfortable winner and Greville would have been acclaimed for riding a brilliant race. In that case, I am sure he would have kept the ride on the horse and won the Arc, in which Pat Eddery rode an identical race to Greville's at Epsom. This time it paid off because of the stronger earlier pace and more suitable track.

In the meantime, encased in plaster from ankle to hip, I learned that it was likely to be as long as six months before I was right again. All the time I was in his charge I hounded Mr Haw to hurry things up. I had the bright idea that, if he could design a support made of plastic rather than the conventional Plaster of Paris, it could be removed to enable me to exercise my leg in the pool without putting any weight on it. I rang him to suggest my plan but it was firmly dismissed! After the First Aid accident I had realised the importance of not allowing my muscles to waste away, which gave me the confidence to work hard on my self-devised physiotherapy. The first thing I did on my return home was to tie two socks containing pebbles over my ankle, and whenever I sat in the armchair I exercised my leg by lifting it up and down with the weight on. When the plaster was removed just under a month later the specialist was pleased, but told me that I wasn't to put any weight on the leg and to continue using crutches. I spent hours in the swimming pool, lowering myself into the water with the help of a rope-ladder hung from the roof, lying in a tyre and kicking my way up and down. I also upended an old tricycle long discarded by the children, and, seated on a stool, pedalled away without putting my weight on the leg. From that I graduated to a full-size bike propped up on drums to allow a larger rotation of the joint. To break down the contusion around the injury I massaged the joint regularly with goosefat, an old country remedy. I also attended the physiotherapist at Malton Hospital on a regular basis.

Only a month and a day after the plaster had been removed, I rode my bike on the road for the first time, riding about four miles, even though I still wasn't allowed to walk without crutches. A week later I popped into the County Hospital at York to see Mr Haw, who was pleased with the progress I had made. The crutches were dispensed with but I still had to use sticks to keep some of the weight off until an X-ray scheduled for the following week could show how I was progressing. Before that I took a gentle walk along the road on Goldie, a quiet pony, and two days later a very short and slow canter in the paddock. At the end of August I had two more canters on Goldie and did plenty of trotting. So far so good. The same day I went for a swim and cycled to the top village and back. That involved a stiff uphill climb and was my usual pre-season exertion to help me get race fit. As soon as I felt I was ready for it I drove over to Highfield and rode a canter both lots before going on another bike ride. As I felt no ill-effects I rode at Highfield again the following day and called in at the hospital on my way home to cancel my appointment with the physiotherapist.

I pestered Mr Haw to allow me to ride and when the day came I started off with a winner at Ripon. That evening I 'phoned him to tell him the good news. He nearly had a fit. 'I didn't mean ride in a race!' he exploded, 'I meant start riding gently at home!' I confessed then that I had been doing that for days. Nevertheless, he was delighted for me and intrigued at my keenness to start working again – some of his patients wanted to lengthen the time off rather than return to work as quickly as possible. I had returned to the saddle 11 weeks and a day after the accident: there's nothing like the thought of missing winners to spur on the progress! He was so impressed at how will and motivation could speed up the healing process that he wrote a paper on the subject in the medical journal *The Lancet*.

I had been back for only a week when I had another scrape at Thirsk. I had just ridden out on to the course when my horse, Panorealm, cocked his jaw and bolted. If I had been able I would have turned him at the bend and let him go round the course, but with both the steering and brakes gone he galloped on to the end of the six-furlong straight. In such circumstances it is sometimes the lesser of two evils to bale out, but that takes a lot of courage at any time, not to mention when you have just returned from injury, so I elected to stay on board. If you fight a horse that is bolting with you it will run into a brick wall, so at the last minute I gave him his head and, confronted by a barrier of corrugated sheets, he dug in his toes and slithered to a halt. Naturally I kept going, and didn't come to until I was in the ambulance. The result was a further visit to my home-from-home York County Hospital, where I was detained overnight for observation after precautionary X-rays were taken of my head. Again, I was lucky to escape relatively unharmed.

While I had been side-lined Bruce Raymond had ridden a three-year-old colt, Lochnager, to win the Northumberland Sprint Trophy at Newcastle. The combination was fancied to follow up in the Ayr Gold Cup but could finish only third to Roman Warrior and Import. Had they won that race I would probably have never sat on Lochnager, but I was offered the ride on him when he next appeared in the Bovis Handicap at Ascot in October. He won most impressively, reversing Ayr running with Import. Lochnager was trained by Mick Easterby. Our association had started way back in August 1961, when I had partnered Steal A March to success at Ripon, the first of 115 wins for Mick. Steal A March was almost as much of a character as his trainer. Before that day at Ripon, he had finished second in all six of his previous races and his enthusiasm was much in doubt. I had watched the horse run and felt that he would win if he was covered up, ridden tenderly and produced at the very last minute, which proved to be the case. The minute he hit the front he stopped. I loved the challenge of riding horses like Steal A March and trying to get it right – there is an extra thrill when you are occasionally able to outwit them. It is not always the top-class horses that give a jockey most pleasure. It takes confidence to ride a horse like Steal a March; if you win it looks good but if it fails to come off you risk being blamed. Mick, himself a horseman who had ridden in point-to-points, understood these problems and we were usually on the same wavelength.

Lochnager, on the other hand, was a straightforward ride. A dark brown, he was a great big powerful horse and a very sensible sober sort, the opposite of what you might expect from such a speedy performer. After he had won the Bovis Mick put him in a large box on one of his farms and he didn't come out again until the beginning of February. When I asked Mick why he had done this, he explained that he would have been fresh on the roads in winter and in danger of breaking loose and injuring himself. It was hardly surprising that after such an idle winter Lochnager would need a couple of races to get him right. For his third race, Mick couldn't decide – or wouldn't tell me – whether to run in the Amoco Handicap at Doncaster on the Saturday or the Temple Stakes at Sandown on the Monday. For me, Saturday was no problem but Monday was a Bank Holiday and I had been offered many rides at different meetings. Mick led me to believe that he favoured Doncaster and told me to plan around that. The horse had given me such a feel when winning at Ascot that I left my options open to the last minute because I didn't want to risk missing the ride and probably losing it for ever.

It was only on the Friday morning that Sandown was decided upon, and due to his two seemingly disappointing runs, both Faliraki and Roman Warrior were preferred in the betting. Lochnager was never in danger, though, and won comfortably. He didn't need covering up as such, but you couldn't ask him to go on too soon as he tended to idle once he hit the front. In the King's Stand Stakes at Royal Ascot, his next appearance, he took on the best France, Italy and Ireland could produce and beat them all roundly. It was imperative to wait longer over the six furlongs of the July Cup at Newmarket. The slope into the dip on the July Course is not as noticeable as it is on the Rowley Mile but it was still essential to gain the extra momentum on the descent to enable him to hold on up the hill. I delayed asking him until approaching the dip, when he went into overdrive and strode away to win well.

The evening before Lochnager's next appearance, which turned out to be his last, in the William Hill Sprint Championship at York, Mick, his owner Mr Spence and I walked the course and discovered that after watering, the fastest strip of ground was up the middle. Taking the trouble to walk the course may have proved the vital factor between winning and losing in what was a very keen and closely-fought race. Lochnager showed tremendous courage and again came out on top in a blanket finish, the distances half a length, a neck and half a length, with Faliraki, Polly Peachum and Three Legs taking the minor honours. The race had proved lucky for me. I had previously won it on Blue Cashmere, when it was known as the Nunthorpe, and the following year, 1977, I was to win it again on Haveroid for trainer Neil Adam.

Stable-mate Polly Peachum was a top sprinter, but Lochnager was always just that vital length better. I had won the Palace House Stakes on her earlier in the season. It was also planned for Lochnager to run at Longchamps in the Prix de l'Abbaye, but after I rode him in his last gallop he disappointed and when he later gave the odd cough, it was decided to retire him on his merits rather than risk him being beaten. So Lochnager retired the champion sprinter of Europe. The last horse to have achieved the coveted sprint hat-trick of the King's Stand, July Cup and William Hill Sprint Championship was Abernant in 1949.

Before the start of the season Susan Piggott, through her agency, offered Charles Spence and his son, David, the colt's owners, a good deal of money for their horse. Luckily for me, they refused to sell. After the July Cup she had walked alongside us to the winners' enclosure, giving admiring glances which I assumed were meant for the horse rather than for me. Had Susan bought him, I would almost certainly have lost the ride to her illustrious husband.

In these days of expensive syndications the top jockeys are rumoured to receive a nomination or, better still, a share in the stallion whose reputation they have played a not unimportant part in making. My reward for riding the European sprint champion to three group race successes was not the hoped-for share, or even a nomination, but half a salmon, which by the time it reached us had gone off! I was very grateful, though, to have had the opportunity to ride such an outstanding horse. Such jewels in the crown come all too rarely in a jockey's life.

Mick Easterby is one of racing's most colourful characters, a real down-to-earth Yorkshireman who, rather than call a spade a spade, would term it a bloody shovel. Mick was virtually penniless when he married Alice back in 1957 and rented a small five-acre farm. He has lived for some years at Sheriff Hutton, just a quarter of an hour's drive from me, and has combined farming and training most successfully. In fact, he now farms something like half of Yorkshire while his brother Peter farms the other half, thanks to their philosophy: 'If you don't get on in the world, don't blame anyone but yourself. You make your own chances and your own luck. If you use your head, luck comes your way'. The successes of Lochnager and Polly Peachum helped Mick to become the first trainer in the North to top the £100,000-barrier in 1976. He was also one of the first, if not the first, Northern trainer to install an all-weather gallop. I attribute the success of both Mick and his brother Peter to the fact that they are both instinctive and very good judges of horse flesh. Mick was certainly unpredictable, but he knew his horses. Sometimes I thought a horse fit enough to win when Mick thought otherwise, and more often than not he was right.

Mick was difficult to ride for because he wouldn't make up his mind until the last minute about what he was doing, and I was never sure that I was riding for him until I saw the declaration sheet pinned up with my name on it. Mick's riposte if I complained was that he didn't know I was riding for him until he saw me walking round on one of his horses down at the start, and even then he wasn't sure I wouldn't jump on to something else if I thought it had a better chance than his! But I enjoyed riding for him even though we were always having a friendly dig at each other. Only recently he said to me, 'By, I wish you were still riding for me'. I replied that I still might have been if he'd treated me better!

Mick's greatest talent came into its own at the sales ring. I am sure he derived more enjoyment from wheeling and dealing than from training. More than once he suggested to me that I could train the horses for him when I finished riding. As I was never sure that Mick's left hand knew what his right was doing, I felt that that would have been taking on too much. One famous example of Mick's sales spiel was to tell an owner that he had only one horse left and that he was going to save it for himself. 'Wouldn't sell it to anybody', he would vow, 'I'd rather part with me wife.' A few minutes later, the bemused patron would usually find that he was the proud possessor of a horse that only seconds before Mick wouldn't trade for love nor money!

Once Mick bought a job lot of ten horses from Lord Grimthorpe and always claimed afterwards that this was because he recognised the qualities of one filly foal. He sold her on to one of his owners, Mrs Edith Kettlewell, who, with her husband Bill, ran the Aysgarth Motel in Wensleydale. One of their elderly regulars who used to come in for a Bacardi always asked for a Mrs McArdy, so that's how the filly came to be named. After her first three outings as a two-year-old, it was difficult for me to appreciate just what Mick had seen in the filly as she showed me very little. Then, towards the back-end, she began to improve and won her last four races in the hands of Neil Crowther.

Mrs McArdy, a shapely, attractive filly, made her reappearance at Doncaster on the opening day of the 1977 Flat season, but I was on the stable's Tudor Jig, who won comfortably by four lengths with Mrs McArdy out of the first six. Allotted 7 stones 7 lb in the Free Handicap at the end of her two-year-old year, Mrs McArdy easily won the race itself with Taffy Thomas riding. Although that race is often a good classic guide, the 1,000 Guineas was a big step up from winning off the lowest mark and she started at 16–1. This time I was back on board, and right from the stalls she was always going well emerging the comfortable winner, beating Freeze The Secret by two lengths. In a television interview afterwards, asked by Brough Scott what instructions he had given his jockey, a beaming Mick replied, 'I just said help yourself!' His one regret was that he had a two-year-old half-brother to Mrs McArdy at home which had already been gelded!

Although she was by the sprinter Tribal Chief, it wasn't primarily lack of stamina that led to Mrs McArdy's poor show in the Oaks; she just wasn't herself that day and was very free cantering to the start. Unusually for her, she was sweating, and trailed in last but one behind the Queen's Dunfermline with Freeze The Secret second again. After that, Mick took the unusual step of running her in the Fen Ditton Handicap at Newmarket in July, and she put up a good performance to win under top weight. She was no match for the colts when sixth in the Sussex Stakes but won the Strensall Stakes at York and then ran third to Boldboy at Doncaster. Mrs McArdy's final appearance in this country was in the sales ring at Newmarket in December when she was sold to Bert Firestone for 154,000 guineas, then a record for a horse out of training at Tattersalls.

I didn't ride often for Bill Watts at that time because John Lowe was retained as his first jockey. John had been apprenticed to Bill since the early days at Richmond and had worked his way up to number one. However, Bill approached me to ride In Haste, a horse he planned to run in the 2,000 Guineas, in his preparatory race, the Free Handicap, and we came to a verbal agreement. Shortly after that, Richard Galpin of the N.B.A. offered me a retainer on behalf of the owner to ride the Queen Mary winner Cramond, trained by Ron Boss, in both the Free Handicap and the 1,000 Guineas. Had I not already come to an agreement with Bill, I would almost certainly have accepted Richard's offer, which, as it turned out, would have meant finishing 17th of 18 behind my eventual ride Mrs McArdy. It is strange how things sometimes work out in racing.

At Ayr in May, I rode a four-timer to take my domestic total to 1,999. I had big hopes of achieving a five-timer in the last race but found one too good. The champagne was put on ice again after I rode another three seconds on the Monday, including being beaten a head on Bally Knoud, a horse I had bought from Robert Armstrong and had leased to one of my brother Tony's owners, John Leader, to help him get started in his first year training in England. Reaching my 2,000 on that really would have been something. Eventually, I reached the target on Triple First in the Musidora Stakes at York. The filly was trained by Michael Stoute and owned by Clifford Turner.

Towards the end of May, Peter O'Sullevan rang me with regard to riding Vincent O'Brien's Be My Guest, his likely Derby second string, in work at Epsom the day before riding him in the big race. My acquaintance with Peter went back a long way; in the 1950s Father had asked him to keep an eye on me and to let him know what he thought. Ever since then, Peter and I have been good friends and I have always felt that I have him to thank for getting me this particular ride in the premier classic. I rode Be My Guest a fairly sharp four furlongs, taking in the descent to Tattenham Corner, and then rode Vincent's other Derby runner, Marinsky, in a similar spin, leading The Minstrel with Geoff Lewis up. I don't know where Lester was that morning, but unfortunately for Geoff he was on The Minstrel when it counted and rode one of his strongest finishes to beat Hot Grove. Be My Guest gave me a good ride up to a point – we were in with every chance early in the straight – but he soon faded and didn't see the trip out. He later proved a high-class miler, winning the Waterford Crystal Mile where he beat Bill Elsey's Don.

I had ridden Bill Elsey's Don in the St James's Palace Stakes at Royal Ascot when we had beaten Lester on Marinsky. Marinsky wore a muzzle because he was inclined to try to grab other horses and often had his mind on things other than knuckling down and racing. The ground at Ascot had been softened by an inch of rain, which as I have said before, makes it harder work for the horses, and this is where you have a marked advantage with a horse endowed with courage. The conditions suited Don, who was blessed with big feet and a heart to match. Early in the straight Marinsky got away from me and, if it had remained good ground, would have won, but Don plugged on through the heavy ground and his opponent gave it away. The lesson is don't trust duck-hearted horses to do their best in testing conditions. In such circumstances, a less-talented but more courageous horse can pay to follow. At the end of the day, it was most satisfying to be associated once again with a good winner from the old stable.

It was at that meeting that Captain Marcos Lemos offered me a retainer to ride for him and the other owners attached to the Clive Brittain stable. Three weeks later Sue and I went down to Newmarket to have dinner with Clive and Maureen Brittain and the next day arrangements were finalised for me to ride for the stable for the next two years, 1978 and 1979. After six wonderfully successful years as a freelance, it might be asked why I reverted to accepting a retainer. Apart from the obvious attraction of a good financial offer, one of the main reasons for my return to the South was the chance to be associated once more with a better class of horse. There were about 80 horses at Clive's Carlburg Stables, which were backed up by Captain Lemos' powerful studs along with those of other powerful owners.

In the first half of the season progress had been slow for the Brittain stable, which had led to the termination of Richard Fox's contract as first jockey. As luck would have it, the horses started to fire just as I began to ride more often for the stable, and before the end of the season I had ridden 18 winners for Clive, which was more than I rode for any other trainer that year. Another reason why I accepted the retainer was that while looking around Clive's yard, I had been particularly impressed by Julio Mariner, a full brother to the 1975 Oaks winner, Juliette Marney, who had cost 40,000 guineas as a yearling. He was a shapely and attractive individual and one of the nicest two-year-olds I had seen for some time. Certainly he was the sort of horse that I was unlikely to have had the chance to ride in the North. At York in October, Julio Mariner provided me with my 100th winner of the season and then ran a promising second to Dactylographer in the Futurity Stakes at Doncaster. He was an exciting prospect for the following season.

– 15 –
Travel

IN our early married days, as I have mentioned, Sue and I enjoyed the odd day's hunting with the Derwent. On one occasion when I was otherwise occupied, Sue had a frightening accident when her horse fell into a deep ditch, trapping her underneath for some time. Luckily, she escaped with a badly-broken leg, but as a result of the fall she became claustrophobic, suffering particularly in aeroplanes, so much so that for a few years she wouldn't fly at all and I had to endure endless journeys by train and boat. I never achieved a Channel crossing without being sick.

One day, in desperation, I gave her a travel brochure. 'Choose anywhere in there for a holiday', I said. 'I can't stand the thought of another boat or train.' The brochure must have been very well-produced because after much perusing she announced: 'I've decided. Let's go to Thailand.' I nearly had apoplexy. I certainly hadn't expected to have to take her across the world, but having made the offer I couldn't very well withdraw!

Before the holiday the doctor gave Sue a sedative to steady her nerves, and the night before we set off she knelt down by the bedside to say her prayers. About half an hour later I thought, these prayers are going on for an awfully long time. On investigation I found she was fast asleep. The 'plane journey seemed endless but we eventually arrived at Bangkok. More recently we have come to know the Far East well and to appreciate the high standard of service and facilities in the hotels, but this was our first visit and we were overwhelmed by the sumptuous Siam Continental and its acres of grounds. We had also never come across such a climate. Even though it was the cool season, not only was the temperature up in the 80s even at night, but the humidity was very high, a condition we found enervating.

One of the great advantages of being connected with racing is the contacts you make all over the world. Owner Eric Morris, who had horses in training with Rufus Beasley, lived in Bangkok and he took us all over the city, showing us a side of Thailand we would never have seen on a package holiday. We went to watch morning exercise at the two racecourses, both in the centre of Bangkok. At one of them, in stables across from the racecourse, stood the stallion Proper Jet on which I had won two races in England for Eric Morris. We also had a highly entertaining day at the races at the Royal Bangkok Sports Club. We sat in a comfortable air-conditioned box, which we appreciated all the more when we discovered there were 14 races! As the runners were pulling up from one race the contestants for the next were already being led out, so there was no chance of a jockey riding in consecutive races.

There were three divisions of a race for country breds, two for thoroughbreds and the rest for Thai ponies. In one of the thoroughbred races the weights ranged from 7 stones up to 11 stones 7 lb, but the Thai ponies carried 6 stones 5 lb to 8 stones 1 lb. The starts, although from stalls, were rather ragged and the field spreadeagled right across the course coming into the straight, but the large crowds were very enthusiastic and shouted and leaped about, willing their chosen horses home.

Eric took us to visit a stud at Petchaboa, way up towards the Cambodian border. It was also a silk worm farm and we were fascinated to be taken around to see how silk was produced and gathered; what was not so fascinating was the sound of gunfire in the nearby hills. The farmhouse was very cool and furnished with low chairs and tables. Lizards seemingly the size of small alligators roamed the bedroom walls. It was surprising to come across a big stud farm, with 150 mares and three stallions, some of them familiar names from England, in such an isolated place, 240 miles from the capital city. We thoroughly enjoyed seeing the 'real' Thailand and staying with a Thai family, who were charming and hospitable. The hustle and bustle of Bangkok contrasted markedly with the empty roads we had travelled. It is said that Bangkok has so much traffic that before long it will take just one more car to bring everything to a standstill. We passed some horses in transit to the races in open trucks, standing sideways with their heads sticking out over the side, a boy monitoring each horse.

We went on to Pattya where pineapples were in abundance and only cost nine pence each. We had them with nearly everything; our usual lunch-time snack was a pineapple filled with lobster – delicious. One day we went for a ride on an elephant. I wasn't too happy sitting so far from the ground, and liked it even less when I shared the 'saddle' with a 20-stone friend. As we sat there, side by side, I spent most of the ride anxiously awaiting the moment when the saddle would tip up. My most lasting memories were of the beautiful sylphlike Thai waitresses in the hotel. With their tight skirts slit from ankle to thigh they quite put me off my meals!

Over the years Sue and I have travelled to many countries in the world where horseracing takes place. One of the perks to have come my way through my success as a jockey has been invitations to ride in South Africa. I doubt if I would have had the opportunity to see this country's magnificent scenery otherwise, and I certainly would not have been the recipient of such lavish hospitality. I was first invited there in 1978 when, along with Greville Starkey, I represented the United Kingdom in an international team event. With us were Philippe Paquet and Freddy Head from France; Gianfranco Dettori and Giovanni Fois from Italy; Hugo Dittfach and Lloyd Duffy from Canada; Greg McCarron and Michael Venezia from the United States and 'Muis' Roberts and Michael Cave representing the host country.

Greville and his wife Chris joined Sue and me at Heathrow for our flight out there. We were sitting on board prior to take-off when Greville performed his party trick – his famous barking dog impression. When the perplexed stewardess came along looking for the dog, Greville pointed over his shoulder and told her it was behind us. After a thorough check that no dog was on board we were able to set off on our first visit to the Southern Hemisphere. Sue was still suffering from her 'fear of flying' syndrome and the doctor had given her some tranquillisers to take if necessary. On the journey from Yorkshire to London she had taken one and, as it didn't seem to have had any effect, took another . . . and another. I hadn't realised this and while awaiting take-off gave her a slurp of brandy from a small bottle I had brought with me to help me get her on the 'plane. She fell asleep and woke up in Johannesburg 17 hours later! It was one way of shortening the journey, but the realisation of what the consequences could have been scared her into being wary of medications ever after.

The whole visit was organised with expert precision. There were receptions, dinners, lunches, visits to places of interest and early morning work-riding, not to mention the racing itself. I was a bit apprehensive about how apartheid would affect us, since my sole knowledge of the situation had been gleaned from the newspapers at home. I was pleasantly surprised when we arrived at the Holiday Inn to find that it was fully multi-racial.

We raced at Germiston near Johannesburg. I think what impressed me most were the excellent tracks at all the South African venues we visited. They were wide, well-designed, galloping courses with well-kept turf. On our first day's racing the heavens opened and the management worried that racing might have to be cancelled. They asked us if we were prepared to ride in such conditions and were relieved to be told that we often rode on far worse going at home.

After the racing at Germiston we moved on to Hluhluwe in Zulu-land, where we were taken round a game reserve. This was interesting although not without its moments of alarm, even from the safety of a mini-bus. At one point we stopped to study a rhino, an animal which, though nearly blind, has very keen hearing and sense of smell. We were warned not to get out of the vehicle as the rhinos were easily upset and deceptively fast if they charged. Suddenly, the old boy sensed our presence and started rumbling towards us. The driver quickly tried to start the engine – it stalled. Luckily, we were parked on a hill and he managed to start the engine by running the bus down the incline, and we were able to get out of the way just before the animal gathered too much speed.

We moved on to Swaziland by coach, which made the journey much longer, but it also enabled us to see more of the countryside. To help pass the journey we played cards and dice. Greville took it upon himself to teach Giovanni Fois a little English, with the result that when he arrived in the paddock at Greyville Racecourse, Durban, the young Italian touched his cap to the owners, gave a bright smile and said 'Pees Orf'!

At Durban we stayed on the sea-front and our hosts continued to treat us royally. While the wives were taken on a sightseeing tour the jockeys went to the Apprentice Academy, a multi-racial school for boys from the age of 14. It is run on the lines of a boarding-school and the pupils, who are there for a five-year apprenticeship, are given a full academic education as well as learning riding and horseman-ship. When they reach a required standard they are allowed to ride for trainers and after a year of that, if they are capable, are given the chance to start race-riding. Their weight is carefully monitored; in fact, anyone who looks as if he might grow too heavy is not even taken on in the first place. One of the Academy's old boys is Michael Roberts, who is now riding so successfully here and who we first met on our trips to South Africa.

The Durban Turf Club owns a training ground at Summerveld between Durban and Pietermaritzburg. It covers about 400 acres and because of its altitude, 2,200 feet, the climate is much better than it is on the humid coast. All the facilities for training are centred there: stabling, lads' accommodation, watered grass, sand tracks, a club-house with a viewing stand, walks, paddocks; everything you could possibly need to train a racehorse. We were taken up there to ride out and get to know our horses. Greville rode one piece of work for a trainer and came back despondent at the thought of riding the horse later on; it seemed lifeless and didn't give him any feel. He couldn't believe it was the same horse when he rode it in the race – it was keen, full of verve and highly-fancied. The trainer must have been some sort of a magician!

One of the trainers I rode for was Fred Rickaby, brother of the popular English jockey, Bill. Fred trained in South Africa for many years and has now returned to Newmarket where he is much sought-after by trainers to help them cure horses with back problems.

South Africa won the series with the United Kingdom second and Canada third. When the official tour was over, Sue and I went on to Cape Town for a few days. We were put in touch with representatives of the sponsor, Connoisseur Brandy, and they took us out to Paarl, the centre of the wine-growing district. This was picture-postcard country, much more cultivated and mellow than the wild scenery of Zululand and Swaziland, with the attractive Cape Dutch-style home-steads nestling in among the vineyards. We went up the cable-car to the top of Table Mountain, and round the coastline – miles of golden sand and surf. At home we tend to mock the tourists who flock to York but we enjoyed seeing all the 'touristy' sights of South Africa and we were left with memories of a vast and beautiful country.

Our second trip to South Africa came in 1982 when Willie Carson was unable to go as he was still recovering from his horrific fall at York. I was asked to take his place in a British team along with Pat Eddery, Joe Mercer, Paul Cook, Greville Starkey and Walter Swinburn, with Jimmy Lindley as our manager. This time we flew first-class, with the hump of the South African Airways jumbo to ourselves. Just as well, really, as our party would have kept the whole 'plane awake. The catering was superb, and we started with a choice of caviar or smoked salmon. Knowing Joe's love of caviar, we tipped off the chief steward to tell him there was none left when it was his turn to be served. Joe's face dropped a mile, but it was soon wreathed in smiles when he realised he was the victim of a prank.

The boys played poker all through the night and anyone trying to drop off to sleep was soon prodded and woken up. The poor passengers down below were greeted early in the morning by Greville, wearing his Gatsby hat and usual dead-pan expression, walking through the cabin with a banana sticking out of his fly. The journey out set the tone of the trip: it was great fun and our hosts enthusiastically joined us in having a good time.

As before, we rode at Germiston and at the Durban track at Greyville, and again we were given the best possible attention. The people we met were courteous and friendly and couldn't do enough for us. The only disadvantage was that I had to forego a few meals and spend some time in the sauna to fulfil my riding engagements.

I played a good deal of golf. The courses, like the racetracks, are first-class and very well maintained. During one of my games my caddy was so disgusted with my lack of ability that day that after two holes he put down my bag and walked off. Walter Swinburn had won the Derby on Shergar the previous year, but when he went to pay his green fees they insisted he only paid half-price because they thought he qualified for the junior fee!

At a buffet lunch one day Sue asked Joe about a particular dish. 'Oh, that's delicious,' he remarked, 'but make sure you chew it well.' She took a mouthful and started chewing, her eyes flooded with tears and you could almost see the steam coming out of her ears as fireworks exploded in her head. Joe had conned her into chewing some hot chillies. The waitress took one look at her and rushed over with some bananas in milk to try to put out the fire!

The party moved on to Sun City in Bophuthatswana, travelling through the platinum mining town of Rustenburg. This brought back memories as I used to ride a horse of that name belonging to Mr Jim Joel. Sun City is an incredible place, a massive playground in the midst of arid bushveldt. The whole complex is geared to gambling. The space-age lobby is a kaleidoscope of flashing lights, mirrors and ringing bells as money pours in and out of the hundreds of slot machines. All around the edge were the different gambling rooms: roulette, blackjack, poker and so on; there was dancing, discos, a lavish cabaret show and sumptuous dining facilities.

Outside was a Gary Player-designed championship golf course, where I had the chance to play. There were swimming pools and a lake where we spent many an amusing hour on the jet skis. I was very much a wobbly novice on these and Pat Eddery, who was particularly good on them, took great delight in riding me off mine, leaving me gurgling in the lake. Pat is renowned for his prowess at poker and one night, when racing commitments had ended, I left him, Muis Roberts and others in a game. I came along in the morning to find them still playing. I noticed that even after a night without sleep and of concentrated effort Pat's mind was as alert as ever.

One of the advantages of such tours is that, as well as enabling you to visit other countries, they give you the opportunity to get to know your fellow jockeys better. At home, although you mix in a business way, after racing you go home to lead your own lives. On these tours you all live together, and the wives are also given the chance to forge relationships.

My lasting memory of the journey home was of Pat, very inebriated, walking up and down the aisle in the hump of the 'plane while the film was being shown, blocking the projector and amusing himself with his shadow on the screen. He was wearing bulky headphones and moving them towards and away from his ears. This was highly amusing to Pat and to us, but it didn't go down so well with our fellow passengers, who were trying to watch the film. The trip ended as it started, in a party atmosphere. The fact that on the racing side we had been well and truly trounced didn't really seem to matter!

– 16 –
Headquarters

EVEN after 27 years in racing I found the prospect of going to work at Headquarters exciting. There has been horseracing at Newmarket at least since the days of Charles II, and it has long been renowned as the world's leading training centre as well as the home of racing's governing body, the Jockey Club. At Captain Lemos' Ashley Heath Stud, I was provided with a three-bedroomed cottage which had a pleasant outlook on to the paddocks. I had a sauna installed in one of the bedrooms, a smaller edition of the one I had in my attic back at the farm.

Owing to an early Easter the 1978 season started unusually at Kempton that year, but I was back on home ground at Newcastle on the Monday when I rode a treble, including the Northern Free Handicap on Brother Kempinski, and my first winner for Clive Brittain as his retained jockey on The Sandford. Clive had mentioned that he would be running a number of horses in the North because of my knowledge of the local tracks, and this was one of the factors that persuaded me to accept his offer.

In May the Huntercombe colt Radetzky returned to Carlburg Stables. At the end of the previous season he had been retired to stud, more or less in disgrace after a series of incidents. Before the Hungerford Stakes at Newbury he had dropped Pat Eddery twice, first in the paddock and again on the way to the start. Later, in the Waterford Crystal Mile at Goodwood, he had delayed the race by a quarter of an hour by refusing to go to the start, but fortunately when I rode him in his last three races that year he behaved a lot better, although it was still decided to end his racing career. However, at stud he was sent only eight mares, seven of which he got in foal, and since this was obviously not enough to make him a viable proposition as a stallion, he came back into training the following season.

Less than six weeks after his return I rode Radetzky in the Queen Anne Stakes over the straight mile at Royal Ascot where he made all the running to gain a very impressive win. In contrast to his antics the previous season he did everything right that day and later confirmed that he was a horse of great ability when finishing third to Gunner B in the Eclipse and runner-up to Jaazeiro in the Sussex Stakes. Clearly, Radetzky's pleasant experiences at stud had made a difference to his outlook on life, but a great deal of credit for sweetening the horse up must go to Clive. Rather than risk his lads with him he had ridden Radetzky out at home himself, and had often taken him out on his own, having many a battle with him along the way. On one embarrassing occasion the horse took Clive into someone's garden and it reportedly took a fair amount of persuasion to get him out again.

The Queen Anne win was also memorable because I received a message that day from Hayley Mills asking me if I would like to go up to her box and read more bedtime stories to her! Unfortunately, by the time I was able to get there, Hayley had left for Richmond where she was appearing in a play.

Because Julio Mariner was a brother to Oaks winner Juliette Marney, it was decided that the stable's potential star should by-pass the Guineas. Instead, he was trained for the Derby and made his reappearance in the Mecca-Dante Stakes at York in the middle of May where he ran a close second to Shirley Heights. However, we weren't to know that Fulke Johnson Houghton's colt Ile de Bourbon would win the King George that summer. As York was Julio Mariner's first run of the season, we went to Epsom full of hope that we would at least finish wherever Shirley Heights did. He looked in great shape on the day and went down to post in good style. Unfortunately, on the return journey he could manage only sixth of 25 behind Shirley Heights. Instead of improving on his Dante run he had undoubtedly gone the other way. There followed another below-par performance in the King Edward VII Stakes at Royal Ascot, where he was well beaten by Ile de Bourbon.

Julio Mariner next ran in the middle of July in a small conditions race at York over a mile which it was hoped would boost his confidence. He won by four lengths but I had to get to work on him and he was tending to hang in towards the rails. As a result, blinkers were tried on him in his next race, the Benson and Hedges Gold Cup, but he ran very free tracking all-the-way winner Hawaiian Sound and was beaten after only seven furlongs.

There was no doubt that the horse had ability – he had shown that in the Futurity as a two-year-old and in the Mecca-Dante, and just before he ran in the St Leger he did a really good piece of work with the four-year-old Remezzo. When Remezzo won a decent handicap over a mile and a half under 9 stones 12 lb the day before the Leger, we knew that Julio Mariner was in good form. If only we could get him to produce what we knew he was capable of in the last of the season's classics I was sure we stood a good chance. The big threat was Ile de Bourbon who was the horse everyone had to beat.

There was drama at the start of the Leger when the French challenger, Easter King, reared up in the stalls and crashed over backwards, fracturing his skull. A 20-minute delay followed while the vet was called and his connections were consulted and he was put out of his misery. Through it all, my horse remained calm. After the York débâcle the blinkers had been left off and the plan was to relax the horse in the early stages. The betting public were not impressed by his chances and let him start at 28–1. Turning into the straight the horse was travelling nicely at the back of the field. I'd intended to follow Ile de Bourbon throughout the race but three furlongs out it became apparent that he wasn't going to win anything. Still going well, and with the odds-on favourite beaten, we had a chance. We had a good run towards the inside to get in front approaching the last furlong and ran on well. Joe Mercer and Le Moss stayed on strongly to be second but never looked like overhauling us – coincidentally, Joe came second in both my Leger wins.

Captain Lemos had first come into British horse-racing in the mid 1960s and had bought Warren Hill and Ashley Heath Studs as well as leasing Carlburg Stables to Clive. He gained significant wins with Petingo in 1967 and 1968 but classic success eluded that horse when Sir Ivor defeated him in the 2,000 Guineas. Morston and I had been responsible for depriving his Cavo Doro of victory in the 1973 Derby. The victory in the St Leger after all these near-misses in other classics was doubly sweet for the Captain, and he asked if he could keep Julio Mariner's St Leger race saddle as a memento. I had planned to ride on it the following week, but it seemed a small price for winning the Leger and I paid it willingly.

When you go through a bad patch nothing seems to go right. Conversely, when things are going well the luck often seems to accumulate. After the success in the English St Leger I flew to Vienna to ride High Noon in the Austrian version the following day. In Austria I finished third of four but, incredible as it may sound, I was given the race after a stewards' inquiry. It was the only time I was ever awarded the race after finishing third, but in the stewards' view I had been hampered by both the first and the second. To cap it all, on the way home I was stopped by a policeman for speeding. Not only did he let me off, he even asked for my autograph. Some weekend! The icing on the cake came when I was named the Wilkinson Sword Jockey of the Month. My September tally had included 16 wins besides the St Leger. At the final Doncaster meeting I was also presented with a case of champagne for the best riding performance of the Leger meeting. With 45 winners including a classic for the Carlburg stable everything was going too well to last.

At Lingfield in October, I was riding Mercy Cure for York trainer Vic Mitchell and was leading, racing three or four horses wide of the inside rail, when she ducked sharply right into the rail about a furlong and a half out and threw me. The horse's front leg made contact with my right leg and the pain I felt was all too familiar. I didn't need telling that I had broken my leg again. As had been the case with Prins Eugen at Haydock, the accident was caused by an over-intelligent horse. Mercy Cure had worked on the track that morning and had entered the course through a gap about a furlong and a half from home. I am certain she remembered it and was looking for the short-cut back to her box when she dived into the rail.

I was brought back by ambulance to the weighing-room, where I informed everyone that it was broken. I didn't yet realise quite what a thorough job Mercy Cure had made of it, but I did know that my foot seemed to be moving independently in its boot. An X-ray at the hospital showed the reason: both bones in my lower leg had broken straight through. I had a couple of screws inserted to keep the other company. Later on, one of these screws started to unwind and it became necessary to operate again to remove the 'Lingfield' screws. The 'York' screw, however, is still in place and no doubt it will stay there now. One of Clive's owners, Mr Rabbi Khan, sent his chauffeur and Rolls along to the hospital to bring me home to Huttons Ambo in comfort. It was a very thoughtful gesture and much appreciated.

I wasn't in too much pain but had another problem this time. Because of the locations of the breaks the plaster encased my leg from my thigh to my toes and I was plagued by the most intense itching at the back of my ankle which there was no way of scratching. It was beginning to drive me mad when Sue came up with what she thought was a brilliant idea. She produced an extending car aerial and suggested that if she poked it down the top of the plaster it would eventually get to the irritating spot. It seemed worth a try, so she wriggled it about, laughing uncontrollably as I instructed 'down a bit, left a bit'. It worked a treat – that is until, the itch relieved, she tried to remove the aerial. Unfortunately, what she hadn't realised was that under the plaster there were layers of bandages, and the aerial was now firmly trapped in the gauze. When gentle manipulation failed to disengage it she lost patience and gave it a tug. The round knob on the end of the aerial broke off and lodged just under my heel. My sense of humour, already strained by Sue's refusal to take my itch seriously, now completely deserted me. I thought I was going to go crazy as this tiny piece of metal pressed into my foot. In the end we had once more to call on my old friend Mr Haw to rescue me, which he did by cutting a sort of window in the heel of the plaster, After that I suffered my itches in silence.

After the York incident I had been in a hurry to get back as plenty of the season remained, but this time, with the whole winter before me, I had a bit of breathing space in which to recover in time for the following season. I had ridden 88 winners, and if it hadn't been for the accident would have been close to the century, but the Brittain stable's form, flatteringly for me – although it may well have been coincidence – had tailed off a bit in my absence. This prompted Captain Lemos to write me a letter in which he suggested that I should endeavour to avoid breaking my leg the following season 'as it is rather obvious we need your services'.

After presenting Jimmy Bleasdale with the Cock of the North Trophy, I went to Barbados to recuperate. I had first been there in 1973 with Pat and Michael Stoute to stay with Michael's parents. I had ridden a horse trained by Michael for his fellow 'Bajan' David Seale, and I was invited to stay with him. How lucky we were to have friends in the right places! David Seale is the leading owner-breeder of Barbados and possesses the island's largest private stable at his stud farm, Hopefield. David's horses are split between local trainer Ron Burke and Scobie Breasley. Hopefield is a magnificent complex with its own private gallops, equine pool and paddocks. We stayed on the plantation at the Seales' guest cottage, which stood next to a swimming pool made from a converted syrup vat. The pool was set into a steep slope above the complex, and by standing on the verandah which surrounded the pool you could look down at the gallops and stables. It was quite idyllic. David and his wife Anne are two of the most generous people I know, and all of us have been there many times to stay. I couldn't have chosen a more pleasant place to recover from a broken leg.

Exactly six months to the day after the accident, I rode my first winner of the 1979 season at Beverley on the filly La Dolce who was later to make herself famous as the dam of Pebbles. All racing eyes were focussed on Salisbury the following day where the young American jockey Steven Cauthen was due to ride for the first time in this country. Steve was retained by Barry Hills, who laid out Marquee Universal for him to win his very first race. Half an hour later, I won the Guineas trial on Johnny Winter's Tudor Maid, and in beating Steve into second became, for what it's worth, the first jockey to beat him in this country. Steve is a very likeable and intelligent young man. He saw at once that the extra streamlined style that jockeys use in America is not suited to the kind of lazy horse that is more often found in England. Nor is it suitable for English tracks, which vary so much from the standard American left-handed tracks. So he adapted his style and the rewards for his skill and versatility came quickly.

Although there is no doubting his ability in the saddle I'm sure Steve would be the first to acknowledge the help he has received in his career from his agent, John Hanmer. John has for years been one of the top Raceform readers and is also a paddock commentator for BBC Television. He is one of the best jockeys' agents around. One thing Steve undoubtedly remembers about his British debut at Salisbury that day was his first encounter with the foibles of British stewards. There had been heavy rain before the meeting and the stewards in their wisdom had piled into a car and driven down the course before racing to inspect the ground. Inevitably the car got bogged down in the mud in the middle of the course. Despite this, when they eventually returned – on foot – to the weighing-room they passed the course as fit for racing. Fortunately for us, by the time of the first race the car had been dragged off the course or Steve's first impression of English racing might have put him off for life.

I had ridden a colt called Foveros for Clive in Marquee Universal's race but he was unsuited by the going. He ran next in the Crawford Handicap at Newmarket – a race for those horses that weren't allotted a weight in the free handicap – and finished a soundly-beaten third to Henry Cecil's Chalet who gave him 10 lb. After that, Clive wanted to run Foveros in the Blue Riband trial at Epsom. I strongly disagreed with this. I felt that as he'd been beaten with everything in his favour at Newmarket the risk of him running close up at Epsom without doing any good, thus spoiling his handicap mark, was too great to be worth taking, especially as he was in the Esher Cup at Sandown later that week with 8 stones 1 lb. Despite my opposition, Clive stuck to his guns and Foveros ran. As luck would have it it turned out to be a moderate year and he won, beating Main Reef, who was having his first run of the season. After the race Captain Lemos, who owned Foveros, came around to the yard and spoke to Jock Brown, the head lad, who was very good indeed at his job. 'Clive was right, you know', he told Jock. 'None of you wanted to run the horse at Epsom. You do your job in the yard, let the jockey do his job and leave the rest to Clive.'

In many ways that race was a turning point. All the previous season I had been consulted over where horses should run. After the Blue Riband trial my opinion was rarely sought on such matters. Placing the horses became a matter between owner and trainer. Later, the yard was to employ Major Swannell, the ex-top Jockey Club handicapper, to assist them in the placing of their horses. The victory affected Clive's policy over where and when to run. Now that the gamble had paid off once he was much more interested in trying for the big time in the hope that he'd be placed even if he couldn't win. There was a lot of sense in this approach from the owner's point of view. To be placed in a group race was often enough to enable a colt to be sold as a stallion abroad, so its value was greatly enhanced. Foveros was a prime example of this. He never won again, although in all he ran 12 times, but thanks to his performances in good company, which included two good runs against Kris, he earned a Timeform rating of 121 and was sold as a stallion to South Africa.

Over the years Clive was often criticised for running his horses in races that looked beyond them, and until his success with Pebbles there were plenty of people who were prepared to have a go at him. But he kept his owners happy with his policy, and it worked for him, too. How can you criticise a man who, after 21 years of 'doing his two' for Sir Noel Murless, now trains over 100 horses and enjoys a lifestyle that is more comfortable than that of most of his critics? The fact that the Carlburg stables, which he now owns, are full every year bears witness to his popularity and success. But the new policy, although fine for the horses' connections, was not so good for me. There were two reasons: first, if a stable's horses are consistently placed just a little bit out of their class you obviously don't get as many winners. As far as most jockeys are concerned, and I was no exception, winners are what racing is all about. My prediction that running Foveros in the Blue Riband trial would cost us races was also proved correct.

Foveros went up 10 lb in the handicap as a result of his Epsom win. At the Newmarket July meeting he took on Chalet again and, on 11 lb worse terms for a five-and-a-half lengths defeat, ran the Cecil colt to two short heads. Had we been at the same weights as before we would have coasted home. I was disappointed both for the horse and for myself, and my mood wasn't improved when a close acquaintance told me he had heard the Captain say after the race, 'Edward isn't riding as well since he broke his leg'. He may well have been right about my riding, but he chose a bad illustration and a bad day to comment on it!

The second problem was less obvious. Clive had never tied me down with orders, but if I was riding a horse that I didn't think had a chance because it was out of its depth it put me in a dilemma over how to ride it. If I gave the horse a good chance early in the race and rode it from behind it was never going to get there because it wasn't good enough, but if I had it up there with the pace it would almost certainly drop out before the finish. Whatever happened, the owners were likely to blame the way I had ridden it rather than accept that their animal just wasn't good enough. To account for this, whenever I felt we were out-classed I made a point of discussing with Clive in front of the owners in the paddock how he wanted the horse to be ridden. It then became a shared responsibility and there were no misunderstandings afterwards.

One day that season when things did go right for me was at Lingfield in May, when for once the fact that I was growing a bit long in the tooth paid dividends. Flat jockeys with experience of flag or barrier starts were thin on the ground by this time. Many of my younger colleagues had never known anything but stalls starts, and some of the starters had forgotten what they had known about the old-fashioned ones. So when the going proved so heavy that the stalls had to be abandoned and a flag start introduced I found myself with a distinct advantage.

My mount, a two-year-old called Willing to Learn, was lucky to be drawn right next to the rail, and with the starter standing above me on his rostrum I was almost out of his line of vision. Realising that his attention was on the far end of the line and not on me, I was able to creep forward in the line, and while I wouldn't admit to jumping the flag I certainly got a flying start! Len Thomas, reporting the race in the *Sporting Life*, described it as poaching four lengths. Willing to Learn was never headed and eventually won by three lengths. The starter later told me that if I hadn't won so easily he would have reported me to the stewards for pinching the start!

News must have filtered back to Bill Watts that all was not going as smoothly as it might have done between myself and Carlburg stables, and in the middle of June he offered me a good retainer to return North to ride for him. I decided to mull it over for a little while. In mid-July it was good to have a winner on my local stamping-ground at York where I rode Tesoro Mio to take the Magnet Cup for Jimmy Etherington. It was a chance ride as Johnny Seagrave was side-lined. Johnny was a good, tough, dependable jockey who never gave an inch. He was a master of coaxing a horse to run well, often above its form, and in a truly-run race he could drop a horse out and then ride it through the field to pinch a place in a way few other jockeys could match. Not too many people took a chance on getting on the inside of Johnny in a race. He was supposed to be slightly deaf in one ear as a result of an accident, but whether he was or he wasn't he often cocked a deaf'un. Little shouts on his inside weren't often heeded. Despite this he was very well-liked by his colleagues. Since he retired from the saddle he has done well training greyhounds.

By the time August came round I had decided to accept Bill Watt's offer of a retainer. Neither Clive nor I were really happy about the way things had worked out that season and in the end it didn't take a lot of thinking about. Over the years, the Goodwood August meeting has become the place where plans for the following season are announced and the disclosure of my proposed defection back to the North followed this tradition. From a riding point of view, the meeting itself wasn't too bad. The Stewards' Cup was never a lucky race for me and I was second again on The Sandford to stable-mate Standaan. However, I had a nice win on Braughing for Bill Gredley, beating Known Fact. After that, the Brittain stable went down with the cough and our association spluttered to an end in more ways than one!

- 17 -
Back in the North

IN March 1980 Bill Watts received the following letter from one of his patrons, Rowena Sutton (Mayday Melody's nervous owner), in response to his request for a contribution towards my retainer. 'Dear Bill, Have just received account for February. I have a query – as I seem to be buying a share in Edward do I have to use the nomination myself or can I sell it? Rowena.' Bill posted his reply the same day. 'Dear Ro. Thank you for your letter regarding the share in Edward Hide. The nomination is only for your personal use and is not to be sold or lent. I apologise for the strict terms of this agreement but as you can imagine we do not want him to come into contact with outsiders especially as such things as metritis etc. are still with us. I would like you to know Edward passed all the tests before starting here. Yours Bill.'

Sadly Rowena, who is now Mrs Peter Nurse, never took up her option on the agreement.

It was a particularly wet spring in 1980 but with the help of his new all-weather gallop on the old Richmond racecourse Bill was able to have his early runners unusually fit. Although only four furlongs long, owing to the lack of space, this gallop was a big help, particularly in the prevailing adverse conditions. Few of the other Northern trainers had access to an all-weather gallop and so that year Bill had a double advantage: not only were his horses fitter than normal for the start of the Flat, but the opposition were hampered by their unusually wet training grounds. He had five winners before the end of March, starting off with Murillo on the second day of the Doncaster meeting. I was unaware then of the fitness edge we had over the rest and when I asked Murillo to quicken to win his race a furlong out he did it so well that at the post he was eight lengths ahead of his nearest rival, O I Oyston.

It's always a relief to have the first winner of the season under your belt, but I kicked myself for winning by so far as it meant he would go up pounds in the handicap. While the betting man understands all about handicap races, not everyone may be so fully acquainted with the subject, so perhaps this is the place to discuss it further.

The theoretical intention of the handicapper is to get the whole field to cross the finishing line in a dead heat. He tries to achieve this by slowing the faster horses down through making them carry more weight, and speeding the slower ones up by giving them a lighter burden. For example, if I were to run against, say, Steve Cram, the only possible chance I would have of keeping pace with him would be if he were handicapped by having to carry something like a sack of coal. Whether for our next race he had more or less coal to carry would depend on the result of the first encounter. Similarly, if the weights horses have been given don't result in their finishing together, then those weights will be readjusted in future races and the further apart they finish the greater the adjustment will be.

Basically, over sprint distances, every length between horses at the finish is reckoned to be worth 3 lb, which is why I regretted my eight-length win on Murillo. Since that race was over seven furlongs it meant he would shoot up in the weights. The penalty for winning by a wide margin in longer races is not so great. By the time you get to two-mile races a one-length margin at the finish is reckoned to be worth only one pound. The fact that, despite all the painstaking juggling of weights, few handicaps even get close to the aim of a multiple dead-heat is what makes this kind of race so interesting. If the handicapper always got it right no one would bother watching, let alone betting on the result.

In the middle of the last century Admiral Rous worked out the scale of weight for age which reflected the relationship between the relative maturity of horses of various ages with respect to distance. The basis of his formula, with slight amendments, has stood the test of time and is still in use today. In trying to assess how good a horse is the handicapper has to interpret the way each horse runs. In this respect a good but lazy horse has an advantage in handicaps because he will produce only enough to win, and the handicapper has to guess at how good he really is (as long as the horse keeps on winning). By contrast, he will soon have the measure of a free-running horse, which gives its all each time it runs. I always bore in mind that it was to the horses' future benefit not to win further than neccessary. However, very occasionally this would backfire and I would be beaten on a horse that should have won.

Most trainers appreciate a jockey keeping a bit up his sleeve when possible, but I vividly recall riding for Bruce Hobbs one day at Ponte-fract and winning hard held by half a length. Mr Hobbs didn't think this was at all clever and told me in no uncertain terms afterwards that should I ever do this again it would be the end of our association.

At the end of the 1979 season, Mr Hobbs had offered me a retainer to ride his classic colt, Tyrnavos, in all his races as a three-year-old. I wasn't able to accept this, because while Bill didn't think he had any classic material, if one of his did prove good enough he would obviously have required me to ride it. However, Mr Hobbs was happy to accept a gentleman's agreement that I would ride Tyrnavos whenever I was available.

Like Julio Mariner, Tyrnavos was a son of Blakeney, but unlike 'Julio' he was considered to have enough speed to be trained for the Guineas. I rode him when he made a winning reappearance in the Craven Stakes at Newmarket and he ran a respectable seventh in that controversial Guineas in which Nureyev was disqualified and the race was awarded to Known Fact. Tyrnavos followed that with a close fourth to Hello Gorgeous in the Dante at York, but we could finish only 12th of 24 behind Henbit in the Derby after being buffeted about early on. His next race was to be the Irish Derby, but I was claimed by Bill to ride at the big 'Pitman's' Derby meeting that day. My agreement with Bill was that he would let me off for English classics if he didn't have a runner in the race himself. In addition, because he liked to go to Royal Ascot, he had also agreed to let me ride there rather than claim me for any of his runners in the North on those four days. But the Irish Derby didn't qualify for a release, although I'm sure if Tyrnavos had been more concerned in the finish at Epsom I would have been keener to ride him in Ireland and Bill would probably have released me.

As it turned out everything went his way that day at The Curragh. With no one else wanting to make the running Tony Murray was able to dictate his own pace to secure a clever and well-ridden victory. After his disappointment in the Epsom Derby we had worked Tyrnavos in blinkers but as they hadn't appeared to improve him they were left off for the Irish Derby, although they had probably sharpened him up. I appreciated Bruce Hobbs' gesture in giving me the ride back in the King George where we tried a repeat of the tactics used at The Curragh. This time, though, Tyrnavos wasn't left alone and he dropped out when headed in the straight to finish eighth of ten behind Ela Mana Mou. After that, he was retired to stud.

Tyrnavos was out of that great broodmare Stilvi whose previous foals had included the Guineas runner-up Tachypous and the champion two-year-old of 1978, Tromos. Her two-year-old daughter Tolmi, by Great Nephew, also owned by George Cambanis, had won the Princess Margaret Stakes at Ascot, the race preceding the King George. I had written in my notebook that Tolmi 'could be nice' after I had ridden her work for the first time, and she confirmed that by winning really well on her debut at Newmarket.

Racing is full of 'might have beens' and 'if onlys', but in Tolmi's

The end of one era and the beginning of the next: (TOP) Riding Pink Foot to victory in the Farewell Handicap at the last meeting of 1960 – and it was goodbye to the Captain who was retiring at 80. His son, Bill (BELOW), took over as guv'nor at Highfield.

L–R: Don Morris, Johnnie Greenaway, Joe Sime, Dennis Ward, Brian Connorton, Jimmy Etherington, me, Cliff Parkes, Walter Bentley, Lionel Brown, Johnny Seagrave and Tony Rawlinson and our wives meet for the Northern Jockeys' Dinner in 1964.

Another racing tip – straight from the horse's mouth!

Edgar Britt and I reminisce about our times with Captain Elsey at Highfield. Edgar was a great help at the start of my career.

A brilliant piece of training by Bill Watts enabled me to win the 1,000 Guineas on Waterloo in 1972.

E. G. Byrne, London.

My greatest moment – winning the Derby on Morston in 1973. It was my 13th Derby ride and he was number 13 on the racecard.

Lochnager wins the William Hill Sprint Championship in an exciting finish from Faliraki (not in picture), Polly Peachum and Three Legs (far side).

Alec Russell, York.

The Press Association Ltd, London.

These two photographs, taken at the same moment, show the foreshortening effect of a head-on view from a telephoto lens. This is a good illustration of the problems facing the stewards.

The home-made exercise bike that helped me to confound the doctor's prediction that I would be out of action for six months (LEFT). 11 weeks after a broken leg I was back — and with a winner!

Mrs McArdy and I working together before her victory in the 1,000 Guineas in 1977.

Hong Kong was not all scandal and frustration – there were happy times with my family (Will, Sue and Lizzie) and on the racecourse. Gay Eighties (BELOW) was the biggest winner of my two years there.

case the fates really did seem to conspire, both directly and indirectly, to prevent her winning the 1,000 Guineas. The 'direct' part of the bad luck came when her preparation was interrupted twice by injury. At the end of her two-year-old season she sprained a joint which caused her to miss the Cheveley Park Stakes, and she suffered a further setback the following spring when she pulled a muscle at the end of March. It meant that she missed vital work and it was touch and go whether she would be fit in time.

The other bit of bad luck that befell her was due, oddly, to Lester, who recovered a lot quicker than was expected from an accident. Shortly before the 1,000 Guineas Lester had been lucky to escape with his life after a very nasty incident at Epsom. His mount, Windsor Boy, panicked after being put in the stalls and somehow managed to squeeze out through the gap at the bottom of the gate. In the process Lester nearly lost his right ear, which needed 31 stitches, and also injured his back. Few who saw him being stretchered off that day imagined that he had much chance of riding in the 1,000 Guineas only a week later. Lester's determination to win did get him to Newmarket to ride Fairy Footsteps. He still didn't look 100 per cent, but he put up an amazing performance. Lester knew his filly well. He knew what pace to set to suit her and he had the confidence to make the running, which takes some doing when you're riding a fancied horse in a classic. Then when the chips were down Lester rode a virtuoso finish, strong and determined as only he knew how, which just kept Fairy Footsteps in front to the line to beat us by a neck. It was one of the closest and most exciting finales there has ever been to the 1,000 Guineas, with only one length covering the first five horses home.

I have often thought back to that race and the neck that separated us from the winner. If Lester had been unable to ride and someone else had taken his place would that neck's difference have existed? Likewise, if Tolmi had not pulled a muscle and instead had been 100 per cent fit for the race would Fairy Footsteps still have beaten us, even with Lester on board? We'll never know for certain, but I have a strong opinion on the matter!

Subsequently Tolmi disappointed in bad ground at Kempton when in season. We had tried to come wide on her to avoid the cut-up ground on the inside. In her following race, the Coronation Stakes at Royal Ascot, we adopted different tactics. She was always going well but I kept her covered up until the last minute and produced her just before the winning post to win cleverly. Sue rushed down to see me come into the winners' enclosure and overheard one top-hatted gentleman say to another, 'Hide nearly made a cock-up of that one as well'. Although she usually ignored comments about me, whether good or bad, in this case she appreciated that I had in fact ridden a particularly good race. She saw red and told the gentlemen exactly what she thought of their knowledge and judgement before she noticed by the names on their lapels that they were Jockey Club stewards. One of them told her that they were entitled to their opinion. 'Someone in your position should know how to read a race', she retorted. She later saw Bruce Hobbs and apologised to him after confessing what she had said to the two men, whom she knew were friends of his. 'You were absolutely right', he replied. 'I'll tell them myself!'

At Ripon during the August Bank holiday meeting I had a nasty experience which could easily have been much more serious than it was. There had been a false start in the race, and while I and a few other jockeys had responded to the fellow waving the red flag and had pulled up, the rest of the field carried on regardless. It was obvious that it would take some time for the stewards to decide what was to happen next, so while we waited at the start we dismounted and led the horses around. Suddenly, one of the other horses which had been standing in the centre ran back towards my mount, Swaying Tree, and let fly with both barrels. His hooves caught me full force in the back and the pain was enough for me to realise some damage had been done. However, since I could still bend and walk I told myself nothing was broken so it couldn't be serious.

Eventually the stewards decided that the race would be re-run half an hour after the last. After cantering back up the course I decided to pay a quick visit to the loo to see what damage had been inflicted on my back. There was nothing much to see in the mirror but I decided that another test was advisable. To my dismay, instead of the usual fluid I produced blood! Terry Lucas took me to hospital where they diagnosed badly bruised kidneys and kept me in for a couple of days. Apparently these things can go either way; sometimes the kidneys give in completely, and sometimes after a while, they gradually start to work properly again. The treatment was to rest and wait and see. Fortunately for me mine went the right way. While I lay on the hospital bed wondering if my end was nigh Jimmy Bleasdale stood in for me on Swaying Tree and won the re-run of the race.

Later in the week, while I was still recovering, I also missed a winning ride on Bill Watts' promising two-year-old Engulf when he put up a smart display to beat Sula Bula eight lengths at Ayr. I was, however, back in the saddle when he next ran, in the Laurent Perrier Champagne Stakes, although I soon wished I hadn't been. Willie Carson, riding Church Parade for the Queen switched left to make his challenge at the same time as Geoff Baxter challenged on my other side. I ran out of room, becoming the meat in a sandwich, and was brought down approaching the final furlong. It was a nasty incident and I was lucky to escape without injury. In fact, the next day when I was interviewed on ITV by Brough Scott he introduced me by saying he was delighted to be talking to someone when only the day before he had expected to be going to his funeral! For some reason best known to themselves the stewards decided not to apportion blame to anybody. Bill Watts was furious.

But Willie Carson shrugged off the whole matter. He was quoted by George Ennor as saying 'Nothing happened. It was just unfortunate'. Nothing happened? Willie's remarks added insult to injury. The one who suffered most from the fall was Engulf, who up to then had looked like being a top-class horse. He was bumped and bruised all over, bled profusely from his nose and had bruises on his head which didn't show themselves until two or three weeks later. Although he was able to run again he never showed any form and was eventually retired to the Apprentice School at Newmarket. I didn't expect a public apology from Willie, but even though it was an accident I felt some private expression of regret for the part he played in the incident wouldn't have gone amiss.

About a year before I had bought a tee-shirt bearing what I thought at the time was a particularly appropriate slogan for Willie. I had been saving it for the right occasion and felt, after reading Willie's comments about the incident, that the moment had arrived. The slogan? 'It's hard to be humble when you're as great as I am'! Willie and I shared the same corner in the weighing-room and often exchanged friendly insults. If it's true that you only insult those you like then Willie and I have been great buddies for years! He was forever calling me 'Ugly' and 'Bump-bump', and why I didn't retaliate with at the very least a play on his initials, I'll never know. 'Ugly' I could accept, but 'Bump-bump' used to really wind me up when it was said outside the weighing-room in front of my connections. It was a reference to the fact that often, when riding in a race, if I was checked I would involuntarily drop and sometimes my seat would touch the saddle in getting my horse going again. When Willie married Elaine during Chester week a few years ago, Sue and I were invited to the reception. It hadn't dawned on me that it was a black tie job and although I enjoyed it, I felt a bit of a wally as I was the only one there in a lounge suit. Elaine and Willie have stayed with us for the odd York meeting and I often told him one of the biggest mistakes I ever made was not drowning him in our pool. He could be very irritating, but now I share most people's opinion that Willie has mellowed considerably – maybe I have as well.

Willie was the first jockey in this country to employ an agent. Because of this he was able to avoid the bookwork and background graft that I had to go through in order to pick up my rides. That's not meant as a criticism – as I was a jockeys' agent myself I appreciate their role better than most, and Willie was one step ahead of the game in using one so early on. Now he has come full circle, and Elaine books his rides. But he was sometimes very vague about the details of the mounts his agent had found him. More than once as we left the weighing-room he asked me how far the race was and what the opposition was. On the odd occasion he even asked me what he was riding, although I concede that it's possible he was having me on . . .

Willie's lack of homework before a race was more than counter-balanced by his natural ability in the saddle and his instinctive flair for doing the right thing at the right time. Perhaps the fact that he has won the Jockeys' Championship five times proves that in his case he doesn't actually need to know what horse he's riding!

A game of musical stables took place among the leading jockeys at the end of the 1980 season. Pat Eddery moved from Peter Walwyn to take over at Vincent O'Brien's, and young Walter Swinburn was offered the Walwyn job but decided instead to go to Michael Stoute's. Michael was known to be very ambitious and many people, myself included, thought Walter had made the wrong decision. We felt that if things didn't work out Walter would be the one to suffer. Time, though, was to prove him right. Joe Mercer ended his successful partnership with Henry Cecil and took up the Peter Walwyn retainer which left Lester to go to Henry Cecil's. Meanwhile, Brian Taylor left Ryan Price to go to Jeremy Hindley and Brian Rouse took over at Ryan Price's.

A long time before any of these decisions was made, I was sitting on my own in the weighing-room one afternoon at Haydock when Pat Eddery came and sat down to discuss the offer he had been made to ride for Robert Sangster and Vincent O'Brien. It was obviously a very important career move for Pat, and I've always considered it a compliment that he asked my opinion. It was a big decision for him to leave Peter Walwyn, who was flying high at the time having twice been Champion Trainer in the 1970s. In his early days it was apparent that Pat had great riding ability, but I didn't credit him with too much between the ears. I soon revised that opinion and now regard him as one of the shrewdest jockeys that has ever ridden. His is a natural talent. It is a well-known fact that although Lester could use his whip in his left hand when necessary he preferred using it in his right. Pat, however, is able to use his whip equally effectively in either hand. Although he can ride a very strong finish he is one of the few modern jockeys who can win as cheekily as Lester often did.

On the front of the menu for our annual Northern jockeys' dinner and dance that year was a picture of me taken in the sauna, reading the *Sporting Life* with telephone in hand. It was captioned 'The trials and tribulations of a jockey'. Guests were invited to pen a humorous caption and submit it for a prize. Among the printable ones were:

'St Peter? Edward here. Which side of the track did you say it was going to rain on?'

'Mark? I'll take you to Pontefract this afternoon . . . will it be all right for a lift to Edinburgh on Monday?' (Pontefract, for the information of Southerners, is about 40 miles from Huttons Ambo, while Edinburgh is close to 200 miles.)

'Bill [Watts], Bruce Hobbs wants me to ride five at Ascot. Now, about that one at Edinburgh.'

The competition was such a success that they ran it again the following year. This time the photograph, entitled 'Well, it was like this guv'nor', showed me gesticulating with my whip in a post-race conference with trainer and owner. Bill Watts had his dark glasses on and there was an interested onlooker in the background. Here is a sample of some of the entries that year:

'I know I went the wrong way but the ground was much faster in the car park!'

'You told me to hold it up and I got done for flashing on the way round!'

'If you took those f***ing dark glasses off, you'd see for yourself what happened!'

'Will you hold this a minute while I prove to him I'm "Cock" of the North!'

'If you think I'm Cock of the North you should see . . .' And so on.

1981 belonged to Shergar. One morning in the spring, I had the leg-up on the great horse in a morning gallop before he made his winning reappearance in the Sandown Classic trial. Shergar blew up in his work that day, but in spite of that I was tremendously impressed. I must have gone on about the horse because a father of one of Will's schoolfriends asked him what he thought would win the Derby. Will, who had absolutely no interest in racing, told him the only name that had registered in his mind: Shergar. The lucky man had his pound on at 25–1.

While Shergar was completing the Derby double in Ireland, I rode the Aga Khan's Dalsaan, a half-brother to Doyoun, to win the Van Geest Stakes at Newmarket. The following month I had another success for the Aga on Shademah, who later gained more fame as the dam of Shahrastani, in the Bill Elsey Stakes at Thirsk. Rhein Bridge gave the Watts stable one of its best wins that year in the Lancashire Oaks at Haydock after disappointing in the Epsom equivalent. She was owned by Robert Sangster, in whose colours I also won the Flying Childers Stakes on Peterhof for Vincent O'Brien at Doncaster.

Winning on Streaker at Newmarket for Bill in October gave me my 100th winner and the last century of my career. I was also engaged to ride in the Arc on Harry Wragg's Pelerin, who had probably the best chance of any horse I had ever ridden in the race. The day before, Sue told Anne Mercer she was going to Longchamp to watch me ride in the Arc. Anne replied that unless she had a booked seat she would never go as you couldn't see a thing. That didn't worry Sue – she could always see the race on the recorder when she got home, but she was looking forward to the day out. As usual, on arrival I abandoned her and in atrocious French she tried to inquire where the jockeys' wives went. She was directed to an escalator and went up and up into an elegant room with armchairs on the balcony, which was almost deserted apart from a few other elegant ladies. If these facilities were provided for jockeys' wives then France was very different from England. It gradually dawned on her that she was in the stand reserved for the wives of the Jockey Club Members but, always one to grasp an opportunity, she sat quietly watching Marwell winning the Abbaye and Gold River the Arc before descending once more among the rabble!

Pelerin had a rough race, being bumped, and was disappointing. I had been apprehensive beforehand, because in his last bit of work he had gone exceptionally well. This might sound strange, but if horses do that at the end of the season it can mean they have gone over the top. This was probably the case with Pelerin.

My first two years back in the North had gone well. My tally, of 211 winners, was considerably augmented by the Watts stable, which sent out 98 winners in the same period. But in 1982 and 1983 there was a decline; the stable sent out only 54 winners over the two seasons and, to make matters worse, Bruce Hobbs had taken on Geoff Baxter as his first jockey and called on me far less often. I could manage only 65 winners in 1982 and 53 in 1983. Other factors also played their part in my dwindling fortunes, not least the continuing slump in the quality of horses based in the North compared with those in the South. Much of this coincided with the rise of the bloodstock agent as a power in racing. With the influx of money, particularly Arab money, into the bloodstock market in the early 1980s, yearling prices at the top end of the sales had shot sky-high and bloodstock was beginning to be treated very much as a commodity for investment by wealthy speculators who often had never had any previous involvement with racing. Obviously, these men required guidance in this new form of investment and most of them employed bloodstock agents to manage their interests and to advise them which animals to buy and where to have them trained. Most of these agents were based in London or Newmarket, and it was obviously more convenient for them to have the horses they managed placed with trainers whose premises were readily accessible to them. This is why, during the early 1980s, many quite ordinary Southern trainers suddenly found themselves 'highly recommended' and their stables full of expensive, beautifully-bred, often American-bought, horses. And a very pleasant experience it was for them, too. Unfortunately, the trainers 'up North' did not have such a good time, since they were left mainly with the humble commercially-bred yearlings after the speculators had creamed the top off the market.

Of course, there's nothing wrong with having your horses trained at Newmarket. The training facilities there are second to none, but the Elsey, Watts and Easterby gallops have all proved more than adequate to prepare classic winners in the past and it would be entirely wrong for people to assume that the decline in the North's fortunes is due to poor facilities or indeed to lack of ability on the part of its trainers. Given the right horses, the Northern men can still do it – in 1982 Dick Peacock proved it again with Fearless Lad. A three-year-old chestnut son of Import, Fearless Lad already had two wins as a juvenile to his credit when I rode him in a small but competitive five-furlong race at Beverley. He won it easily by five lengths, which encouraged Dick to go for the King's Stand Stakes at Royal Ascot. This, too, he won impressively, beating Chellaston Park by two lengths. At the end of the season, Fearless Lad gave me a great ride when going down by only a head to Sharpo in the Prix de l'Abbaye and was then exported to South Africa as a stallion.

This marked a great revival in the fortunes of the Manor House stables. Dick's last Royal Ascot winner had been Tudor Melody in 1958. He was the third generation of his family to have trained at Middleham. His grandfather, Dobson Peacock, had set up there in 1894, and on his death Dick's father Matt took over at Manor House, while Matt's brother Harry set up at Hurgill Lodge at Richmond where Bill Watts is now. Matt Peacock trained Dante to win the 1945 Derby. He was the first Northern-trained Derby-winner since Pretender in 1869 and, to this date, the last. Dick took over in 1951 on his father's death and trained there until he died in 1984. His stables, though, were not exempt from the depressed fortunes of the North and by 1981 he had only 16 horses in training, including Fearless Lad.

In his office Dick had a motto framed and mounted on the wall. It read simply: 'God save me from my owners' friends'. It is a thought which most trainers must have uttered at some time. The owner who rings his trainer to say 'My friends think you should run the horse more/less often; give it more/less work; run it over further/shorter distances; get Cauthen/Eddery to ride it – your jockey can't lie straight in bed' is unfortunately all too common. Owners' friends usually know very little about racing, but for some reason owners often prefer to listen to them rather than to the trainer, who is a professional at the game. The most dreaded friends' advice is, of course, 'Try another trainer because yours couldn't train ivy up a wall'.

In the 1982 Derby I was booked by Gavin Hunter to ride his Chester

Vase-winner, Super Sunrise, which, as a two-year-old, I had partnered to victory. Lester's intended Derby mount, Simply Great, trained by Henry Cecil, was withdrawn due to injury on the Sunday before the race, and when Lester didn't have a Derby ride, nobody slept well. There was no way I could see myself in the saddle with Lester watching from the stands! Apart from Super Sunrise, Lester was interested in the French-trained Persepolis, but owner Stavros Niarchos insisted he would honour his contract with Yves Saint-Martin. Gavin Hunter assumed that Lester would replace me on his horse but Lester asked for another 24 hours, obviously to try again for the Persepolis ride. No doubt if he had felt that Super Sunrise had a winning chance Lester would have accepted immediately. Finally, owner Jack Maxwell tired of the cat and mouse game. In his opinion Lester's waiting was unfair to all concerned, and he confirmed that I would be in the saddle. It was very rare for Lester to miss out on the Derby. There was no happy ending, though, for Super Sunrise could manage only 12th behind Golden Fleece!

In the meantime, horses like Say Primula and Atlantic Traveller kept the flag flying for Bill Watts and for me. Some Southern trainers were very complimentary in the press about my riding in the Goodwood Stakes aboard the latter, and I was hopeful that one or two of them might remember the S.T.D. code for Malton when they had a spare ride. But nothing came of it and I continued to struggle to find winners for the rest of the season. One of the troubles now was that many Southern stables that had previously supplied me with good rides had expanded to such an extent that they could employ their own second jockey to ride their runners in the North, and my services were seldom required.

I rode for my brother Tony whenever I was available. He had ridden 21 winners as a jockey but became too heavy, and after Father's retirement he had spells as assistant to Major Nelson at Lambourn and with Bruce Hobbs at Newmarket before his appointment in 1973 as private trainer to the Marchese Della Rochetta's Dormello Olgiata Stables, where the Marchese and Federico Tesio had bred both Nearco and Ribot. For the three years Tony was there, everything went very well, and out of his 200-odd runners there were 68 winners, an impressive ratio. His best horse was Mannsfeld, which won the 1974 Premio Parioli (the Italian 2,000 Guineas), the Group Two Prix Eugene Adam at Saint-Cloud and ran a close fourth to Nonoalco in the Prix Jacques le Marois at Deauville.

Tony returned to England in 1976 and set up on his own at Machell Place, Newmarket, owned since 1910 by the Leader family, to which Tony's wife Sue is related. One story told of the Leaders is that they always include one particular hymn in all their family wedding services, known to them as 'Leaders, Heavenly Father, Leaders . . .' but

I couldn't vouch for the truth of that tale! Machell Place is a nice 40-box yard overlooking the heath, but unfortunately the boxes have seldom been full. This is a surprise to me as I've always felt that Tony is a very capable trainer. Somehow he just hasn't caught the public's imagination, even though he has shown with such horses as Doc Marten and Celestial Dancer that he can come up with the goods if given the right material.

Doc Marten won the Taby Open Sprint Championship at Stockholm in 1982 but Celestial Dancer, a big, rangy colt, is the best horse that Tony has trained to date. The horse possessed a lot of ability, but once in front was inclined to give it away, so it was vital to cover him up and produce him as late as possible. In the valuable William Hill Trophy at York, Celestial Dancer and I were always travelling like winners but it was again a matter of not getting to the front too soon and keeping him covered up. Inside the final furlong, I felt there was a legitimate gap between Willie Carson on Blue Emmanuelle on my outside and the horse on my inside, Cyril's Choice, ridden by Michael Wigham, and I went for it. Had Willie given me an inch there would have been no problem, but Willie hasn't ridden the number of winners he has through giving much away, and you couldn't blame him for tightening me up. I got up to win by half a length but it had been very close and I suppose it was inevitable that there would be a steward's inquiry. The chief steward maintained that Willie had kept a straight course, although my reading of the film clearly showed Willie to come back into me. That's all water under the bridge now. The race was awarded to Cyril's Choice and I was found guilty of reckless riding and given a ten-day holiday. It did at least mean I could take a short midsummer break in Spain and I made the most of this opportunity to relax.

On our return from Spain we were horrified to hear on the car radio that a policeman had been shot dead in Malton and that several hundred policemen were searching the countryside near our home for the gunman – especially as Elizabeth was at home on her own. There followed a few very frightening days: whenever we were in the house we kept all the doors locked and the horses were all turned out so that we didn't have to go into the farm buildings. Many rumours prevailed, including a very strong one that the gunman had been in our village – someone's goat was dry at the morning milking time. Helicopters with heat-seeking equipment droned overhead day and night, going up and down the hedges and ditches. One evening the horses were suddenly startled and had obviously seen something, so we 'phoned the police who arrived in force and surrounded the farm, crawling up the fields and across the lawn on their stomachs with guns at the ready – all very dramatic, but it was for real. Eventually the man took a family hostage in Malton and shortly afterwards he was cornered at the tennis club behind their house and shot himself. They were a horrid few days.

Celestial Dancer really came into his own as a five-year-old, providing me with my only win on French soil in the Group Three Prix de Meautry at Deauville, beating Parioli a head with Petong and Sayf El Arab behind. It was third time lucky for the horse, who had finished fourth and fifth in the two previous runnings of the race. He started at 50–1 but he showed the win was no fluke when he went on to justify favouritism in the Group Three Golden-Peitsche at Baden-Baden, beating the previous year's winner, Gabitat.

Towards the end of 1982, I suffered one of those bad runs that most jockeys have to endure at some stage in their careers, going a full month without one win on home soil. I was in good company in suffering this experience: Doug Smith once went over 100 rides without a winner when he was Champion Jockey, and Steve Cauthen experienced a similar bad run in the States just before he came over to Britain. But knowing that didn't bring me much comfort at the time. If you don't keep up the winners you don't get the rides, and with the difficulties that being based in the North was already causing me I could see the situation spiralling downwards if my losing run didn't soon come to an end. Fortunately, the situation brightened a little just before the end of the season when I had a treble at Edinburgh. The second winner, Chrome Mag, trained by Walter Bentley, gave me my 2,500th winner in Britain.

Even so, the experience of that losing run had given me a jolt. People would be only too ready to dismiss me as a has-been at the age of 45 if I didn't maintain a high profile. There was no way I was going to retire yet, not until I had crept a little further up the all-time winners' table. I was confident that I was riding as well as ever and was as fit as ever. Perhaps what I needed was a change of scene.

– 18 –
Pastures New

THE idea of riding abroad for a winter season had been tempting me for some time. I had had a chance to go to India very early on in my career, but Father had been very much against it, largely because he had got it into his head that because Gordon was so successful I should follow his example. Since Gordon always took a complete break from racing during the winter to 'recharge his batteries' he felt I should do the same.

Something that had prejudiced him against foreign riding was the experience of Wally Swinburn. In 1954 Wally had ridden By Thunder! to victory in the Ebor carrying 6 stones 11 lb. He was struggling to build up his weight by eating chocolate and drinking milk, believing that he was too light to be given the better rides. Shortly afterwards he went off to India to ride for a winter season and Father always maintained that the hot sun made Wally blossom like a flower! Whatever the reason, after that winter in India Wally soon had a problem doing 8 stone. The prospect of watching me go the same way was enough to make Father refuse those early offers so firmly that I soon gained a reputation as a jockey who 'didn't ride abroad'. During the 1960s and 1970s the November Handicap signalled a mass exodus of British jockeys to racetracks in sunnier climes. Unbeknown to me, my reputation worked against me on at least one occasion. I learned only recently that Rada Sigtia, well-known in Britain as the owner of Sodium, who won the Irish Derby and St Leger in 1966, made inquiries in the 1970s to see whether I would ride for him in India, only to be told by Sam Hall that 'Edward doesn't go abroad in the winter'. In fact, at that time I was unlikely to bloom any more and would have welcomed a change of scene!

Within minutes of winning the Derby on Morston I was approached in the weighing-room by John Brown, a former assistant to Jack Clayton at Newmarket, who then trained in Hong Kong. He wanted me to ride for him over there during our off-season, but the offer came at the wrong moment and from the wrong country from my point of view. Racing in Hong Kong had turned professional in 1971 but it was still far from top-class. The track at Happy Valley was notorious among the jockeys for being extremely sharp. It was only about six and a half furlongs round, but the horses had to race against the camber and sometimes had difficulty negotiating the bends, and some spectacular accidents resulted. Having just achieved the pinnacle of English racing with a victory in the Derby I felt my future looked too rosy to take the risk and I turned down John Brown's offer.

By the early 1980s though the situation had changed. Racing standards in Hong Kong had improved beyond all recognition. Not only had the old Happy Valley track been made better and safer, but a new ultra-modern course had been built at Sha Tin on 250 acres of reclaimed land from the South China Sea. This was a fantastic piece of engineering and, according to colleagues who had ridden there, the facilities had to be seen to be believed. After a discussion with Sue I decided to take a trip to Hong Kong to see what the possibilities were. If everything was favourable I would apply for a licence to ride while I was there.

My first attempt at finding overseas employment ended in disappointment. On a reconnaissance trip to Hong Kong in December 1982 I came up against a stone wall in my application for a licence. There was not even any interest in having me over to help instruct the young apprentices. For some reason, both Jamie Barber, director of racing, and Jim Marsh, chief stipendiary steward, were extremely hostile towards me. Marsh told me, 'We have enough of your sort here already', and accused me of 'trying to take the bread out of the mouths of the local boys'. This attitude was not new, nor was it reserved especially for me. It has always been a sore point with British riders that while it is comparatively simple for foreign jockeys to come and work in England we frequently meet with stern opposition when we want to ride abroad ourselves.

At a race meeting at Happy Valley I was introduced to a Chinese owner who felt that he could raise the necessary support among his fellow owners for me to obtain a licence to ride for his trainer, Brian Kan. With this in mind I returned to the Jockey Club to collect the necessary forms and was directed to Jamie Barber's office. I was somewhat taken aback when Barber, a tall man who I understood was renowned for his mild manners, completely flew off the handle on hearing what I wanted. 'I thought we had made it quite clear to you that we don't want you here', he yelled. I was surprised by the strength of his feelings and wondered what he might have heard about me to make him react in such a hostile way. I never did find out for sure, but I had to accept that for the time being there wasn't an opening for me in Hong Kong.

However, I had sown the seeds for the future by making it known that I was interested in riding abroad, and in February Eric Collingwood rang offering me a job riding for him in Hong Kong for the 1983–84 season. I had ridden for Eric when he trained at Middleham and had known him for a long time. Unfortunately, it was impossible for me to accept an offer for a full season since racing in Hong Kong ran from late September to May and my retainer with Bill Watts precluded me from accepting the offer. It seemed at this stage as though I might after all finish my riding career without achieving my ambition to ride abroad for a winter season.

In 1983 I had a chance to look at another part of the racing world where there was a possible opportunity for me. Before the English season started I was invited out to Hyderabad in India for a few days to ride in a big race. I rode a horse called The King, which was trained in Bangalore by Eddie Cracknell, in the Charminar Challenge Indian Turf Invitation Cup. This was a prestige race between the best horses from each racing centre in India. We finished in the middle. The race was won by Wally Swinburn, who might just as easily have ended up in hospital. I was tracking him when his horse clipped the heels of the horse in front and pitched on his head. Somehow it found a fifth leg and recovered with happy results for all concerned.

My first impressions of India gained that day did not leave me keen on the country. Hyderabad was just as I had always imagined India to be from my school geography lessons; cattle in the streets, squalor and unbearable heat. If racing at Hyderabad was typical of racing in India then I didn't wish to return. Fortunately, when the racing was finished I flew to Bombay with the Swinburns, Wally and Walter. Bombay was a different kettle of fish. True, parts of Bombay had their squalor, too, but other areas of the city were spectacularly beautiful, the magnificent architecture dating from colonial days and earlier. The weather seemed ideal when I was there – not as hot as Hyderabad – and Wally, who had ridden there for several seasons, said this was typical. In addition the racecourse at Bombay looked a very nice course to ride on. It had a good, level galloping track and well-built stands. Another attraction for me was Beach Candy, which was a sports and leisure club next to the sea with a swimming pool, restaurant and various facilities where many of the ex-pats seemed to spend their off-duty hours. The lifestyle seemed quite attractive and held considerable appeal for me.

The icing on the cake was that there were a couple of good golf courses nearby. Golf has been a hobby of mine since I first had lessons from the professional at Ludlow racecourse as a boy. I am no expert, but I play well enough to enjoy the game, and the negligible costs involved in playing in India would be a big incentive to play more often: you could have your green fee, a caddy and a boy to go ahead and spot your ball for less than the cost of playing a round of golf in England carrying your own bag. I decided that if an offer came my way to ride in Bombay I would seriously consider it.

The 1983 season at home now loomed, so any thoughts of working abroad had to be put on ice for a while. At the end of the previous season, Paul Kelleway had rung asking me to ride for him in 1983 but as I was committed to ride for Bill Watts, we came to an arrangement where I would ride for him whenever possible. Indeed, we had a handful of winners in the spring of 1983. Our association then cooled, though we teamed up again successfully later in the season. 'Pattern race Paul', who rode the great jumper Bula in his riding days, is another trainer who is not afraid to run his horses in the best company – hence his nickname – but he is very capable, and has had top-class successes with Swiss Maid, Madam Gay and Risk Me.

A race that gave me a lot of pleasure that spring was the Yorkshire Cup, which I won on Line Slinger. She was owned by Noel Hetherton, Bill Elsey's longest-standing patron, and she was the fifth generation of the very good family I had been associated with. Line Slinger was a 33–1 outsider in the field of ten but relished the heavy ground. As no one else was keen to go on we made the running. Three-quarters of a mile out, aiming to get the others at it and trying to pinch a length or two, I kicked for home. In the straight we came up the centre of the course to get the better ground. Two furlongs out Khairpour challenged and actually got a neck in front but showed a lack of enthusiasm. My game filly was struggling on and would probably have got in front again anyway, but Khairpour ducked violently right making our task that much easier. Some more pattern race success came my way in July from Robert Sangster's Chapel Cottage in the Cherry Hinton at Newmarket for Mick Easterby and the same owner's Beaudelaire for Vincent O'Brien in the Beeswing Stakes at Newcastle.

Arthur Stephenson is better known for the prolific winners he trains over the jumps, but one of the 20 winners I rode for him on the Flat was at Edinburgh around that time. Arthur is another tough Northerner who doesn't mince his words, and he didn't please me in the paddock by intimating that he thought I was a bit old to be going round such a sharp track! I raised a figurative two-finger salute by going out and winning the race.

Arthur and Mick Easterby have a lot in common, not least the fact that they are both very sharp horse-traders and love to barter. The story goes that shortly after the war Arthur found himself in possession of a job-lot of 50 army folding bikes. They had apparently been designed to be dropped with paratroopers into enemy territory so that on landing they could unfold them and pedal away to the nearest cover. Because they needed to be light they had no mud-guards or 'extras' and were extremely flimsy – they were only supposed to be used for a few miles before being discarded. Arthur soon realised that he had been sold a pup – I believe the trickster was Willie Stephenson – but he was determined somehow to pass them on.

His opportunity came one day when he heard Mick trying to persuade someone to buy a horse. Knowing that Mick loved a deal he offered him 'Fifty bikes for the horse, unseen' which Mick, after some argument, accepted. They tossed for who should transport the goods and Arthur lost. This inconvenience did not prevent him from chortling at the thought of putting one over on Mick when he drove into the Easterby yard with the bikes in the back of his horse-box. The bikes were duly unloaded and the horse was brought out for his inspection. Sure enough, as Mick had promised, it was a beautiful animal. It's only drawback was that it was blind . . . Some people maintain that this is an apocryphal story, but many of us who know both men find it easy to believe.

At the end of July, I rode the two-year-old Bamaribo for Michael Jarvis to win first time out at Newmarket. I may have been high in the handicap in Michael's estimation afterwards, but my rating must have plummeted the next time I rode the colt at Yarmouth where I managed to get shut in in a three-runner race and was beaten a short head. This feat isn't quite as impossible to achieve as you might imagine.

I was drawn on the rails and Tony Ives, on the eventual winner, made the running. I was tucked in behind with Geoff Baxter on my outer. Geoff was going well enough to sit on Tony's tail and keep me in. My alternatives were to push my way out, which would almost certainly have meant disqualification, or to wait and hope he would weaken in time to let me through. In the end, as the winning post approached and Geoff showed no sign of weakening, I had to pull back and come round him, and try as I might, I just failed to get up.

I rode Teleprompter when he started his three-year-old career in the humble surroundings of Edinburgh, not the ideal track for such a big horse since the bends are very tight. The obvious reason for sending him there was to get him started at the right end of the handicap. If a horse runs in bad company or on a second-class track the handicapper does not penalise the win as heavily as he would in other circumstances.

After winning his second start at Edinburgh, Teleprompter won at Carlisle, proceeding to Royal Ascot where he landed the Britannia Handicap under 7 stones 13 lb with Willie Carson, Lord Derby's jockey, in the saddle. I've always felt that his run at Redcar later in the season sowed the seeds for my departure from Hurgill Lodge. In the paddock beforehand, in Lord and Lady Derby's presence, Bill Watts stressed that as he was such a long-striding horse I was to challenge on the outside to give him plenty of space to use himself. However,

Teleprompter suffered from an intermittent back problem which occasionally caused him to hang in his races, and after turning into the straight he hung back in as I tried to get him to the outside. I finally decided to let him have his own way. He veered to the inside and, although he ran on well, was beaten a head. Another two strides would have made all the difference. Nothing was said afterwards although the owners looked daggers. The next day Bill told Tim Richards, 'No one can blame Edward. Teleprompter may have pulled a muscle or done his back in during the race. Something is bothering him as he isn't 100 per cent this morning'.

In fact he never lost this tendency to hang. As a four-year-old he won at York with Willie Carson up, but he hung left and won only by a neck. Obviously in an attempt to help his jockey keep him straight he wore blinkers on his next outing in the Royal Hunt Cup at Ascot and always wore them thereafter. The use of blinkers overcame the hanging problem and he developed into a top-class horse. But back in 1983 I think the blame for his difficulties as far as the owners were concerned lay with me rather than with Teleprompter.

I had a chance to make amends on the big horse at Yarmouth in early September but again came off worst by a head after he hung left in the final furlong. The following Sunday, Bill rang me as usual to give me the week's plans but had far more important and disappointing news. Due to a reduction in the number of horses in his stable, his owners would not be retaining me the following season. It was true that things hadn't gone too well for the stable over the last couple of years and it obviously reflected on me. I am sure that there was nothing between myself and Bill that a few more winners wouldn't have put right. Not long before our split Bill had said in a Timeform interview: 'I think he's a marvellous jockey and we're very lucky to have him riding for us. His experience makes him invaluable; he's always up to every trick in the book, finding the best going and shortest way round'. Ah well, such is racing; up one moment, down the next.

Although I didn't have much luck with Teleprompter at Redcar, I rode 193 winners there, 40 more than at any other racecourse. However, in the past I have criticised both the bends as occasionally they weren't safe to navigate at racing pace. The racecourse's managing director, Lord Ronaldshay, pinned the following on to the noticeboard in the course's recently refurbished weighing-room, under the title 'With Apologies to a Great Jockey'.

There's a certain Northern jockey
Who with quite a lot of force
Is inclined to come to Redcar and
To criticise our course.

If it isn't the rough going
Or the sharpness of the bends
It's the lack of decent sandwiches —
So we've tried to make amends.

We've built up both the cambers
And put in hand repairs
Till the bends ride like those walls of death
You see at country fairs.

We've taken on the catering
Specifically to see
That this great figure of the turf
Receives a proper tea.

We've modernised the jockey's room,
(You should have seen the bill!)
And laid down carpet for his feet
So he'll not catch a chill.

So in this game of hide and seek,
(I'll mention not his name)
We like to feel we've helped this star
Of international fame.

And if this year he still complains,
Our efforts he refutes?
We'll fix him up a special peg
On which to hang his BOOTS!

I thought this was a very clever and amusing way for Lord Ronaldshay to make his point. Jon Freeman, the Northern racing journalist,
penned his own witty reply, 'Dedicated to a Master Tactician', in the
Sporting Chronicle.

There is a certain Northern jockey
(I'll mention not his name)
Who with years of sterling service
Has built up wide acclaim
He's been to every racecourse
From Ayr to Bath and back
Knows every blade of grass by name
On every British track

Come with him as he takes you on
His mystery guided tour
This star treks those uncharted routes
Where no man has been before
The time will come, Lord Ronaldshay,

To write a new refrain
When your stewards find him guilty of
Excessive use of BRAIN!

Although it had been a relatively quiet season, I was Cock of the North for the 16th and last time in 1983, beating John Lowe by one with Mark Birch only one behind him. John was unlucky: he had sustained an injury that put him out for the last fortnight of the season although, to be fair, I had lost 12 days due to suspension. David Nicholls had arranged the end-of-the-season jockeys' 'do' at Wetherby in expectation of John's success — these events need a great deal of organising as I discovered when I arranged one for Mark Birch in 1982 at Malton. This year, Michael Dickinson presented me with a carriage clock amid a barrage of light-hearted jeering from Messrs Birch, Charnock and Nicholls.

It was Mark who stepped into my boots as Cock of the North — literally! A little while ago Rose Carr, wife of trainer Frank, organised a collection of Northern racing memorabilia to display in Malton. We all donated a few items and a closer inspection of 'Mark Birch's' boots revealed not his name but mine inside them!

– 19 –
India

IN November I learned that Walter Swinburn junior was unable to fulfil a contract he had made to ride in Bombay because of other commitments. He had been due to ride for two big owners, brothers Cyrus and Zavareh Poonawalla, who were involved in the pharmaceutical industry, but he was having to delay his departure until January. I arranged for someone to let the brothers know I might be interested if Walter had to drop out of his contract. Cyrus Poonawalla rang me at Huttons Ambo from his stud at Poona at about five o'clock one morning and after discussing the situation for ten minutes he said he would come back to me in two or three days to let me know. An hour later he rang again to say they wanted me to go, and less than three weeks later I found myself airborne, heading for the sun.

I flew initially via Bombay to Poona, where the brothers had a training track installed on their stud. Racing had finished for the season at Poona and all the horses based there were about to be shipped up to Bombay for the winter season. There was no such thing as a between-season rest for most of these horses! I had never met the Poonawalla brothers before, although I knew they were big owner-breeders and were members of the Indian Jockey Club. They sent their Rolls Royce to the airport to pick me up and I was suitably impressed. I was even more impressed when I arrived at Cyrus's house and found myself being introduced to no less a person than Dr Jonas Salk of Salk polio vaccine fame. Apparently, there was a medical conference in Poona and several speakers, including Dr Salk, were guests of the Poonawalla brothers, who had a serum laboratory at the stud where 300 workers manufactured anti-diptheria and anti-snake venom vaccines. Now that polio has all but been eradicated in most of the world it is easy to forget what terror this crippling disease held for people as recently as 30 years ago. The discovery of the vaccine which offered protection in just a few drops on a sugar lump was so momentous that the name Salk became almost a household word at the time. A photograph taken that night shows seven men, including me, sitting around a coffee table listening in awe as the great man spoke. It is one of the treasured items in my scrapbook of India.

I stayed for four or five days at Poona, riding some track work and playing a lot of golf. It was a bit of relaxation and a chance to get to know some of the horses before the season started. The brothers stood three stallions at their well-run stud and the quality and condition of the stock pleasantly surprised me. There was little grazing in the dry paddocks but there were plenty of shady trees and the horses did not seem oppressed by the heat. The irrigated training track adjoining the stud was constructed on such a lavish scale that they could almost have held a regular race meeting there.

I was supplied with a car and a chauffeur, Bhiku, and at the beginning of December I drove up to Bombay and saw some of the spectacular Grand Canyon-like scenery that lies between the two centres. When I arrived I was taken to a private house where I was to rent a room, and found myself thrown into the preparations for the start of the season. The job, I have to admit, was not exactly arduous. The ex-pat jockeys would arrive at the track at around 6.45 a.m., when dawn was just breaking, ready to do track work. Some of the trainers liked to start work in the dark but luckily for me the Poonawalla's trainer, Uttam Singh, wasn't one of them.

The training complex was impressive; there was an equine swimming pool and drying-off sand ring, and a grass and two sand training tracks on the inside of the racetrack. The stables were well-built Victorian barn-type structures which, although a bit run-down, were adequate for the job. Each trainer had his own ring where his string would circle round before and after work, so if you were riding for a few trainers there was never any difficulty in finding your next horse. You just went to the appropriate ring and it would be brought to you by one of the 'syces', or grooms. These lads didn't ride themselves and half the time they didn't even walk the horses round; they would just squat down, holding the horse – which stood, docile as a seaside donkey – on a long piece of rope. After we had ridden whatever bits of work were required all the jockeys and trainers would meet at the café at the track for breakfast and coffee and a chat. Most days we would sit outside: there wasn't a drop of rain the whole time I was there, every day the temperature was ideal and the skies clear blue. Among the jockeys with whom I breakfasted were Ernie Johnson, Mike Kinane, the Champion Irish jockey, and Stephen Crane.

The food in India was my main cause for concern before I left England. Breakfast was no problem, but I wasn't looking forward to the main meals. I have never been able to stand curry – the slightest hint of curry powder brings me out in a sweat – and I was worried that I might have to send home for food parcels if I couldn't find a restaurant serving European food. Fortunately, it didn't come to that! I made the acquaintance early on of a racing restaurateur, and although he never understood my conservative taste in food he managed to supply me with meals that were, if not English style, at least only mildly spiced. As a special treat I would have steak on a platter at a restaurant near Beach Candy. If I overdid it and needed to lose a pound or two, I would park my car in the sun in the middle of the racecourse an hour or so before I had to be in the weighing-room and go for a jog around the track in a plastic suit and a tracksuit. Then I would sit in the car for as long as it took to sweat the weight off. There was no need for a sauna in India!

There were usually two race days a week in Bombay. Racing was popular and there was quite a lot of betting. The authorities took amazing precautions to ensure that the jockeys and punters didn't get together. Every jockey, even those who only had a ride in the last race, had to be in the weighing-room two hours before the first. Although the horses had been declared in the morning, the declarations were not made public, nor was the draw made until all the jockeys were all safely locked away. In Japan they can be even more extreme – I have read that for Sunday racing the jockeys are sometimes locked away from Friday onwards without a telephone or any contact with the outside world!

However, in Bombay they did help the punters in other ways. One novelty to me was the photo form book, which I think would be a good thing in this country. It would probably be too expensive to be feasible except where there is weekly racing at a track. The system worked in the following way: along the whole course, starting at the stalls, photo-finish-type cameras were positioned at intervals to photograph the field. Finally, of course, there was a shot of the finish itself. The end result was a picture sequence of the race which included three photographs taken in the final furlong, which gave you a very good idea of each horse's performance during the race.

Another aid to the punters was the publication in the programme for each meeting of times and distances for track work done the previous week. I had a leather casing made for my stop-watch so that I could wear it over two fingers and switch it on and off as I passed the track markers. I felt this would be more accurate than the timing of someone on the ground, whose angle of vision to the posts would introduce error. Even so, I was never convinced that timing was as valuable as the punters seemed to think, and something that happened towards the end of my season in Bombay confirmed my doubts.

I rode a top-class sprinter, Klairon Gold, in his last bit of sharp work before a big race. The grass track was too firm for work so we went on to the sand to avoid jarring him up. We worked over three furlongs and I really asked him to stride on and use himself. Later, I rode another horse over the same three furlongs. They recorded identical times. The two horses ran in races on the same afternoon a couple of days later, and while Klairon Gold won the country's top sprint the second horse couldn't find the pace to lay up with the field in a mile-and-a-quarter race! Admittedly, the surfaces were different – the slow horse probably had a bit of knee action which helped him handle the sand – but even so it shows that times shouldn't always be taken at their face value.

On my first day's racing I started as I hoped to go on. I had four rides and finished the day with three winners and a second. The local press made quite a thing of it. One of the quotes I particularly liked read: 'Hide, although now a bit old, is like wine and is riding better with age'. No one seemed able to forget that I was now 46 years old. Another correspondent wrote: 'For a man who is getting on in years Hide displays a youthful enthusiasm which would make most of his youthful counterparts look octogenarian'! This plaudit was apparently due to the fact that I had been seen walking the track before racing. It was a habit of mine, ingrained over the years, when I was riding on a track which I hadn't ridden on before. Only one of the winners I rode that day, a filly called Petula Clark, belonged to the Poonawallas, but even so they took me out to dinner at the Taj Hotel to celebrate. They seemed proud to show me off. This was something I was not used to, but in India and later in Hong Kong I realised that it was quite the norm to enjoy being seen in the company of a jockey, particularly after a successful day. However, I soon came to realise that after a bad day I would be seated away from the public or, more likely, not taken out at all!

My relationship with the brothers started to deteriorate that first race-day night. One of them – I think it was Cyrus – informed me that they did not wish me to ride work for anybody else while I was in India in case I was injured and unable to ride their horses. When I informed them that I had already ridden work for other trainers and had arranged to do so again the next morning their hackles rose. I backed down and said that since they felt so strongly I would respect their wishes on this occasion. I would cancel my arrangements for the next day but I couldn't guarantee that I wouldn't ride work for others in the future. Their argument seemed ridiculous to me: I was just as susceptible to injury riding their horses as anyone else's. I was used to the English arrangement whereby if you are retained by a trainer he has the right to have you at whichever meeting he wants riding the horses he wants, but after that you are free to ride for anybody else that might want you. I had assumed that the custom would be the same in India.

I rode for them until January but I don't think any of us was too sad when the contract came to an end. I picked up plenty of rides from other trainers since most of them knew me because I had ridden track work for them, and after a series of good wins I was in quite strong demand. Between race meetings, in the plentiful free time after track work was finished, I played golf, lay around the pool at Beach Candy and did some sight-seeing. I had recently bought myself a camera with a close-up macro facility, and I took the opportunity to further my interest in photography while I was in India. The many public gardens in Bombay with their colourful displays of dahlias, chrysanthemums and more exotic blooms made ideal subjects for me to practise on and I filled several albums. Another favourite subject was the topiary at the hanging garden, where careful training of privet hedges over many years had produced life-sized living sculptures of various animals, ranging from a giraffe and rhinoceroses to ostriches and sacred cows.

In many ways it was as though you were living in the days of the Empire – the hotels, the parks and the racetrack itself certainly gave an impression of European-style affluence – but I found the contrasts of India disturbing. While the well-off had modern conveniences like washing-machines the poor still washed their clothes in great open-air concrete stalls in an area reminiscent of a cattle market. In parts of Bombay whole families lived and slept on the pavements, surrounded by all their worldly possessions, with only a tree for shelter. In spite of their poverty they were still proud and disliked being photographed, which was understandable I suppose. No one in that position wants to be treated like just another tourist attraction. Even worse than the pavement families were the beggars. Every time your car stopped at traffic lights there would be a knock at the window and a child with one arm or one leg would hold out a hand, or worse, a stump for money. I was told that begging was a business for some families and that they maimed their children early on in their life so that they could send them out to beg. There were so many of them that you either had to give to all or none. Once you gave to one, three or four more would instantly appear, seemingly from nowhere, all appearing to be equally deserving cases. It was distressing to see and horrifying to think about.

After riding track work on the few days that I was in Poona I became aware that many of the horses I rode had a marked tendency to hang in towards the rails, particularly if you were trying to settle them. In some cases this habit was bad enough to be dangerous, and on one occasion the horse I was riding was hanging so badly that for the one and only time in my career I needed both hands on one rein to try to keep it straight. I was convinced that this was due to the fact that horses in India only ever galloped right-handed. All the tracks in India are right-handed and all work is done the same way. Inevitably, the result is that many horses get very one-sided. I was surprised by the furore my comments on the matter caused among trainers: perhaps the main reason for the row was the solution I suggested, which was that on one or two days when the horses were doing slow work they should be worked left-handed around the track. Two editorials in the racing newspaper *The Turfite* supported my cause and gave an example of how reversing the direction of work had helped cure one of John Lowe's mounts of hanging a couple of seasons before. But it was all in vain, and my idea died a quiet death. I was reduced to taking the really bad horses into the centre of the track and schooling them by doing figures of eight. Apparently, horses at Bombay had been working right-handed for 100 years, which proved to most trainers that it must be a satisfactory system!

Fortunately, although I rode quite a few one-sided horses that winter I managed to avoid any accidents caused by hanging. The one spill I remember was caused by something quite different. I was riding track work one morning while a television company was doing some filming at the course. They had strung a cable over the track at one point about 20 feet up. It posed no apparent threat to horses or riders but it was obviously low enough to be seen by my horse. We were going at three-parts speed when he spotted it and put the brakes on. His worked better than mine and I carried on going, escaping with only a few bruises. Afterwards I was annoyed with myself for not having predicted the horse's reaction, because I'd had experience of this fear of overhead wires before. In the days of the old-fashioned starting gates, they would take the tapes down if possible whenever a gate wasn't in use, but would leave the release wire up. It was half the thickness of my little finger, but it was amazing the number of horses that could spot it. You would be riding along and you would sense the moment they saw it – you could feel them tense and squat as you passed underneath the wire.

At evening stables it was usual for the horses to be led out for a while. This was a time for socialising for the owners and their friends. Often I was there for a couple of hours – you never knew how many people would turn up. It was 'open house'; the trainer would be seated and the connections would draw their chairs around him and discuss matters of interest. Despite my differences with the Poonawallas I continued to ride for them and managed a winner or two after my 'understanding' with them finished. I had a good season in India and ended up with 20 winners, finishing second in the jockeys' table behind Pesi Shroff, the leading Indian jockey, which wasn't bad considering that foreign jockeys were usually allowed to compete in only four of the seven races on the card. Three of my wins came in Calcutta: I used to fly there quite regularly with some of the other jockeys when meetings didn't clash. It was a sharper track than Bombay, and the buildings were dirtier and more run-down, but we enjoyed the change of scene. On one memorable occasion Mike Kinane and I arrived back from Calcutta and were met at the airport by Bhiku, my chauffeur. As we set off to drive into town we were perturbed when, instead of keeping his eyes on the road, he kept turning his head and talking to us in the back. We realised that he had been on either drink or drugs when we approached a set of red lights and it was apparent to both of us that he was going to plough into the stationary traffic. We both screamed at him to stop. Mike quickly jumped out and dragged him out of the driver's seat. We slung him into the back before climbing into the front ourselves. It was the end of my association with the chauffeur . . . from then on I drove myself.

Towards the end of my stay in Bombay I won the big invitation sprint, the Sprinters' Cup, on the horse I mentioned earlier, Klairon Gold, who at that time was without doubt the fastest horse in India. It was a particularly pleasing win because the horse, which had also won the race the year before, had nearly died eight months earlier after staking himself badly in an accident. It was a real triumph for Sandeep Mangalorkar, his likeable trainer, who had begged that the horse should not be put down and asked to be given a chance to try to save him. In the race we were drawn 12th of the 13 runners, right on the outside. At Bombay there is a maximum of a two-and-a-half-furlong run from the jump-off to the turn, but Klairon Gold had so much speed that I was able to get out clear in front and had room to cross to the inside rail before the bend to lead into the straight. Nothing ever headed us.

Once again the press were flattering about my riding, crediting my 'unrivalled skill' and 'brilliance' with having kept the horse going as he began to tire. It gave this old man confidence that perhaps he had a few years left in him yet! At any rate, it sent me back home for the 1984 English season with a determination to try to go abroad again the following winter.

– 20 –
Hong Kong

MY main aim in 1984 was to gain the 33 winners I needed to pass George Fordham and move into sixth place in the all-time list of winning jockeys in Britain. As I had ridden more than that number in each of the previous 30 seasons I was entitled to think that, barring an accident, I should comfortably achieve this. In the Lincoln Handicap I was engaged by Jimmy Fitzgerald to ride Vintage Toll, a horse with a fair amount of ability but little inclination to show it on the race-course. In this, his first run of the season, being both fit and fresh he ran the race of his life, but on the day found one too good for him in the Dermot Weld-trained Saving Mercy, partnered by Walter Swinburn. An early big-race success would have been a boost to my return to freelancing. Despite my retention of the Northern Jockeys' Championship the previous season, winning rides – indeed any rides – were increasingly hard to come by. If a jockey who had ridden only a handful of winners had won over 50 races everyone would have said what a wonderful season it had been for him. But I had on numerous occasions more than doubled that score, and the 53 winners I rode seemed a poor effort.

I could imagine people saying what I had heard said about other jockeys over the years, that I was either past it, too old or had lost my nerve. While I felt none of this was true, striving to be successful was harder than ever. In my opinion both Lester and Joe were riding as well as they ever had, but they too were noticing the decline in good rides. How fickle people are. Towards the end of his career Lester remarked that during one Sunday – the traditional day in which plans for the week are sorted out – his 'phone hadn't rung once.

Although I rode Vintage Toll at 8 stones 3 lb in the Hunt Cup at Royal Ascot keeping my weight in check was becoming increasingly difficult. If I didn't have a light ride for two or three days and hadn't used the sauna I often found I weighed at least 8 stones 7 lb stripped. When all is going well there is more of an incentive to keep on top of your weight. On top of everything else I was becoming more and more disillusioned with the domestic scene. When Eric Collingwood returned to England early in June he repeated his invitation to me to ride for him in Hong Kong. One advantage such a move would hold for me was that the weights in general were higher there, most horses carrying 8 stones 8 lb or more, and there would be less need to keep to strict eating habits. As Happy Valley and Sha Tin are only ten miles apart there would be very little travelling involved. With Eric's support I should have little trouble this time in obtaining a licence to ride in Hong Kong. In the end, it wasn't a difficult decision to make.

The two courses in Hong Kong opened for track work some seven weeks before the official start of racing but, having won group races on Celestial Dancer in France and Germany, I wanted to ride him for Tony in the Vernon's Sprint at Haydock, so with Eric's approval, I delayed my departure until shortly before the Hong Kong season opened. The very firm ground was against Celestial Dancer, and after meeting with interference we finished five lengths behind Petong, Habibti and Never So Bold.

The first surprise awaiting me in Hong Kong was the gaggle of reporters and press photographers at the airport who swarmed around me as I looked for Eric Collingwood. I was surprised: I had not expected this and failed to see why the media should be interested in my arrival. I was hardly the first English jockey to come out to Hong Kong for the season. At the back of the crowd of Chinese faces I instantly spotted Eric's familiar ruddy complexion and grey hair and I struggled towards him. He rescued me from the clutches of the press and led me to his car. The heat and humidity as I stepped out of the air-conditioned comfort of Kai Tak airport into the outside world was a physical shock. We sped off in Eric's car to the Lee Gardens Hotel where I was to stay until an apartment was fixed up for me. While I sat back and enjoyed what was only my second view of the concrete jungle that is Hong Kong, Eric explained the reason for the press attention.

It appeared that, because of the enormous popularity of racing – or more accurately, betting – in the colony, people involved in the industry were given almost a celebrity status, and the trainers and jockeys were the brightest stars of all. I was recognised by strangers on the street. People would turn to look as we went window shopping or just out into the streets and I would hear little whispers of the Chinese translation of my name, 'Ho Tat, Ho Tat, Ho Tat', rippling back through the crowd as we strolled among them. Admittedly, my decidedly Anglo-Saxon features must have made recognition easier for them, but even so I found it surprising. I'd never considered myself famous before. It made a change from England, where away from the racecourse very few people recognised you.

At my hotel Eric filled me in on the details of how my days at the track would be organised. The following morning, after passing the compulsory medical examination, I started work at Sha Tin where his horses were trained. Sha Tin is one of the most impressive race-courses in the world from the point of view of facilities for both horses and the betting public. There were three tracks; the main grass race-course on the outside, the sand track for racing and training and the inside all-weather track.

The horses were stabled in two-storey blocks with their own exer-cise yards, communal swimming pool and veterinary clinic. Most of the trainers, including Eric, lived out at Sha Tin in Jockey Club flats and many of the ex-pat officials also lived at the course. My first view of this ultra-modern complex came at five o'clock in the morning when most of Hong Kong was still asleep. I was collected from my hotel by Alex Wong, Eric's assistant, who had spent some time with Scobie Breasley at Epsom.

The early start, a lot earlier than I was used to, had been necessary in the days when all the horses were stabled at Happy Valley. Before Sha Tin was built the horses were actually kept in tower blocks due to the desperate shortage of space in Hong Kong. For walking exer-cise they would go up ramps on to the flat roofs of the blocks where they were led around, while for fast work they would be taken down the steep Shan Kwong Road to the track, their feet muffled to avoid waking the locals from their slumber. The course was floodlit so that all work could be finished and the horses safely reinstalled in their tower blocks before the morning rush-hour traffic reached its peak. Now that most of the horses were stabled at Sha Tin this early start was strictly speaking unnecessary, but the practice was continued for the benefit of the native grooms, known as 'mafoos', who nearly all had secondary jobs such as taxi-driving later in the day.

It was quite eerie driving through the deserted sky-scraper-lined streets at that time of the morning – like being in another world which, compared to the rural calm of Huttons Ambo, Hong Kong certainly was. Then suddenly the track appeared like a floodlit oasis, a huge hive of activity in the middle of the sleeping city with the mafoos leading their horses around awaiting their riders. I walked over to Eric's pitch where his first horses to be worked were waiting, hearing for the first time the 'dawn chorus' of the mafoos as they hawked and spat, a sound that was to become so familiar over the ensuing months that it will forever be associated with Hong Kong in my mind. This habit of the mafoos of spitting approximately every few minutes meant that you always had to tread carefully first thing in the morning!

That morning I took five horses around the track for Eric. Fast work was done on the inside of the sand track, slower work on the outside and steady work on the all-weather track. To reach these you had to go through a tunnel under the main grass course. The all-weather track had been replaced owing to problems caused by the high humidity, and now consisted of a deep sand surface. For fast work most of the Australian and Chinese trainers worked the horses singly against the clock. But Eric leaned towards the English way, working two or three horses together 'upsides'. He trained 25 horses of all ages and classes. Horses are graded according to the assessment of the handicapper. There are seven classes plus the 'griffins', as the new two-year-olds are known. Depending on their degree of success they move up or down in class, and any horse in Class 7 that doesn't win by the end of the season is compulsorily retired. In the very early days of racing in Hong Kong they had an ingenious way of handicapping. They used ponies imported from China; 12-hand ponies carried 7 stones, and 7 lb was added for each inch of the animal's height. At one stage the horses racing were said, tongue-in-cheek, to be divided into four categories: those that could gallop and wanted to; those that could gallop and didn't want to; those that couldn't gallop but wanted to try; and those that couldn't gallop and didn't want to anyway.

In all there were about 800 horses in training, mainly at Sha Tin, the rest at Happy Valley. All horses are bought in. Hong Kong soil deficiencies and the shortage of land make horse-breeding difficult, so for some years the racehorses have been imported from England and Ireland or Australasia, either as horses with known form or as unraced two-year-olds. There is never any difficulty in finding owners for the new horses. Competition for racehorse ownership is so keen that ballots have to be held by the Royal Hong Kong Jockey Club to select the lucky owners from its members. I don't think such a system would go down too well with the big buyers over here! Most of the horses purchased with known form are no better than good handicappers, while the yearlings are all good, sound commercial colts costing on average about 8,000 guineas. What the Hong Kong racegoers want is competitive racing, and this is what the club's purchasing policy aims to provide. Of the 460 races run in a season, all but 20 are handicaps.

In the days that followed, as I settled in and became familiar with the system, I was offered the chance to take two or three horses around for other trainers as well as Eric's usual four or five. I was anxious at first about how I would adapt to the methods of the Chinese and Australian trainers, who worked to the clock. In England an aura of mysticism surrounds their methods, as if the American and Australian jockeys have clocks built into their heads. In reality I found it was just a question of adjustment, and learned to equate their times with the equivalent half-speed, three-quarter speed and full gallop that I was used to. The trainers timed their horses with the aid of a light which flashed on when the horses went through a beam. These were placed at each furlong marker around the track. The electronic timing facilities had only recently become available to trainers. I heard of one trainer who used to take his horses down to the course at Happy Valley before dawn and work them in the pitch black, the jockeys blowing their whistles at certain prearranged markers. This method ensured that the rest of Hong Kong was kept in the dark about their form too!

He would not have got away with it a few years later. By the time I was there, secret trials were not possible. All the gallops had to be conducted under the eagle-eyed scrutiny of the stipendiary stewards. Hong Kong horses are branded, and each horse has to wear its identifying brand number under its saddle at track work. The imports of different years wear different coloured number cloths so there's little chance of anyone training a 'dark horse'. Gallops are fully reported in the newspapers, with individual times against each horse. Recordings of the work are shown on Chinese television later the same morning. The public interest in all these facts and figures never ceased to amaze me.

One day a week there were barrier trials at both Happy Valley and Sha Tin. Colours were worn and, although the trials were timed, few trainers wanted their horses' form exposed and they were no guide to racecourse performance. Until a horse had passed a barrier trial it couldn't run, and if it misbehaved at the start or during a race, it was necessary to go through the whole process again. Some horses were exercised in the large indoor equine pool, but even the number of laps a horse did was reported in the Chinese newspapers! As in India, photo form books were available so that punters could study each horse's performance in previous races. There was another form book called 'Lowens', in which I was amused to read the description of one horse: 'Depending on how it feels on the day, this horse runs both hot and cold, although it does have ability. It is also reputed to be able to read the Tote board on the way down to the post, so the state of the betting is probably the best guide to its chances'.

Because of this intense public interest in racing the newspapers have paid informers in all the stables. While the constant gaze of the public eye puts a certain stress on trainers, there are plenty of advantages associated with training in Hong Kong which help to compensate them. All the best feed is provided by the authorities, who also organise stable staff and accommodation. The Jockey Club runs an apprentice school and allocates work riders to each stable from the pool of boys who are trained there.

Probably the advantage the trainers appreciate most is their freedom from major financial worries. There are no such things as bad debts from owners because the Jockey Club is responsible for collecting the training fees, and after deducting the required amounts for expenses, they pay the trainers direct. To some struggling English trainers who have to spend valuable training time chasing non-payers, it must sound like Utopia. Perhaps the other principal differ-ence in a Hong Kong trainer's life is not so welcome: he is under immense pressure to supply his owners with successful tips. These can make or break his reputation, and so deciding what advice to give is a constant worry. It is bad enough to tip a loser, but the worst thing a trainer can do is to tell an owner his horse has no chance and then watch it go on to win. If that happens he can expect the horse to be removed to another trainer immediately; it enables the owner to prove to his friends that he was as deceived as they were. They hate the idea that anyone might be trying to put one over them and can't tolerate losing face. Even tipping a winner isn't always good enough – one trainer told me he had once advised an owner that his horse had a good chance and, sure enough, it won at 20–1. Instead of thanking him, the owner came up in a foul mood afterwards, complaining that he had not been given the correct horse to put with it in the Quinella – Hong Kong's equivalent of our dual forecast bet.

In a country where the people are gambling mad it is surprising that it is nearly all illegal. The only legal gambling is run by the Royal Hong Kong Jockey Club, a registered charity, on horseracing and the Mark Six, the national lottery. Betting is what racing is all about to the average Chinese. To the British race-goer the amount of money bet and the crowds that go racing over there would be mind-boggling. On an ordinary day 30,000 spectators can bet over £5,000,000 at one course, while at the other another 12,000 or so spectators watch the racing on a giant video matrix screen with full betting and dining services at their disposal. And that's on an ordinary day – on special days they go mad! On the last day of the 1987–88 season at Sha Tin 53,000 people wagered a record £52,000,000, an average of £980 each. To draw some comparison, the crowd on King George Day at Ascot in 1988 was a mere 30,849. I have not seen figures for an average flutter there, but I would be surprised if it was a tenth of the Hong Kong figure. In addition, there are 124 Jockey Club-run betting shops open all over the colony, and 300,000 punters bet by 'phone. 87 computers process 1,500 bets per second on a race-day. On one evening, the turnover would be way above that of the entire Royal Ascot Meeting! And that's only the official betting – it is rumoured that nearly as much is bet again through illegal bookmakers.

A week after I arrived in Hong Kong Eric provided me with a flat in Kowloon Tong, midway between Happy Valley and Sha Tin, and a car with which to transport myself to the track. John Lowe had used the flat on a previous occasion. It was comfortable enough but rather dark, being on only the second floor and surrounded by high-rise flats. You had to crane your neck out of the window to see the sky. Our neighbours were nearly all Chinese and all night the clack-clack of the mahjong tiles provided background music to my attempts at sleep. When Sue arrived she found she had to follow the traditional method of hanging out the washing on bamboo poles. Unfortunately, since we were on a low floor, she would often find that just as our clothes were ready to be brought in somebody above us would hang out their dripping wet laundry and soak ours all over again.

Until our visit to Hong Kong Sue had never been interested in betting, but during our stay I was amused to find that she became quite hooked on it. She would go to the races and find her way to the rows of Tote betting windows which lined every floor of the grandstand. The marketing of the betting is ingenious, and there are all sorts of combination bets available. The most popular is the Quinella, but there are many other possibilities such as tierce, quartet, doubles, trebles, accumulators and six-up – even 'exotic' bets. At first Sue found it quite complicated to work out how to mark off the computerised cards and know which bet was which, but there are dozens of girls on duty whose only job is to assist people and explain to them how to risk their money. With their help, Sue soon got the hang of it and would come back home in a state of great glee after the races, recounting how she had got the 'Double Q' or some such bet for a minimum outlay.

Racing started seven days after I arrived. I had two rides for Eric's stable on that first day but I didn't exactly cover myself in glory on my debut. The first horse finished tailed off; the other arrived at the start without me, having cocked its jaw and ducked left, depositing me on top of the rails. I had badly bruised ribs as a result but had it happened in England I would probably have carried on and ridden after the horse had been caught. In Hong Kong though, loose horses are automatically withdrawn once they have cantered around the track, so my first day came to a premature and rather humiliating end.

Ten days later I had better luck when I rode my first winner, a horse of Eric's called Marksman, on the sand at the Happy Valley track. We were unlucky not to complete a double that night as our other runner, Wynnwith, planted himself as the runners left the stalls and gave the rest of the field half a furlong's start. In spite of this, he stayed on to take second place, beaten by much less ground than we'd lost at the beginning. As a result Wynnwith had to face a compulsory barrier trial – he did the same thing again so they had to fail him. He had no difficulty entering the stalls, it was leaving them that was the problem, so I suggested to the starter, Colonel Tedford, that we put a blind on him and remove it at the last second. I had tried this tactic a few years previously on a horse at Hamilton with successful results. The trick worked, and Wynnwith passed his barrier trial and went on to win his next race with the help of a similar ploy.

Evening meetings are held under floodlights which, after trial and error, have been perfected so that there are no shadows on the track. The majority of these races are run on the sand, which is regarded as a necessary evil to preserve the grass tracks. No one likes them, though, least of all the horses, who are often half-blinded by the sharp sand being thrown back and leave the track with their eyes red and swollen. The punters don't like it because so many horses just won't face it, and others often show entirely different form on sand. The hooves scoop out the sand as the horses gallop, leaving a hole in which a bare half-inch of sand covers a rock-firm base. After rain the surface is much worse; the track is very fast and riding on it could be likened to racing on a road with sludge thrown on it. On the turf, many horses produce their best form when covered up during a race, but on sand they resent the kick-back and you have to take them wide. It's a no-win situation because they won't succeed either if they see too much daylight. Different tactics and form books are necessary for sand and turf. No jockey likes riding on the sand for obvious reasons. When it is wet two pairs of goggles are not enough as they are soon covered in slush, and once these have been pulled down the eyes are covered. When I was riding I needed all the oxygen I could get, but I was given mouthfuls of sand instead. I scoured the Hong Kong toy shops until I eventually came across a small mask to cover my nose and mouth, which I found a help.

Before I left England Peter O'Sullevan had asked whether it would be a help to me if he dropped a line to George Moore, the former Australian jockey who was by then one of the leading trainers in Hong Kong. Normally George's son Gary rode for him, but both Gary and George were away in Paris for the Arc meeting and so I picked up two spare rides as a result of Peter's letter. Both obliged at 50–1 and 12–1 respectively. Peter wrote to congratulate me. He had seen George at Longchamp; 'I've owed you a good turn for a long time, matey', George had said to him, referring to my winning double. However, judging from the winning prices, there must have been a marked lack of stable confidence and I doubt whether George's followers would have been as pleased!

Another winner or two followed before the Sha Tin Trophy meeting in mid-November. That was unfortunately where I had my first confrontation with the stewards and my first taste of Hong Kong justice. The problem was over a horse called Gobi Star, a four-year-old trained by Eric Collingwood, who was making his seasonal reappearance in a Class 5 six-furlong handicap. The previous season he had been twice ridden by Brian Taylor, stable jockey to Eric at the time. In his first race he had been unruly at the start, unseating Brian before finishing last of the ten runners. On his next outing, despite having been dismounted as a last resort, Gobi Star had refused to enter the stalls. After this Brian made it clear that he never wanted to ride the horse again. Wally Hood took over for the third and last run of the season, and although Gobi Star finally consented to take part he was again soundly beaten.

Eric's pre-race orders to me were 'Let's hope he goes into the stalls. If you are not there with a chance don't knock him about as it's important to try to gain his confidence'. As a three-year-old Gobi Star used to run backwards and fall over, and neither of us, particularly me, wanted him to revert to doing that. He started at 50–1 and finished a well-beaten eighth of the 11 runners. I wasn't hard on the horse, but whatever I had done he would not have been placed. Nevertheless, I was hauled in by the judiciary panel for being too easy on him. The panel consisted of the Chairman, who is always one of the 12 stewards of the Jockey Club; a voting member and three professional Stipes: the Chief Stipendiary, Irishman Jim Marsh; Senior Stipe, Brian Sullivan and fellow Aussie and ex-Hong Kong jockey, Geoff Lane. I asked for Brian Taylor and Wally Hood to be allowed to express to the stewards the unflattering view they both had of the horse, and to explain the caution with which he had to be ridden. This was also confirmed by his trainer. But although the stipendiary stewards were fully aware of Gobi Star's characteristics I was given six days for failing to give him a full opportunity to obtain the best possible placing in the field. In England six days would have meant only a week off, but as they only raced twice a week in Hong Kong it was equivalent to a three-week suspension. As for Gobi Star, after I left Hong Kong he descended to the bottom of Class 7 and despite racing off the lowest handicap mark he never won a race and was compulsorily retired.

In England there are often complaints of inconsistencies in the decisions of the stewards, but to a certain extent this is understandable under British conditions, which feature a large number and variety of courses and many different panels of stewards. In Hong Kong there is no such excuse. The three Stipes attended every meeting; they had only two courses and saw the same horses, jockeys and trainers all the time, at morning work as well as at the races, so they had plenty of opportunity to familiarise themselves with each individual. There are six patrol cameras sited round the course, one giving the view of the whole race and the others different angles. The whole system seemed designed to provide every assistance to the exercise of fair and consistent discipline. And yet there were glaring inconsistencies in the panel's decisions, often over apparently similar incidents.

Stewards' decisions are much easier to accept when they appear just or even only consistent. Even harsh penalties are tolerable provided everyone else is penalised on the same scale. As is customary, I was allowed to take part in the following meeting before my suspension started and rode a winning double for our stable which put me in a happier frame of mind for my enforced holiday. Sue and I decided to take the opportunity to visit Brian Connorton in Singapore. Brian, whose house was adjacent to the racecourse, was a contemporary of mine but an accident had finished his riding career. He was now running the apprentice school in Singapore and was also assistant starter.

Singapore is lush with vegetation, the wide roads and cleanliness contrasting strongly with the concrete jungle of Hong Kong. The racecourse at Buckit-Timah was more like a British track, set in the countryside with similar stands and parade rings. Apparently, though, riding there can have its drawbacks. Numerous stories and reports of jockeys being beaten up or receiving death threats and other incidents have been rife for some years. Singapore doesn't have the same sophisticated off-course betting system as Hong Kong and there is a big illegal bookmaking problem, which can often lead to violence. Australian jockey Malcolm Johnson was badly injured when he was attacked on his way to track work during a stint on the Malaysian circuit a few years ago. It was said that another Australian jockey, Terry Lucas, who was retained there by Ivan Allen, never stayed at hotels under his own name! On one occasion Ivan Allen himself was shot and had to have several bullets removed from his body.

At the races we met up with Tim and Anne Thompson. I had known Tim when he was reporting for the *Daily Mail* and later as manager of Doncaster racecourse. He went on to Hong Kong where he was closely involved with the new Sha Tin racecourse. He was head-hunted by Singapore and has been general manager there for some years. We were also introduced to Philip Johnson, the Chief Stipendiary Steward on the Malaysian circuit. Philip had been in Hong Kong, where he was well-respected. He was later lured back to the colony to take charge of their Stipendiary Board – probably one of their better moves. In conversation Philip mentioned that he had been turned down by the English Jockey Club for a Stewards' Secretary's position. It puzzled me how they allowed a man of his undoubted ability to slip through their fingers.

Brian Connorton is now back in England helping to run the Racing School at Newmarket. This is an excellent concept; trainers nominate apprentices to take a course of general stable management and riding. Sue Camacho, wife of Malton trainer Maurice, was so concerned at the deteriorating standard of labour in racing that she started a similar school. Her pupils, however, come straight from the inner cities with no racing and generally no riding experience. Sue starts them from scratch, teaching them riding, stable management, banking, accounts, how to dress and behave and so on, and then finds them jobs in stables. She is doing what trainers used to do in the old days, and those that have used her pupils are full of praise for the job she does.

Having returned from our short break in Singapore we attended the races at Sha Tin on 8 December. The meeting was the last of five celebratory meetings commemorating the centenary of the Royal Hong Kong Jockey Club. But the celebrations turned to tragedy with the fatal fall of Brian Taylor. At the end of the eighth race Brian was easing up a T. C. Cheng-trained grey gelding, Silver Star, when, for no apparent reason, the horse pitched and fell just after the winning post, catapulting Brian head-first into the turf. Watching from the owners' and trainers' stand I could see that Brian was lying ominously still on the ground.

Silver Star had proved a jinx horse only ten months previously when an almost identical accident in track work resulted in severe injuries to his rider, Philippe Paquet, which had left him in a coma for three months. He underwent brain surgery before recuperating in Australia. In another bizarre twist to the story, Brian had actually given evidence at the hearing into Paquet's accident. He had also been working at the track that morning and stated that Silver Star's front legs appeared to go from under him for no apparent reason. Because of illness Brian had missed the previous four race-days but had returned to ride a brilliant race to win on All Able earlier that afternoon. There had to have been a doubt about his fitness and Brian must have been apprehensive at the thought of riding Silver Star. He had asked Wally Hood to stand by but had clearly felt well enough after the seventh race to take the mount. Later Wally said 'I wish I had ridden the horse, as everyone's fate is different'. One of Brian's closest friends, Newmarket trainer Johnny Winter, said: 'Brian was our personal friend for 20 years. He was a brilliant jockey and one of the world's gentlemen. He brought fun and laughter into the house'.

Brian was about the only jockey to successfully mould himself on Lester, who had actually won the race in which Brian was killed. Later Lester said, 'Brian and I were good friends for many years. We always occupied the same corner of the jockeys' dressing-room. I missed him a lot when he went to ride in Hong Kong. He was a fine jockey and a wonderful person, a great pal, marvellous company with an irrepressible sense of humour who will be very sadly missed in racing'. Obviously I had known Brian for many years as a weighing-room colleague, but it was only in Hong Kong that I had got to know him away from the racecourse. He was a natural all-round sportsman; his prowess on the golf course was well-known; he was an excellent shot and he also enjoyed training his gun dogs. He too, had been hoping to hang up his boots shortly; indeed, he had bought a stud near Newmarket to which he hoped eventually to retire.

One of Eric's horses, Witty Witty, had shown much promise over the straight 1,000 metres (five furlongs) at Sha Tin before I arrived in Hong Kong. He had gone into most people's notebooks as a future winner and Frank Carr had even mentioned to me before I left that he was one horse I ought to win on. Witty Witty's owner therefore came up with what he thought was a clever idea. To fool the betting public he would run the horse over nine furlongs in order to get a bigger price for his bet! To my mind, as well as to that of the betting public, there was never a chance of the horse staying the trip, but few of the Chinese owners understood horses as horses. To these people, a horse was like a motor car with a go and stop pedal. One trainer explained to his owner that his horse couldn't run as it was coughing. 'Do horses cough?' he asked.

The owner's notion unfortunately led me into another confrontation with the stewards. The only chance Witty Witty had of lasting the distance depended on settling him and getting him to switch off. Unfortunately, he had other ideas and took off, virtually bolting with me. Drawn wide and so racing on the outside, I hoped that a few on my inner would soon pass me enabling me to get in behind them and attempt to relax the horse, but this didn't happen until nearing the bend by which time Witty Witty had run himself into the ground. Although I rode him hard in the straight he continued to weaken and passed the post ninth of the 13 runners, beaten 12 lengths. I was brought before the stewards and questioned about covering unnecessary ground in the back straight and on the home bend. Despite my protests that being drawn on the wide outside I would have covered exactly the same amount of ground had I crossed over soon after the start, I was warned to watch my future riding. Witty Witty's only victory in Hong Kong was when he eventually reverted to the straight 1,000 metres.

Fortunately it wasn't all gloom and stewards' inquiries. I had a number of winners, including a double at Sha Tin. One was a grand old horse called Zamber Boy. He was a bit shouldery, and the first time I rode him in the morning he pitched on his head and nearly lost me. I realised he was prone to do this and in future was ready for him, giving him plenty of rein. In a race, however, he tried his heart out, and although he was no world-beater I thought highly of him for his character and courage.

I also won two races on one particular horse who had failed to win in recent seasons. I discovered that the best way to ride him was to weave my way through the field, not letting him see daylight until the last moment. On one occasion when Eric and I felt he had a good chance his owners decided that 16–1 wasn't a big enough price for them and I was told to challenge on the outside of the field. Eric and I were furious, but I had to follow the instructions or the horse would have been moved elsewhere. After looking a threat inside the last furlong, he didn't go through with his effort and was narrowly beaten.

I was enjoying Hong Kong enough to think I would like to come back. Before the end of the current season jockeys have to re-apply for a licence for the next. Apart from his duties as a Stipe, Brian Sullivan was Secretary to the Licensing Committee, which put him in an extremely powerful position. I handed over my licence application for the following season to him before the start of a night meeting at Happy Valley.

In the fifth race I was booked to ride an animal called Villa Pine. Up to this point in his racing career he had run 16 times in Hong Kong and still hadn't won. Furthermore, he had finished tailed off last the only previous time he had run on sand. Like many horses in Hong Kong, Villa Pine was a very free-running horse whose only chance of lasting 1,400 metres depended on settling him in the early stages. Unfortunately, he pulled so hard that night that his saddle slipped forward and he made life even more difficult for me by hanging out quite badly turning into the straight. Thereafter I was able to ride the horse out, waving my stick at him and actually hitting him three times. The winner was never in any danger after quickening clear at half-way and won easily by two and a half lengths. I was just touched off by a short head for second place. In Hong Kong, a jockey is required to report any incident in a race that may have affected his horse's chance, so as soon as I dismounted, I reported to Marsh and told him about the saddle slipping.

Later that evening I was had in and questioned about my riding of Villa Pine. It appeared to be a kangaroo court: no matter what I said, it seemed to me that the Stipendiary Stewards were going to find me guilty before I went in. I was told later that the race-day stewards had been outvoted three to two by the Stipes at both the Gobi Star and Villa Pine inquiries. In the Villa Pine case I was eventually given another six-day suspension for failing to ride the horse out to the best of my ability over the last 300 metres. A six-day suspension isn't all that serious in itself; the stewards can stand a jockey down for six months or longer if need be. However, as Secretary to the Licensing Committee, Sullivan was more aware than most that two six-day offences could constitute sufficient reason to refuse a jockey a future licence. When I thought about it afterwards, I assumed that it must have been Sullivan who instigated the inquiry because it was clear that Marsh, from what he said during the proceedings, could not have been watching me throughout the last 300 metres. Despite my continual waving of the stick he continually mentioned that I had been riding only with 'hands and heels'. Even after he had watched the film several times I just couldn't get through to him that I had been doing a lot more on the horse than that. Marsh also dismissed the significance of the slipping saddle.

The Stipendiary Stewards' reports on all incidents at the races are published in the following day's newspapers and also in the official form book. Although Marsh had tried to dismiss the slipping saddle, Sullivan had grudgingly accepted it, and so I was further mystified to find that there was no reference to it whatsoever in the Stipes' report. After the Gobi Star incident I had sought advice from one of Eric's owners, Jockey Club Steward Sir Sydney Gordon. He advised me that there was no point in appealing against the verdict unless we had further evidence. The race-day stewards had only to prove they had a justifiable reason for holding an inquiry. Sir Sydney later told me that he had been ticked off for giving me this friendly advice! Undeterred by the fact that nobody in Hong Kong had ever won an appeal, I felt that the decision was so unjust that I had to ask for a re-hearing.

I was obviously worried that I would not now have my licence renewed, but this was overshadowed by my outrage at the implication that I was dishonest. It was the suggestion that I had wanted Villa Pine to be beaten that really made my blood boil. In his previous two starts over the same distance, when he was ridden by Y. P. Chan, Villa Pine had led until weakening early in the straight. Surely if I had wanted him beaten I would not have attempted to settle the horse or have tried to prevent him hanging out when he turned into the straight? In over 30 years of race-riding in England I had never deliberately stopped a horse or been accused of it. Here in Hong Kong it seemed that my good reputation counted for nothing. I was damned if I was going to finish my career with my name blackened. However stacked the odds against me were, I had to fight the decision. Ironically, a few days before the appeal was held, having given me six days for failing to ride out a hanging horse to the best of my ability, the Sha Tin stewards found me guilty of careless riding because I had continued to ride my mount with the whip while the horse was hanging out. They suspended me for two race days – I could do nothing right.

At the appeal itself, I produced a photograph that clearly showed that the saddle had slipped forward. Television commentator Peter Gumbleton, a former Hong Kong jockey, also confirmed to the stewards what he had said on television that night, that Villa Pine had run one of his best races to date. Furthermore, he was able to point out that Hughenden, who had won Villa Pine's previous race on the sand by six lengths, had finished second last in the race in question. I hoped that this support would sway the panel but it was not to be. Eventually the panel decided to dismiss my appeal but reduced the penalty from six days to four days. This was baffling. Jim McGrath, a leading racing writer and television commentator who now works for the *Racing Post* in England, wrote in his Monday column, 'Hide had his suspension cut . . . and yet the stewards announced that they had dismissed his appeal!' An owner of Eric's, High Court judge Archie Zimmern, said that in English law a decision like that was impossible. If I was guilty, the original suspension should have stood. But as there was obviously sufficient doubt in their minds to reduce the original sentence the suspension should have been lifted altogether. To illustrate the inconsistency of the panel's decisions, the following season Villa Pine's saddle again slipped forward during a race. This time the jockey was Y. P. Chan. The Stipes' verdict on this incident? No action was taken because the slipped saddle left him 'at a complete disadvantage in assisting his mount'.

The Licensing Committee met in May to consider applications for jockeys' licences for the 1985–86 season. The Stipendiary Board chose to oppose my application as my 'disciplinary record in the current season fell short of the standards required'. Two six-day offences may be sufficient grounds to oppose an application, but one of my six-day offences had actually been reduced to four. I was serving out my two days' suspension for riding my horse when he was hanging at the time and as there were only three meetings left afterwards, and Eric hadn't many runners, I had decided that there wasn't much point staying in Hong Kong. However, if I wanted to ride there the next season, it was now imperative that I did stay on to attend the Licensing Committee's meeting at which my application was to be considered further.

I informed Brian Sullivan that I wished to attend the meeting but he advised me against it. If I was present and was turned down, the decision would go on my record as a licence refused. On the other hand, if I didn't appear, it would be the end as far as Hong Kong was concerned. I felt I had to take the risk of events going against me; I wasn't about to give up without a fight. Before the meeting I was sent my disciplinary record and was disturbed to read the latest inclusion: 'Jockey E. Hide was warned in regards to his use of the whip forward of the saddle on Blessing.' At the time, this incident didn't merit a mention in the Stipes' report in the newspapers or the form book. I obtained a transcript of the inquiry and I quote it here:

Marsh: We have viewed those films in slow motion and it looks on the film as though you are dangerously near the head. The rules and regulations in this country are that the furthest forward you go with the whip is the shoulder, not up the neck. On both the head-on and the side-on, [which wasn't available to be shown] it gives us the impression that it is very near the head, so please control your stick and be more careful in the future.

Clearly, as these words show, this was not an official warning and furthermore, there is nothing in the Hong Kong Rules of Racing about not using the whip forward of a horse's shoulder. So I went to see Sullivan about this. He told me that it had been excluded from the Stipes' report to safeguard me against prosecution by the R.S.P.C.A. That certainly didn't tie up with the fact that an Australian jockey had made the Stipes' report when actually striking his mount across the head while endeavouring to turn him into the straight. The average Chinese punter couldn't care less what happened to a horse so long as he collected his bets. I'm sure that most had never even heard of the R.S.P.C.A., or at least didn't know what the initials stood for.

The friendly advice of Gary Alderdice, a New Zealander in his late 30s who had been a practising barrister in Hong Kong for 12 years, had been instrumental in reducing my suspension in the Villa Pine affair. I wasn't allowed to have a legal representative at the licence appeal, but I was able to call Gary as one of my witnesses. He began by referring to the Villa Pine case, pointing out that in over 3,000 criminal appeals he had dealt with in the past 12 years, where there was any area of doubt established the conviction was almost invariably quashed. He reminded the committee that an expatriate jockey should have something to contribute to Hong Kong. 'I respect-fully invite the committee to look at his record. I had no idea how impressive it was . . . he has had 35 years of virtually unblemished riding. I feel, as a member of the Club and someone who enjoys racing, that he will be a loss to Hong Kong racing if he isn't given a chance to ride here again and prove himself.'

I had asked Colonel Tedford, the Chief Instructor of the Apprentice Jockeys' School and the Royal Hong Kong Jockey Club starter, whether it was possible for him, in his position, to give me a letter of support. I was overwhelmed when he told me that he was willing to actually come along in person and speak up for me. He said: 'I find that he has considerable experience, and through that experience he has on occasions given very helpful advice to us, the starting team'. He added that if I was allowed to stay on in Hong Kong he planned to invite me along to talk to the Apprentice School at Beas River.

Another working member of the Royal Hong Kong Jockey Club who came along to support me was Graham Rock, at the time the official handicapper. I had known Graham since the beginning of his career as a racing journalist some 12 years previously. He said: 'I have watched you ride literally thousands of times. During that time, I appreciated your skill as a sympathetic jockey and your record speaks for itself . . . Almost without exception, the local jockeys believe that the harder they hit a horse, and the more often they hit it, the faster that horse will run . . . The Jockey Club may feel that they wish to raise the standard overall, particularly the standard of horsemanship, and with regard to teaching young riders that it is possible to make a horse do its best without recourse to the whip, I think you can make a significant contribution'. It wasn't an easy time for me and I very much appreciated the support of Colonel Tedford and Graham Rock. Marsh, however, seemed to find it inappropriate and cut them dead afterwards.

The meeting lasted 40 mintues and the Chairman, John Pearce, informed me that the Committee would let me know their decision the following day when the racing was at Sha Tin. One of my rides that day was for the Deputy Senior Steward, the Hon. Li Fook Wu. I received the Licensing Committee's answer by special messenger – they had turned me down. I was shocked and very disappointed. Although I knew my chances were remote, I was determined to appeal against their decision.

In the *South China Morning Post*, Jim McGrath, in a piece entitled 'Jockey Club Put the Boot in' questioned the legalities of the Hong Kong Jockey Club. 'Putting it as simply as possible, jockeys are now told that two breaches under Rules 131(ii) and (iii) may place their licences in jeopardy. The Stipendiary Stewards, who have three votes out of five on any race meeting stewards' panel, are the key figures in laying those charges and handing out the penalties they consider necessary. However, also consider that the Licensing Committee have as their Secretary a member of that same Stipendiary Stewards line-up. Although he doesn't have a vote on the Licensing Committee, he is their official Secretary. I ask whether it is wise for the Club to have their race-day policing and what amounts to a licensing judiciary linked in this manner, no matter how remote it may be. The Jockey Club have streamlined their control of racing so much in recent years that it seems silly for such a fundamental to be overlooked.'

Peter Gumbleton in *The Standard* added: 'Hide's short history in Hong Kong has been marred by two suspensions under Rule 131 (ii). The two horses he rode, Gobi Star and Villa Pine, have never won a race in Hong Kong and on the face of it, it will be a long time before they do. This doesn't sound like British justice to me'.

It was a worrying time for me but my spirits were temporarily raised by a win on Star of Hong Kong, my 18th and last win of the season, which put me in seventh place out of 45 in the jockeys' table – not bad considering the enforced time off. Eric finished the season with the best winners-to-runners ratio in the trainers' list.

To prepare the case for my appeal I gathered together form books dating back to 1979 and spent innumerable hours going through every race, scrutinising the Stipes' reports to see which of those jockeys that the Club were happy to re-licence had had problems in the past. I came up with several who had far worse records than mine. For instance, local jockey K. S. Wong had in that time been stood down twice for six months and twelve months and had also received a six-day offence, yet he had been granted his licence. M. C. Tam did rather well, too. He had been given two separate six-day suspensions and in the October of the current season had been given six months for the worst offence. There was no opposition to his licence either.

The hearing of my appeal against the decision of the Licensing Committee took place five days before the end of the season. Like the previous inquiry, it was held in the boardroom on the ninth floor of the Club building at Happy Valley. This impressive room is big enough to hold a dance in and the focal point is a large horseshoe-shaped table. The meeting was chaired by Michael Sandberg, Chairman of the Royal Hong Kong Jockey Club and, although they took no part in the proceedings, Sir John Archer, the Chief Executive, and Jamie Barber, the Director of Racing, were also present. I was legally represented by Gary Alderdice, who did a great job presenting my case from the evidence I had gathered. Eric Collingwood and jockey Paddy Young, who had ridden Gobi Star in his last two races, spoke up as witnesses for me along with Graham Rock and Colonel Tedford, who virtually repeated what they had said at the previous meeting. Jim Marsh claimed that if K. S. Wong and M. C. Tam had been expatriate jockeys he would have opposed them. Gary responded that it was wrong to discriminate between jockeys, and that it was also wrong to 'perpetuate incompetent and dishonest jockeys just because they are local – that does nothing for racing here'. He raised the case of Australian jockey Peter Leyshan who, as well as having a worse disciplinary record than mine, had been found guilty the previous October, of improper betting. It was the first time that charges of that nature had been preferred against jockeys in Hong Kong. Gary submitted that that conviction lent weight to 'all the rife and rumour and speculation that goes on, that jockeys are in it up to their eyeballs and know what's going to happen'. Yet there had been no resistance to Leyshan's licence.

After a marathon three-and-a-half-hour hearing, the stewards overturned the Licensing Committee's earlier decision. It was a great relief to me – all the work and worry had finally proved worthwhile. Eric and I celebrated over a meal and, as I was returning to the flat, the midnight news broke the story of the result of my appeal.

Many people congratulated me on beating the Jockey Club but I didn't see it as that kind of a victory because, after all, it was the Jockey Club who granted me my licence in the end. But I did feel that it was a triumph over the Stipendiary and Licensing Boards, who had both opposed me. I was booked to fly out on Saturday evening straight after the finish of racing. Now, at least, I could leave our possessions behind knowing that I would return.

– 21 –
Countdown

I RETURNED from Hong Kong early in June 1985 with one thought in my mind – to get the seven winners I still needed to make sixth position in the table. After that I wasn't sure: retirement was obviously not far away, but if I was still enjoying riding and still being offered rides I wasn't going to hang up my boots just because I'd reached the magic figure. My first task was to pass the Jockey Club medical, something I had first undergone eight years previously when I turned 40. The Jockey Club had soon realised that there were plenty of men fit enough at that age and so raised the age limit to 45. I was delighted to hear from the Jockey Club's medical officer, Dr Allen, that he rated me as fit as I had been eight years before.

The first trainer to offer me a ride on my return was Pat Rohan, on a two-year-old in the first race at Haydock. Shortly afterwards, Barry Hills offered me one with a better chance at Catterick the same afternoon. I didn't want to turn Pat down and as luck would have it, I was able to ride at both meetings. After being beaten on Pat's, I drove the 100 miles to Catterick to win the last for Barry on Valadon.

One day shortly after this I had another winner in a race which holds unpleasant memories for me. It was quite truthfully the only time in the whole of my career that I was approached to play a part in fixing a race. The horse I was riding was a last-minute booking and so I wasn't listed in the morning newspapers as the rider. On leaving the weighing-room I was approached by two jockeys who told me there was only one trier in the race. They asked if I would be in on it. I replied that first, I had no intention of being involved and second, they had made a mistake – as far as I was concerned there were at least two triers, the one they fancied and mine! Winning had always been my motivation and I wasn't about to change course at this stage of my career. I don't know how much money was lost when I came in first but I was far from popular. The 'fancied' horse finished second

to me and the two jockeys who'd spoken to me made an unsuccessful attempt to persuade its jockey to object.

If I thought the matter was closed, I was wrong. In a later race, I was
riding a fancied runner for a Southern trainer when, shortly after
leaving the stalls, one of the 'fixers' made a bee-line for me, cutting
me off and pushing me on to the rail, effectively putting me out of
contention. I was in a difficult position: I didn't want to split on my
colleague but, in fairness to the trainer, who had given me a lot of
support over the years, I felt I had to explain to him what had happened. I asked him to leave me to sort it out. Unbeknown to me he
later reviewed the patrol film at Jockey Club Headquarters. The film
was inconclusive due to poor visibility, but the barging incident had
been noticed and commented on in Raceform. Following the
trainer's complaint I had a visit from a couple of Jockey Club security
officers. Although I had no alternative but to confirm what had taken
place I pointed out that as I was still a jockey I would prefer not to
sign any statement. Much as I deplored the other jockey's action I
didn't wish to assume the role of 'grass'. I did assure the officers that
should I later succeed in becoming a Steward's Secretary, as I hoped
to do then, they could be confident that I would show the same loyalty
to their cause when on that side of the fence.

I would never condone the behaviour of the jockeys concerned,
but I did feel I understood the circumstances that encouraged them
to accept a bribe. The newspapers are full of talk of 'millionaire'
jockeys. A few such men exist, it's true, and good luck to them; those
reaching the pinnacle of any competitive profession deserve their
rewards. But it is only the very top few who are anywhere near that
category. Below them there is a middle core of men who make a
comfortable living out of it – although perhaps 'comfortable' is not
the word for a life which revolves around dieting and saunas. Finally,
at the base of this pyramid, is a large band of men who struggle to
make ends meet. Most of them are self-employed, many of them
have a wife and family to support and mortgages to pay off, and yet
they often find, having driven to somewhere like Ayr for one moderate
ride, that by the time they have paid their expenses they are out of
pocket. Only a relatively small proportion of jockeys are in a position
to command a retainer. Many ride work for trainers purely in the hope
of picking up rides. (Mark Birch was once asked if he had a retainer.
'Oh yes', he replied, 'the guv'nor gave me three broccoli plants once
but two of them died.')

I certainly don't want to give the impression that racing in England
is generally crooked. In all enterprises involving large amounts of
money it is impossible to prevent some dishonesty, but in racing it is
the exception rather than the rule. There is no doubt that there are
many horses over the years who have not been given hard races but

the advent of the patrol film has meant that any real 'stopping' would soon be spotted. I am convinced after 35 years in the saddle that the horses who are capable of winning but are prevented from doing so are few and far between. The fact that in 17,700 rides I was approached to fix a race on only that one occasion speaks volumes for the overall straightness of racing. Perhaps the reason why so many people, particularly unsuccessful punters, claim that racing is 'bent' is that it provides them with a good excuse if the horse they've put their money on is beaten – if they tell themselves it was because they backed a 'non-trier' it is less hurtful to their pride than admitting that their judgement in picking a 'certainty' was wrong.

Such people might do well to accept that in racing there is no such thing as a certainty – if there were there would be no racing. The 19th century trainer John Porter summed it up when he said 'I have known of only three racing certainties, and two of those lost'! Some readers may remember Gordon Richards riding a 20–1-on favourite in a two-runner race at Chepstow: the horse went only a few yards before it stuck its toes in and whipped round, catapulting Gordon to the ground to leave its sole rival to canter home alone! Even the best laid plans can come unstuck. There's a story that Grandpa Edwards liked to tell about a man who went up to a bookie and put £100 on the outsider in a three-runner race. The bookie looked at him and said, 'You must know a lot about that horse'. 'No, I don't', replied the man. 'But I know there are only three in the race and the other two are both mine and they are not trying.' The bookie declined to mention at the time that the other horse was his and was also a non-trier. The man lost his £100!

Jockeys are notoriously bad tipsters. Soon after the Tote introduced their 'Jackpot', for which you had to pick all six winners, I joined a car-full of jockeys going to Lanark. As we all had fancied rides we each decided to put two pounds in the kitty and have a go at this new bet. I had my form books with me and much studying was done – there were no Page Three girls to divert our attention in those days – and we thought it was pinching money. I was riding a 'good thing' which we made the 'banker'. As it turned out, not one of our selections won, and I was even beaten on the supposed certainty by one of the other passengers. On the way home we stopped for fish and chips at Penrith instead of the hoped-for celebratory steaks at Scotch Corner.

It was at Doncaster on 28 June 1985 that I equalled my target. The mount which achieved it for me was Daring Way, owned by Robert Sangster and trained by Michael Stoute. The following day, I put myself into clear sixth position behind Sir Gordon, Lester, Doug Smith, Joe Mercer and Fred Archer by winning in the Commanche Run colours on Tantino at Newcastle. The race may not have been of vital importance to owner Ivan Allen or trainer Luca Cumani, but it meant a tremendous amount to me. Two races later, I rode Insular into fifth place for the Queen in the 'Pitman's' Derby; I would have called it a day in this country had we won but it wasn't to be. Luca Cumani told me that he had never seen me riding better and his words, along with the encouragement of Michael Stoute, Barry Hills and Bruce Hobbs, encouraged me to carry on a little longer. I rode three more winners before calling it a day in Britain and my last and 2,591st winner was on Hi-Tech Leader for Jimmy Etherington at Nottingham on 13 August. I had what was to be my last ride in this country later in the evening on Singing Boy, trained by my brother. It would have been great to go out on a winner, especially for Tony, but fairy-tale endings rarely happen in real life and I was pleased enough with a third place.

At the time I didn't know for sure that I wouldn't ride again in England, but I thought it unlikely. Realistically, the chance of a good job coming my way at the age of 48 was remote. Perhaps it was time to follow the example of Lester and Joe Mercer and retire gracefully to make way for the next generation. First, though, I had a swan-song to sing in Hong Kong.

– 22 –
The Year of the Tiger

WHEN I returned to Hong Kong ten days before the start of the 1985–86 season I had to start flat-hunting all over again. I eventually found a place on the Island side, but it was on the outskirts of Hong Kong and when Sue joined me a few weeks later she wasn't happy with it. We looked around for some time before finding a flat which, although small, was only five minutes' walk from Happy Valley racecourse, the shops and transport. On the 21st floor, it was bright and sunny and had magnificent views over Hong Kong to the Peak and Central district. Unfortunately, it was also more expensive. Eric Collingwood, who footed the bill, had said that if Sue didn't like the first place there would be no problem in moving elsewhere, but neither he nor his wife, Audrey, of whom Sue had seen quite a lot the previous season, ever called in to see the new flat despite our open invitation. I felt that the deterioration in our relationship started over that move.

Eric's stable wasn't firing at all, and we didn't have our first winner until the middle of November with my old friend Wynnwith. At 20–1 it came as a pleasant surprise, if not to the owner, then certainly to the trainer and jockey, who were just happy to get off the mark. Wynnwith had not previously shown any form at Sha Tin, but the other horses had gone off too fast and they all fell in a heap to present the race to him. Prior to this I had another contretemps with the stewards. I wasn't concerned in the finish of the race in question, but close home horses on either side of me were tightening me up and I was in serious danger of being brought down. I shouted for more room and instinctively put out my hand to fend off the jockey causing me most problems. I didn't make contact, but the stewards stood me down for three days for attempting to strike the horse and jockey. In England the other two riders would have been on the mat!

From the beginning Eric had explained to me that, unlike some other trainers, he called the tune rather than his owners. He assured me that I would ride most of the horses but in spite of this it was, as usual, the jockey who was first to shoulder the blame. As our dry spell continued the inevitable happened: I started to lose some rides. Eric didn't tell me I was jocked off a horse; the first time I was aware of any change in policy was when I saw another jockey taking a horse of mine out for track work. The only consolation was that the horses weren't running any better for anybody else. It is at times like this that you know who your friends are.

The Chinese are great believers in luck, and in an attempt to reverse our fortunes a feast was held in the stableyard. There was roast suckling pig, duck, beer and a very potent Chinese wine. Some of the owners suggested that I visited the temple or got the Fung Shui man to look around the flat to see that the furniture, mirrors and ornaments were facing in the right direction, as they believed that this could make a difference to one's fortune. Connections even went so far as to suggest that as my telephone and car numbers didn't have the lucky number 8 in them I should try to get them changed. I thought this was a lot of nonsense, and my response wasn't particularly diplomatic. I felt the lack of form was caused simply by the fact that the horses were too high in the handicap after the previous successful season. Furthermore, Eric was never hard on his horses in their early work and they were noted for taking time to find their best form.

My second winner didn't come until February – little wonder I was losing rides – and that was for an Aussie trainer, Roy Edwards, on a horse called Speedy Wongchoy. I was able to dictate the pace, a ploy which admirably suited this horse, who had finished last in his previous race. Roy was called in before the stewards to explain the apparent improvement in his horse's form. He told them that the horse's earlier performances indicated he was at his best left alone in front and this was accepted. Roy also told the stewards and the press that it was a case of the master competing against the pupils: he kindly reported that I had completely out-manoeuvred the other jockeys, riding a perfectly judged race in front.

Robin Parke wrote: 'Speedy Wongchoy was given a superb ride by veteran Edward Hide, one of Hong Kong racing's forgotten men. Hide's ride was a classic example of winning from the front on a horse that is not over-endowed with courage. It was a timely reminder that Hide still has something to offer local racing'. The Year of the Tiger was just around the corner and, in mentioning this, Shannon in the *South China Morning Post* described me as 'Tiger Hide clawing his way back from the wilderness'. I was obviously delighted to read comments like this but I have never liked the use of the word 'veteran'. I didn't want prospective employers to have visions of me turning up at the races in a bathchair with pension book in hand! Lester, though a year and a half older than me, never qualified for the 'veteran' tag. It was usually 'the Maestro' or 'the Long Fellow'. Roy Edwards, being aware of my feelings, further endeared himself to me by referring to me as 'evergreen'. That was more like it!

Once you're in a rut it's very hard to climb out. In that situation in England, you at least have the opportunities to fight your way out because there are often two or three meetings on the same day, providing more rides for more people. The Hong Kong scene is a completely different story. Unless you're riding winners or, even better, tipping winners you are not given rides. Owners would ask me for a tip, but obviously thought I was crazy when I often replied 'I don't think it has much chance but I'll be doing my best.' They couldn't understand me. To their way of thinking, if I didn't think my mount had a chance then I should make sure it was saved for another day when it did have a chance and they could back it. For them, it was black and white – either 'sure win', or 'don't back it today'.

It wasn't only the owners who thought this way. Most of the Chinese I met had the same touching faith that the jockeys always knew what would win. Some waitresses at the golf club, whenever they saw me, would come over with a big smile and ask me for a 'sure win'. I tried not to encourage them. If I told them anything had a chance I stressed it that was only a 'su su' – small – chance, as I knew that if I showed confidence they would put a whole month's wages on the horse; and not only them, but their aunts and uncles and grannies as well!

At our first flat the caretaker used to wash my car and every race-day he would knock on the door, waving his Chinese racing news-paper, and ask me for my 'tipsies'. He wouldn't go until I gave him a number or two. Some of them came up, although I think on balance he must have lost more than he won, but he never charged me for washing the car. I remember remonstrating with an owner, for whom I had ridden several winners, when I discovered that a Chinese jockey was to ride his horse. 'Ah, but he tipped me a good winner from another stable the other day so he is due to ride my horse', he explained. I was exasperated and retorted, 'I haven't come all the way over here just to ride your horses' track work!' He genuinely couldn't understand my attitude and I couldn't understand his.

It was fine leaving everything to Eric when I was getting the rides, but after being jocked off a few of the stable's runners I felt that it was high time I took action. I went to see two of our main owners, Sir Sydney Gordon, head of China Light and Power, and C. H. Wong, a senior partner in a firm of solicitors, both of whom were stewards of the Royal Hong Kong Jockey Club. They told me they were more than happy with my riding and pledged their support. Sir Sydney's Scotch Silver was one of my first winners in Hong Kong. Eric later remarked on the pat on the back from the grateful owner, and said cynically that apart from my winning percentage through the Jockey Club that would be all I would receive. But I valued the support of those owners at this time far more than a few Hong Kong dollars. Even riding their horses at track work was a great boost to my morale.

I never thought I would be content with racing only twice a week, but it was beginning to dawn on me that there was more to life than living horseracing 24 hours a day. I took the chance to sample some of the diverse attractions that make Hong Kong such a fascinating place to live. It certainly wasn't all despondency out there: we had a lot of fun and made some good friends, particularly during that second year. Maybe it's being less successful that makes you more popular — I don't know, but I certainly felt more relaxed than at any other time during my riding career. Often the 'phone would ring and someone would ask us if we wanted to join a boat trip. We'd stock up with some food and drink and join the others to go off for the day on a junk or an owner's sumptuous motor cruiser. A popular port of call was the island of Lantau, where we would anchor in the bay and the more energetic could water-ski. I've always had a fear of water but I donned a life-jacket and a pair of skis and had a go. I had barely been pulled upright when I was down again and dragged head-first through the water. If you're ever in a similar position, for God's sake let go of the baton. I didn't, and amid much gurgling and spluttering and to the amusement of the others, I sampled the delights of a sea water and pollution cocktail!

We would go ashore to a deserted beach from which a single track led to a remote village and the most unlikely named pub, the Frog and Toad. A barbeque on the roof terrace and a darts match would follow. Apparently, the nearby mud-patch was the scene of the annual all-in mud wrestling competition. It must have been the Australian influence that made 'barbies' the 'in' thing. On other occasions we would go to the beach to set up the 'barbie' and the day would usually end with a noisy game of dominoes. When the weather was poor the nearby South China Sports Club offered ten-pin bowling. A crowd of us would meet there to bowl, chatter and eat and drink the rainy day away.

Clubs are very much the centre of life in Hong Kong. Most people live in flats which are too small for entertaining and prefer to socialise at their club. The Hong Kong Football Club, which became our base, was only minutes away from our apartment. It had excellent facilities: a fine swimming pool, tennis courts, bowls, squash, sauna, snooker, darts, bars and restaurants. It was here that I took up lawn bowling for the first time, and I now play occasionally at the indoor centre at Malton. The Football Club complex was managed by Malcolm Davies, who became a good friend and still keeps us in touch with the Hong Kong scene by sending us *Racing World* magazine and the Football Club's own journal. Jockeys Wally Hood and Pat Trotter and their wives were also members, and other friends and tennis and golf partners included Dave Allison (son of Malcolm); Tommy Langley, who played first division football for Chelsea; Lee Palin, now playing for Bradford and Barry Powell, who is now coaching at Wolverhampton Wanderers. All three footballers played for South China Football Club, coached by Geoff Varden, another good friend. They were all keen race-goers and since our return to England we have stayed with Tommy Langley and his wife for Royal Ascot. Sue used to go to aerobics three mornings a week at the Football Club and also helped with Riding for the Disabled, where I lent an occasional hand leading the ponies round.

Another small and select club was the Monday Club, so named because its 'members' met each Monday at a different restaurant and ate, drank and talked their way through the day. It was a men-only club, and although I attended once or twice I couldn't lay up with the regulars: Wally Hood and a friend of his; Jim McGrath the commentator and journalist; and journalists Chris Collins and Robin Parke. On one occasion 'Parkie' turned up with his binoculars still around his neck from the previous Saturday's racing, not having been home since then!

Hong Kong's shopping facilities are renowned throughout the world. You can still have suits made virtually overnight if necessary but the prices are now beginning to catch up with our own. The place is vibrant at night, the clubs and restaurants entice customers in and the shops stay open until very late, and yet it is still an extremely safe place to be out in the streets. There is so much to do in Hong Kong. Top-class tennis and golf tournaments are held annually as well as concerts and theatres with leading entertainers, and everything is at your fingertips.

Although the weights carried were higher, keeping my weight down was still difficult because of the lavish entertaining and dining facilities which spoiled us for life. There was every sort of restaurant from every nation in the world, with exceptionally high standards and service. The time I feel most nostalgic about Hong Kong now is when I go to our pantry and find that Sue hasn't had time to stock up. We both look at each other and say 'Wouldn't it be nice to pop out to a restaurant and have something really delicious like we used to in Hong Kong?' To help dispose of the unwanted pounds there was a mixed sauna available at the Football Club but there were also several top-grade public saunas dotted around town. After the sauna you relaxed in the lounge where drinks and fresh fruit were provided. You could have a manicure and pedicure followed by a massage from a young, attractive girl. You soon worked out which girls were the best and requested them by number, just like a Chinese take-away!

Probably the two most enjoyable days of the year were those of the Rugby Sevens, when the stadium was filled with ex-pats watching some of the finest rugby players in the world, ably supported by their own fans who had travelled over to cheer on the teams and were intent on having a good time. Jugs of beer and wine were on sale non-stop, and although the atmosphere became decidedly merry, the rivalry was good-natured, with none of the malice associated with our own football crowds.

Anyone who thinks Hong Kong is nothing but high-rise blocks of concrete would be pleasantly surprised to drive out to the New Territories. In the depths of the lovely countryside, surrounded by high hills reminiscent of Scotland, the Jockey Club has its Beas River Country Club, and adjacent to that is the Hong Kong Golf Club, with three 18–hole championship courses, at Fanling. One of the perks offered to jockeys was the use of all Jockey Club facilities, which included the use of restaurants and extensive sports amenities at Happy Valley and at the splendid new club house at Sha Tin, as well as the facilities offered at the Beas River Club where you could stay overnight, ride, swim, play tennis and generally get away from the hustle and bustle of Hong Kong.

Beas River was also the headquarters of the Apprentice School. There boys were taught all aspects of stable-care and riding. At the end of the course they were allocated to trainers for further experience on the track. Some graduated to become jockeys, some made it as work riders and some inevitably dropped by the wayside. There were only a limited number of vacancies at the School and it was rumoured that as soon as a boy was accepted for the course his parents could expect an approach from one of the betting syndicates. If, for example, they ran a shop their business would suddenly take an up-turn although this was soon reversed if their son didn't 'toe the line'.

Some time ago apprentice races were tried. They were the first leg of the popular 'Double Q' bet. However, it soon became apparent, when only a couple of horses started well and the others drifted out of the stalls, that the boys had been 'got at'. Of the ten or so races held it is alleged that only one failed to go according to plan, and the Jockey Club were soon obliged to put a stop to these events. Flash cars were very much a status symbol in Hong Kong, and talk abounded when an apprentice who had ridden only a few winners was seen driving around in an expensive sports car. On investigation he was also found to have a bank account vastly in excess of what he had earned in fees and percentages.

On Thursday 20 February 1986, I left my flat at around the normal time of 4.30 a.m. for track work at Sha Tin. The horses were being led around as usual, waiting for their jockeys to come and take them out, but as dawn broke over the mountains some were still there and a buzz of concern began to spread among the trainers and mafoos. Very shortly, Hong Kong's multi-million dollar racing world was reeling from the shocking news of the arrest of 22 people, all closely involved with the sport.

Between 3.00 and 3.30 a.m. that morning, teams of operators from the Independent Commission Against Corruption (I.C.A.C.) had simultaneously raided the apartments of 22 prominent Hong Kong racing personalities who were taken away for interrogation into alleged racing malpractices. Personal possessions including travel documents, money and bank statements were all seized and taken away in plastic bags.

One trainer not involved described the amazing scenes outside his apartment block. He happened to be up at that time and, looking out of the window, he saw a fleet of vehicles pull up, some with short-wave radio aerials and several people rushing about. Then all the door buzzers in the building were pressed at the same time, followed by a voice announcing: 'The I.C.A.C. are in the building on official business.' The trainer admitted that it gave him a hell of a shock. Another trainer in the same Sha Tin complex was awakened by a 'phone call from his jockey: 'The I.C.A.C. are here, they're trying to break the door down, what shall I do?' He promptly replied 'Let them in, you idiot, before they succeed!'

Apparently, I.C.A.C. investigators had also spent more than ten hours at Sullivan's apartment before taking him away with boxes of documents and his wife's jewellery and furs. At 9.00 a.m the Jockey Club issued the following statement: 'For six months the Jockey Club has been working in close collaboration with the I.C.A.C. to investigate racing malpractices. As a consequence of these investigations a number of jockeys, trainers, owners, one Club employee and some other individuals not directly connected with the Club are now helping the I.C.A.C. with their inquiries'.

It appeared that the aim of the investigations was to smash the notorious 'Shanghai Syndicate', whose members were alleged to have been involved in race-fixing. At one time Hong Kong racing had many large betting syndicates but most of the big racing punters had long since gone to the wall. Only the Shanghai Syndicate and 'The Banker' were still believed to exist. The Shanghai Syndicate had been part of Hong Kong racing legend for decades and was said to be so powerful that it could even influence the outcome of an inquiry by the Jockey Club. Its leader, Y. L. Yang – racing's 'Mr Fixit' – was among those arrested, but he was released 36 hours later on cash bail of HK$1,000,000. The others were freed on HK$50,000 bail in their own recognisance.

The Jockey Club then announced that 'to maintain public confidence in racing' it had suspended the licences of 13 people; two trainers and 11 jockeys. These men were not allowed to go racing or to exercise the privilege of using the Jockey Club facilities. The jockeys included current Hong Kong Champion, Gary Moore, who was due to leave in a few days to take up a retainer with Criquette Head in France, and his fellow Australians, David Brosnan, Rod Staples, Pat Trotter and Greg Hall, along with our own Bruce Raymond and five local riders. One of the trainers was the current leading trainer, Derek T. C. Cheng, a former jockey who had also ridden winners in England. The other trainer was Englishman Derek Kent. Derek was soon released by the I.C.A.C. and was immediately reinstated by the Club. Unfortunately, his health suffered from all the pressures involved with training in Hong Kong and to cap it all he was later disqualified for three years.

A month after the initial raids there followed a mopping-up operation. Two more Australians were arrested – jockey Ian Albuino and my friend, the former Western Australian Champion Trainer, Roy Edwards. Of the 26 senior jockeys licensed to ride in the territory, 11 were now out of action and seven of those were in the top ten of the jockeys' table. Outside the Jockey Club some wag had put up a notice with a large arrow pointing to the headquarters, bearing the words: 'Jockeys wanted – apply within'. Gossip was always rife in the goldfish bowl-world of Hong Kong racing. The integrity of Hong Kong's multi-million dollar racing world had long been under suspicion but officially the racing scene was clean.

Until 1971, that is. According to the stories in the newspapers that year a drug-soaked carrot was found in the stables adjacent to the Happy Valley racecourse. This blew up into the world's biggest horse-doping scandal of all time. Inquiries revealed that no less than 88 horses had been doped by two rival gangs, one feeding the horses 'uppers', the other 'downers'. This, of course, brought about some interesting results, especially when horses who had been given doses of different drugs were in the same race. Some of them ran extremely fast while others moved like the proverbial tortoise! Jockey Joe Pereira and a number of others were arrested and charged in what became known as the 'Joe Pereira doping case'. It was this scandal that forced the Hong Kong Jockey Club to discard amateur riding (termed 'shamateur' by many) in favour of professional racing with its much tighter controls and links with major horse-racing countries.

The newspapers revealed that in the early days of professional racing, the Shanghai Syndicate had flourished. They brought in a leading international trainer severing the links with one of the many White Russian trainers who had been the backbone of Hong Kong's amateur racing for decades. All of their considerable resources were put behind this one stable and a jockey was employed solely to ride the stable's horses. The syndicate alone would decide where and when a horse would be allowed to try to win. The trainer had to adopt a somewhat unconventional training policy to cater for the group's last-minute decisions. In training, horses were brought to a certain level of fitness and then kept ticking over. Rarely would they be tuned up for any particular race because the job of stopping them became a lot harder if it was decided at the last minute not to try. If a horse was not race-fit or was running over an unsuitable distance the jockey had no problem in giving the horse a run round without breaking the rules. However, it was a totally different matter if the jockey was informed only minutes before the start of the syndicate's intentions. If it was 'Yes', the horse was expected to win; if it was 'No' he was to keep out of the first two placings, and what is more to achieve this in such a way that the stewards, with the aid of six cameras, would be unable to recognise or prove any malpractice!

The syndicate's intentions on race-day were said to be the subject of constant speculation among punters, the more astute of whom were well aware of its existence. The subterfuge adopted by the syndicate as a consequence had its humorous moments. The opening of Sha Tin, for example, presented a few problems in planning. The layout of the track and grandstand area wasn't known so this had to be subtly reconnoitred before opening day so that the point at which the 'go' or 'stop' signal should be given could be decided. The spot chosen was above the walkway where the jockeys left the paddock. But the conspirators were unaware that the decorative work had not been completed. On opening day, to their dismay, in front of the designated spot stood scores of potted plants of all shapes and sizes. As the press reported, 'There was so much foliage about that you would have had to be an expert in jungle warfare to get through'.

The I.C.A.C., an elite force answerable only to the Governor of Hong Kong, came into being in February 1974. It was their probe into police corruption that gave them their lead into the local racing scene. They mounted a surveillance on a former senior policeman and two serving officers of the same rank, a trio which was suspected of taking money from illegal betting outfits. During covert investigations, it was discovered that the former policeman had many associates in racing circles, jockeys and trainers included, one of whom was Y. L. Yang. From that point, the I.C.A.C. were on the trail of the Shanghai Syndicate. It was widely acknowledged that the Jockey Club didn't become involved until early November 1985, after the departure, under a cloud, of English jockey Paddy Young.

The I.C.A.C. investigation gathered pace after Paddy had made all the running on Auchenshuggle for his retaining stable at Happy Valley in October 1985. The win was a surprise, not only to the rider but also, more importantly, to Y. L. Yang who, feeling that he had been double-crossed, ordered Paddy to vacate his flat immediately. Relations between Paddy and his trainer were also very strained and, as he was being given few rides, Paddy felt that it was in his best interests to quit Hong Kong forthwith. Before he left, he was interviewed by the Jockey Club and by the I.C.A.C. about alleged race-fixing. After a detailed statement was taken, Paddy was allowed to return to England. As the season progressed, the surveillance of those involved was stepped up. It was said that, on account of the stable he was riding for, Aussie jockey Greg Hall was followed by the I.C.A.C. from the moment he stepped off the 'plane onto Hong Kong soil. If this was true, what happened to Philip Waldren could have been lucky. Philip was all set to take up a retainer with T. C. Cheng when the arrangements were blocked by the Licensing Committee, which said Philip hadn't ridden enough winners in the previous season in England to be able to ride in the colony. The 'good turn' that they did for Greg Hall in allowing him to take the job didn't in the end turn out to be as fortuitous as they might have hoped. It was said that Sullivan was tailed by the I.C.A.C. when he went home on holiday and when he later went to Europe for the Arc.

I have no evidence that telephones were tapped but many people were convinced of it. Apart from their security department, the only people in the Jockey Club who were briefed by the I.C.A.C. were two top-ranking officials. Other leading functionaries were kept in the dark and the events of that morning of 20 February stunned them all.

Y. L. Yang's trial took place the following September. The 63–year-old textile tycoon was described as having a personal income of between £3 million and £4 million a year. According to his defence counsel, Yang's motive was not pecuniary; it was the satisfaction of tipping winners to his friends. He pleaded guilty to six charges of conspiracy to cheat at gambling but his counsel asked for a suspended jail sentence because of his client's medical condition. Yang, who wept intermittently throughout the hearing, was described as suffering from uncontrollable diabetes and secondary bone cancer and predictions of his life expectancy ranged from weeks to months. Apparently, he certainly looked a very frail old man in court. He was given a two-year suspended jail sentence and fined HK$5.4 million, which he paid immediately by cheque, walking out of court with a lightened step. Initially, the judge had considered a five-year jail sentence appropriate. This had been reduced because Yang had pleaded guilty and also because of his age and the fact that he had cooperated with the I.C.A.C. and had shown a willingness to make amends for his earlier wrong-doings. The major reason for consideration was his health; he was dying of cancer and was said to be in need of immediate radiation treatment. He left for America shortly afterwards for that treatment and is still leading an active life, commuting between the States and Jamaica.

Rumours would often sound off the Peak and ricochet round

Happy Valley, and one of them which spread to England, was that the wily Chinaman had deliberately lost weight and had his tailor make a suit two sizes too big for him to intensify his frail, drawn appearance for the benefit of the judge. During the trial Rod Staples admitted to fixing 24 races and pleaded guilty to 78 charges under the Rules of Racing. He was fined HK$540,000 (about £50,000) and disqualified for 18 years by the Royal Hong Kong Jockey Club. Staples was granted immunity from criminal prosecution to give evidence for the Crown. It was said that as soon as he was picked up by the I.C.A.C. he 'sang like a canary', and it hardly seems fair that by putting his friends in it up to their necks he should escape imprisonment. In his evidence he mentioned a senior racing figure, a very prominent member of the Jockey Club, but declined to name him. Perhaps it was the same Jockey Club figure who, when giving rather suspect riding orders to a colleague of mine, said as an afterthought, 'I'm talking to you as an owner, not as a steward'. Staples was quoted in the *South China Morning Post*: 'We're all being made out to be the bad boys. Everyone knows that the whole business was going on long before most of the jockeys involved were even in Hong Kong. We just happened to be on the spot when it blew up'. He refused to pay his fine to the Jockey Club, since as he was finished as a jockey he had nothing to lose. His disqualification was extended as a result but it made little difference to him.

One of the men to whom he did most disservice was his friend, David Brosnan, a former Champion Jockey of Western Australia. He was sentenced to a year's imprisonment and disqualified for 12 years by the Jockey Club, who fined him HK$330,000 for conspiring to cheat at gambling. Greg Hall, fined HK$20,000 received a much shorter ban of only six weeks. Greg is now riding back in Australia and not so long ago said: 'I'm still terribly bitter and upset about what went on. They have bad trainers, bad jockeys, bad owners and good facilities and you can't live by good facilities alone'. Bruce Raymond had his passport confiscated for some months by the I.C.A.C. but was eventually released without being charged. But he, like most of the others, had to face a Jockey Club inquiry. One of the charges of which Bruce was found guilty was breaking Rule 65(c) which stated that a jockey must not bet or have any interest in a bet. It's true to say that if this rule was strictly enforced in Hong Kong, there would be very few jockeys riding there! Bruce is now back here riding for Michael Jarvis, confirming what I've always known, that he is one of the best riders around.

Another jockey who is back, carving out a successful career, is Gary Moore. On the morning of the I.C.A.C. raids the officers went to his flat but he wasn't to be found. He was at his girlfriend's — clearly the I.C.A.C. hadn't done all their homework! Moore was released quickly by the I.C.A.C. He left for France within 24 hours of his suspension being lifted. His treatment was in marked contrast to that of some of the others, who had to wait behind for months. This naturally caused ill-feeling. Even if he was completely innocent of any charges the Jockey Club should have been seen to be consistent by holding an inquiry and announcing publicly that Gary was cleared before allowing him to leave for France. Every other jockey and trainer taken in by the I.C.A.C. that night had to face a Jockey Club inquiry even if the I.C.A.C. had cleared them of criminal charges.

Pat Trotter, who had been riding in Hong Kong since 1981, latterly for English trainer Gordon Smythe, had a particularly tough time. He had his passport impounded and, along with the others involved, had to report to the I.C.A.C. headquarters every month. It was ten months before his case came up and it was dismissed in minutes. In spite of the pressure of the I.C.A.C.'s shadow he maintained his innocence all along. The long stay in Hong Kong with no income and high legal and accounting fees hit him hard, not to mention the traumatic effect on his wife and two children.

Brian Sullivan, who had been due to take over from Jim Marsh as Chief Stipendiary Steward, was dismissed by the Royal Hong Kong Jockey Club. Under the Jockey Club's provident fund scheme he would have been entitled to a sum reputed to be in excess of £100,000 but he lost it all. He is now back in Australia running a wholesale newsagency. By sinister coincidence, not long after his return he met with an accident in which he sustained two broken legs. One can't help agreeing with Chris Collins, chief racing writer of the *South China Morning Post*, that 'the sensational events of the past six months could have easily provided Dick Francis with another best-seller'.

While the I.C.A.C. conducted its investigations the rest of us were left to carry on. Towards the end of February Lester Piggott, Yves Saint-Martin, Pat Eddery and Willie Carson turned up for the Ritz Club Challenge. The expatriate team was made up by those leading jockeys that hadn't fallen foul of the I.C.A.C., chosen according to the number of winners ridden that season. At the eve-of-competition cocktail party, Willie Carson was his usual ebullient self. I was due to ride C. H. Wong's Saturnian who, when racing in England, had been trained by Dick Hern and ridden by Willie. Willie, tactless as ever, disheartened the owner by telling him that Saturnian was held together by string and elastic bands and that he wouldn't ride him around the track for £1,000. Although he disappointed a little in the early part of the season, Saturnian, who had suffered from a joint problem, had showed much improved form when tried in a morning gallop in blinkers. So I was able to inform the Master Scot that he may be forced to eat his words after the racing. Sure enough, Saturnian proceeded to make all to win a £10,000 handicap comfortably, earning enough for C. H. Wong to keep his horse in string and elastic bands for life! Saturnian went on to complete his hat-trick – a very unusual feat in Hong Kong – and ended the season by finishing runner-up at level weights in the Chairman's Prize, the leading sprint race of the season. The Jockey Club would rather have five horses win five races than one completing a nap hand, and I felt their often harsh system of handicapping encouraged cheating. Unless your horse started the season a class in hand you were unlikely to win more than one race.

The winners were starting to flow at last. With many jockeys out of action because of the investigations there were obviously more opportunities for me, and Eric's horses were at last running into better form. Bruce Raymond was a great help, putting me in for many mounts that would normally have been his. Despite the ups and downs, I would have liked one more season in Hong Kong. I went to see Eric about riding for him for a third season but he couldn't see enough support for me to obtain my licence. However should I be successful elsewhere, he said, there could be up to ten horses in his stable which the owners would be pleased for me to ride.

Through my rides on Speedy Wongchoy and through playing golf I had come to know Roy Edwards well. As Rod Staples was his stable jockey Roy couldn't help being caught up in the investigations, and I felt sorry for him. Before the bubble burst Sue was watching a night race at Happy Valley with Roy and his wife Maureen. He told her he fancied the horse and had a big bet on it. From the time it jumped off it was clear he wasn't getting a run for his money. He later had words with Staples, intending to terminate the contract, but his jockey pleaded that if he did he would be out of a job as in Hong Kong contracts can't be changed mid-season. Roy reluctantly relented. When I required another trainer for a third year Roy said that should he be clear of his problems and able to resume training the next season, he would have at least 40 horses for me to ride. (I needed the support of the owners of a minimum of 15 horses in a stable.) However, the Jockey Club wouldn't entertain my application as Roy was still under suspension.

He was an expert at reading blood reports and one thing he learned from them was whether a horse was over-worked or under-worked. After his suspension his assistant, Kenny Kam, took over the team. On one occasion he called round to Roy's apartment to ask his opinion on the blood report of a horse due to run that evening at Happy Valley. Roy took one look at it and exclaimed, 'What have you been doing with this horse? You'll kill it with all this work!' After the races the poor animal dropped dead while being led back to his stable.

The worry of the investigation was probably at least partly responsible for Roy suffering a stroke. He appeared in court in a wheelchair. He wanted to fight to clear his name and it was only because the pressure had affected his health that he agreed to plead marginally guilty. He was fined and sentenced to 12 months imprisonment, suspended for two years because of his illness. The following season Kenny Kam was given a full licence to train, but he too had his problems. He was attacked twice in one month, once in the street and once in his car when thugs wielding iron bars smashed his windscreen. Kam sped to safety and was given round-the-clock protection by Jockey Club security officers.

Towards the end of the season I was told that someone from the Jockey Club had made it their business to inform the Chinese trainers that, due to my age, if they employed me they would be held responsible should I have an accident. This was a malicious and irresponsible thing to say as in no way are the trainers held responsible for a riding accident. I had a fair idea who was saying this and it didn't improve my opinion of the man. Obviously, someone still wanted to see the back of me. The whole time I had been in Hong Kong I had been under this impression – the obstacles put in my path each time I tried to apply for a licence and various other incidents all pointed to the same conclusion. I was not the only jockey in Hong Kong to sense a conspiracy to get rid of him. In the 1987–88 season a top New Zealand jockey, Bobby Vance, who had been third in the Hong Kong Jockeys' Championship in 1987, suddenly found his supply of rides dwindling. In January 1988 he was summoned by the Jockey Club Licensing Committee for an 'interview', the principal feature of which was the reading out of a prepared statement informing him that his licence was being withdrawn in mid-season. The press called it 'shabby' but their protests carried no weight. The way I was treated, the revelations about race-fixing and Bobby Vance's abrupt and unjust ejection from Hong Kong make it very tempting to believe that if your face doesn't fit there or if you are not prepared to bend to the system, then sooner or later the system will spit you out. If, as the newspapers suggested, the syndicate was powerful enough to influence Jockey Club decisions, it was inevitable that jockeys like Bobby Vance and myself would not be welcome in Hong Kong. We were just flies in the ointment to those who had played the system their way for years.

With Greg Hall out of action, I came in for the ride on Gay Eighties in the Champions and Chaters Cup and it resulted in the biggest success of my two seasons in Hong Kong. It was the sort of ride I liked. I was able to dictate my own pace in front and quicken off the bend to gain a decisive lead, holding on by a short head from Yuno When. The runner-up was going for Hong Kong's version of the

Triple Crown, having won the Hong Kong Derby and the Gold Cup. The pleasure of winning was given extra piquancy as the runner-up was trained by leading trainer Brian Kan who, after I had ridden for him and finished out of the money earlier in the season, had told me I was past it. Gay Eighties was owned by Dr Douglas Laing, a much-respected member of the Jockey Club whom I had met some time before through Brian Taylor. He later sent me a scaled-down version of the trophy as a memento, a gesture I much appreciated. My last winner in Hong Kong was also to be the last of my career. It was provided by a horse called American Liberty, trained by Gordon Smyth, who had trained Charlottown to win the Derby. This milestone was another of the many coincidences of my racing life; it took place on 18 May, the date of my daughter Elizabeth's birthday.

If the I.C.A.C. had considered me important enough to follow during the latter part of their investigations, they would have had a healthy time getting to know every contour of the local golf courses! The day before I was due to leave Hong Kong I enjoyed a final round of golf with Gary Alderdice, and on returning to the clubhouse found a message asking me to ring Phil Jones of the I.C.A.C. What on earth could he want? Just a chat with me, he said, I wasn't actually compelled to see him. However, I had the distinct impression that I didn't really have too much choice. Although Jones had said there was no problem I was sure he wasn't asking me down there for the good of my health. Gary asked if I wanted him to come along too. 'Not bloody likely', I replied, 'If you turn up they *will* think I have something to worry about!'

The I.C.A.C. offices are on top of a multi-storey car park. As the lift doors parted, I faced the reception desk, announced myself and was told to wait. After a few moments, the security-tight double doors opened and Phil Jones appeared. He led me down several narrow corridors to a small interrogation room, bare except for a simple table and some chairs. The whole place was intimidating and I could imagine how the people rounded up in the early hours of 20 February must have felt, their possessions confiscated and their lives thrown into total confusion. I was told I was being interviewed because I was leaving Hong Kong and was one of the few jockeys not to have been questioned. It was simply a formality. After a short discussion, I was free to leave and no statement was taken. I returned to the flat to tell Sue that everything was all right and that we could finish packing. Although we felt very sorry for those who had had their passports impounded – they didn't know whether it would be weeks, months or years before they would be allowed to leave – it was a relief for us to be leaving the troubled scene to return to the serenity of our stud farm at home.

In 1988 there was a farcical conclusion to the I.C.A.C. investigations when three jockeys and two Hong Kong businessmen were charged with conspiracy to cheat at gambling. Three other jockeys, Gary Moore, Rod Staples and David Brosnan, flew in to give evidence against those charged after being granted immunity themselves from any possible prosecution. After sensational revelations about the methods and frequency of race-fixing – Rod Staples admitted that when riding for the syndicate he was not trying or 'pulling' horses 99 per cent of the time – the whole trial was dramatically abandoned due to the actions of David Brosnan. The Australian jockey, not surprisingly, felt very bitter about having served eight months for race-fixing when Rod Staples was now openly admitting worse offences in court with immunity from prosecution. Apparently drunk one night, Brosnan approached one of the jurors who happened to be in the same bar and informed her that they had 'the wrong boys in the stand'. He later claimed that he meant that Gary Moore and Rod Staples should have been on trial as well. Because of jury interference the judge ordered a retrial.

Bruce Raymond once said to me that, in view of all the resistance I had encountered on my first visit, he thought I was either stupid or brave to have gone back. It may well have been a mixture of the two, but in spite of everything I'm glad that I took the opportunity to ride there.

- 23 -
Tactics

MY interview for the post of Stewards' Secretary took place just two weeks after my return from Hong Kong. To say I was disappointed at the Jockey Club's rejection was an understatement as I looked at my now uncertain future. Today I feel that they did me a favour in that the job might not have suited me as well as I thought. At the time, however, I was disconcerted and far from sure what to do next. After pinning my hopes for two or three years on that one job I suddenly found I had to consider alternatives. Should I return to the saddle and ride for the rest of the season in England? The idea held little appeal, partly because of my increasingly difficult fight to keep my weight down and partly because I knew that the way that the media now seemed to focus on my age every time I rode would make it harder and harder for me to get good rides as time went by. Not long afterwards Mick Easterby did in fact offer me the chance to ride for him, but there was no Lochnager or Mrs McArdy in his stable by then, and although I was pleased to be asked I was not seriously tempted.

Sue felt very strongly that she didn't want to watch me soldier on as a jockey, going down the hill I had spent so long climbing. She wanted me to retire while I was, if not at the top, at least still riding winners. That way she felt I would be associated with success, not failure, in the mind of the public. Personally, I was inclined to Fred Winter's belief that ultimately it doesn't really matter whether you end your career on a high or low note since in a very short while what you have achieved is no longer of much consequence to anyone except yourself and those close to you. But, in the end, Sue's view predominated. Come-backs are rarely successful: it was perhaps better to give in to my weight problem and retire gracefully. But to do what? Obviously, it had to be something connected with racing. The thought of training crossed my mind but I didn't seriously consider it. There are many aspects of training that appealed to me; the continuing involvement in racing and the training and placing of the horses. But it would have meant moving elsewhere and starting from scratch. It would probably have taken several years to build up a string to the standard I would want, and if I had started at the age of 48, by the time I was established I would have been ready to retire.

Training had other disadvantages, too, many of which I had witnessed at first hand; problems like owners not paying bills, the deteriorating standard of labour and the increasing difficulty of winning races with moderate horses. Wealthy owners these days are prepared to go 'pot-hunting' at even the smallest tracks and in the least prestigious races, and unless you are training for that kind of owner it is bound to be a struggle.

All in all, I agreed with Willie Carson that it was too late to be putting my foot on the first rung of that particular ladder. Admittedly, Lester had done it, but he had been preparing to start training long before he retired and had built stables and laid the foundations for his operation some time in advance. After years of riding for the top owners and breeders he would have had little difficulty in attracting clients and, indeed, started off with 100 horses in his first year.

I could have considered a livery or 'spelling' yard. If Low Farm had been near Newmarket it would have been ideally situated and much in demand. But in the North the amount of money owners or trainers are prepared to pay for livery wouldn't make it commercially viable: there is always a farmer up the road who'll turn a horse out in his fields for a few pounds.

There was, of course, always the option of letting retirement mean retirement and doing nothing. Sue and I could have sold the farm and gone to live in the apartment we had bought in Spain where I could have spent my time playing golf, but I never for a moment considered that a realistic alternative. Financially it was unworkable and mentally it would have driven me crazy. After all that time spent living a life that many would call hyperactive, adapting to sitting in an armchair twiddling my thumbs between rounds of golf would have been impossible. You have to have a reason to get out of bed.

While I was mulling all this over I was approached by two different Southern trainers to assist them and ride work for them. They lived close to each other and it would have been feasible to have taken up both offers, but it would have meant leaving home for the season. Nevertheless I was very close to deciding that it was my best option when, during a holiday in Barbados, we ran into Wally and Doreen Swinburn, who asked if I would be interested in becoming their son Walter's agent. Joe Mercer had taken up that occupation after his retirement and was acting for Brent Thompson and Tony McGlone. Willie Carson had had an agent for years and since Steve Cauthen and Pat Eddery started using them as well the rest have had to follow. Even those jockeys and trainers who were originally against the idea had to accept it in the end. These days it is almost impossible to get regular rides unless you do have an agent. Most jockeys haven't the time to do enough background work to compete with an agent, so even if they can't really afford one they are compelled to use one.

Being an agent involves a great deal of 'phone work, study of the form book and a good working relationship with as many trainers as possible. I was pleased to take on the job as it was more or less what I had been doing all my life. The only part missing was, regrettably, the riding. It was also a job I could do from my home. I was flattered when, after the announcement that I would be acting for Walter first appeared in the press, over a dozen jockeys 'phoned to ask if I would act for them, too. Initially, neither the Swinburns nor I were enthusiastic about my taking on another jockey since there might at times be a conflict of interests, but when Bill Watts approached me to act for Nicky Connorton it was eventually agreed that for me to have a Northern-based jockey as well as one in Newmarket might be to everyone's advantage. I have spent two years acting for Walter and Nicky. In 1989 I moved on to fresh challenges with my appointment as racing assistant to John Gosden, but I enjoyed my brief interlude in the competitive world of the jockeys' agent. These days, everyone else is ringing up trainers for rides, too, and you have to be on your toes to get in first. Even when you manage it you don't always get a direct answer from a trainer; he may want to hear who else would like to ride his horse before making a decision, so it's often a question of 'I'll ring you back'. In some trainers' minds there is a pecking order among jockeys from the top downwards.

To stay in the running, jockey and agent have to work very much as a combination. The jockey must produce the goods when he has the rides and the agent must capitalise on his jockey's success by pressing his advantage at every opportunity. It's a very time-consuming job. Sundays have always been a busy day for jockeys in arranging the forthcoming week's rides. In some ways there was even more pressure on me than when I was riding myself, because other people's livelihoods depended on me. But only in some ways. When people see me at the races they often ask me if I wish I were still riding. If I'm honest with myself I have to reply 'Yes and no'. Of course I loved it while I was doing it and racing gave me some wonderful experiences, but a jockey can't go on for ever, either because of weight problems or injury or simply anno domini creeping up. However successful you are, and however much you enjoy your job, the idea of retirement usually holds a certain appeal – when you do finally call it a day you are rewarded by an instant release from some of the pressures that have been a routine part of your life for so long.

There's more to being a jockey than just sitting on a racehorse for a few minutes. This is the side the public sees; not everyone realises that you have been up since dawn that morning riding work; that you have to travel thousands upon thousands of miles a season and that you must maintain a disciplined, almost obsessional, approach to your weight. Perhaps the biggest relief an ex-jockey experiences is being able to slow down this hectic lifestyle and in particular to stop the daily routine of wasting with which he has tortured his body for as long as he can remember. Most jockeys have a weight problem. However little you weigh there is always the temptation to try to do even lighter, especially if you are offered a potential winning ride on the condition that you shed a couple more pounds. This is not to say that the jockeys who ride at a low weight without wasting don't have problems, since, generally speaking, owners and trainers prefer to use heavier and stronger jockeys for the better rides.

My ideal riding weight was around 8 stones, that is, about 7 stones 10 lb stripped. In the very early days I was extremely strict about what I ate and drank. I have always enjoyed food and regard good dining as one of the main pleasures in life, but until I retired the delight of eating was always clouded by the thought of the weight that would have to be shed again as a result. One big meal and a couple of drinks would have little effect on an average person's weight but for a jockey, who can be two stones under his 'normal' weight, it might put on pounds. I always had to stop and think before I ate anything. As a youngster even in winter I rationed myself severely, refusing all food I thought might encourage me to 'blossom'. Since my know-ledge of the body's needs was very limited, my diet would probably have given any nutritionist nightmares. In pre-sauna days I was strict about my fluid intake, too. Often if I was thirsty I would swill my mouth out with water instead of actually swallowing it.

My first weight-reducing aid was a steam box, in which I used to sit for about half an hour with my head protruding. Pat Stoute made me a towelling suit which I would wear to absorb the sweat on coming out. It provoked great mirth in the family and became known as my 'Andy Pandy' suit. On top of that went a plastic suit and a heavy dressing-gown. Thus attired, I would go and sit in front of a fire and watch television. In an hour and a half to two hours I could take off between two and three pounds.

Away from home, in a few large towns like London and Southport I could achieve a similar result by going to one of the public Turkish baths. If neither the steam box nor a Turkish bath was available I would sweat weight off in a hot bath into which I had tipped a third of a packet of Radox. The secret was not to have the bath too hot to start with, otherwise I couldn't stand it for more than a few minutes. If I turned on the hot tap once I was acclimatised I could gradually build up the temperature until I started to sweat. There I would stay for the hour or so it took to shed a couple of pounds. Once I had started sweating the water didn't need to be so hot – because of the bath salts the process seemed to carry on by itself. For years I never went away without a packet of Radox and a set of bathroom scales packed in the car boot.

The only drawback to the bath was that it tended to drain my energy, more so than the sauna, which was introduced from Sweden in the 1960s and which jockeys recognised at once as an ideal weapon in the battle against the scales. Most people think of a sauna as a place of relaxation. Not long ago I went with Sue for a few days' break to a health farm and was amused to read the instructions for the use of their sauna: 'After every five minutes in the cabin take a cold plunge . . . no one to use the sauna for more than 30 mintues in one session . . .' and so forth. Those rules are clearly intended to make a sauna a pleasurable experience – by contrast the jockey's sauna is often more like a torture chamber!

When we moved to the farm I built a sauna in the attic, with a telephone near at hand, and a shower and television next door together with the all-important hospital scales. Once I was in there I stayed in for as long as it took to make those scales get down to the required weight. For me, and for most jockeys, there was no luxury of a break and a cold shower every five minutes, although if time permitted I occasionally allowed myself a 'breather' by donning a plastic sweat suit and sitting in the heated room next door for a few minutes. One of the worst aspects of this often daily ritual was the boredom. Most saunas are just pine-panelled cupboards, which doesn't matter if you're only in there for 20 minutes. But two hours of staring at the same knot in a plank of wood can drive you mad, so I had a double-glazed window put in so that I could watch the television. Failing that there was always the racing calendar, the form book and my girlie magazines, in that order of course!

The other enemy was the heat itself. Sometimes it became so unbearable that I resorted to plunging my head in a bucket of cold water every so often; anything to enable me to stay in and shed weight. As an alternative I constructed an air tunnel to the outside with a fan and a plastic sleeve attached. When I felt in need of reviving I would switch on the fan, press my face to my improvised mask and take a few gulps of cooler air. The heat can affect your eyes, making them sting, and some jockeys wear goggles to combat this. I remember seeing Gary Moore in Hong Kong using eye-drops after a sauna and wishing I'd thought of that years before.

According to the health farm instructions your spell in the sauna should be followed by 20 minutes of relaxation and recovery. In my case, it was usually followed instead by an often hectic drive to get to the races in time for my first ride. Some jockeys I knew actually drove encased in a plastic suit with the car heater going full blast just to finish off the job the sauna had started. Fortunately, I never had to go to those lengths. Sweating off weight can result in loss of strength, although, if used sensibly, the sauna left you feeling stronger than other methods. In fact, if I had had one or two days off from riding I often felt fitter and blew less if I used the sauna before my first ride than if I didn't. It is most important that you don't end up too weak to do yourself justice. Neither the trainer nor the owner would thank you if you couldn't ride the horse properly and you owed it to yourself to be in a fit state to do your very best.

To achieve this, diet, of course, is all-important. Anything a jockey puts in his mouth results in a weight gain, even a sip of water, so what does go in needs to be of a high energy value. I always tried to have some breakfast, however small, reasoning that if you don't put petrol in a car it won't go. When it was touch and go with my weight I would have what I termed my 'mixture', a raw egg beaten and covered with a little milk, a touch of sherry, plenty of glucose and a couple of lumps of ice. I would sip this in the sauna before leaving for the races, feeling it gave me maximum energy in return for a minimum gain in weight.

The only day of the week throughout the season when I allowed myself lunch was Sunday, with the family, unless I was riding light on a Monday. But the pleasure was always followed by the penance. Quite recently, at the end of a meal, my son William pushed his chair back and, in an imitation of me, said 'Thanks very much, that was very nice but now I've got to go and sweat it all orf'. Apparently, that was for years my catchphrase after Sunday lunch – I had never realised it! One thing I never tried was 'bingeing' and then making myself sick, a practice currently in vogue with some American jockeys. I tried laxatives a few times but stopped when even the thought of taking them made me feel ill. Diuretics or 'pee-pills' are all right if used in moderation and with commonsense, but overuse can lead to dehydration and the cramps.

Over my last 17 years of riding, excluding the two in Hong Kong, I kept a record of the weight I sweated off. It came to 4,374 pounds – that's over 312 stones, or an average of over 18 stones per season, and I didn't regard myself as having a serious weight problem! There are many jockeys who could easily beat that figure. My weight now I have stopped riding has settled at around ten stones. The self-discipline shown by people such as Lester Piggott and more recently Ray Cochrane, whose 'normal' fit weight would probably be even greater than mine, is appreciated by very few people.

In the days when I was doing 7 stones 4 lb, and would slide through a tennis press as a party trick, Lester who was only a year and a half older than me, was doing 8 stones 4 lb. There was a stage when Lester took up jumping because he thought his weight was going to beat him. I was told he once rode over jumps at Sandown at over 10 stones on a three-pound saddle. But at some point he must have decided he was going to make a fight of it. As I matured through my 20s my weight gradually went up a stone, but somehow Lester kept his weight under 8½ stones for the rest of his riding career. People talk about Lester's natural talent and genius as though it all came easily to him, and the hard work and dedication it took to achieve success, the self-sacrifice and single-mindedness, are not always recognised. He never allowed himself even the luxury of a winter break after an accident and an enforced holiday once caused his weight to shoot up. His daughter Maureen recently told me that after that he never dared run the risk of it happening again. This was the reason he carried on, riding in Australia, America, Hong Kong and all over the world, right through the winter.

I sometimes heard less-successful colleagues criticising Lester, maintaining that if only they had his chances they could be brilliant jockeys, too. I often think that those people who are envious of success don't always appreciate the sacrifices involved in making it to the top in any walk of life. People who haven't made it are only too ready to put it down to luck or opportunities. Luck certainly comes into it, but it doesn't come looking for you. I once heard that great golfer Gary Player sum it up. 'It's a funny thing', he said, 'but the harder I try, the luckier I seem to get.'

Reaching for the top is hard work. Staying there is even harder. Racing might be a glamorous life, but you lose out on other pleasures and luxuries that many people take for granted. You miss out, for instance, on social life. Not for you the enjoyment of an evening spent drinking and chatting down at the local pub, or visiting friends for dinner parties. Worse than that, you miss out on family life. When big family events happen, whether it's the birth of children, wedding anniversaries, birthday parties, school open days, weddings or even funerals you're all too often hundreds of miles away chasing the next winner. When you're among the top few in the jockeys' league table you can't afford to take a day off for anything less than a major family tragedy. If you let someone else take over one of your rides you may never get on that horse's back again. In contrast if you're not under the kind of pressure imposed by life at the top of the tree there is time to enjoy other experiences and opportunities. It would be foolish to pretend there are not rewards for being successful but there are compensations for people who are less ambitious, too. Life for them can be fuller, more varied perhaps and in some ways more satisfying because they don't have to be so single-minded. No one can have it all. You have to decide somewhere along the line where your priorities lie and what you are prepared to give up in order to achieve those priorities. Then you must live with the consequences of that decision without envying the guy who decided to follow a different path.

One essential for any jockey who has decided he wants to try for the top is to stay fit. Without having ridden a racehorse few people have any idea of the strength and stamina it takes. But it soon shows in a finish if you're in need of a bit of work! Before the start of each season I did press-ups, skipping, running and cycling and used a wrist strengthener which I kept in the sauna. You might think that riding work before the start of the season would get you well tuned up, but no matter how much you ride at home it's never enough. There is no substitute for race-riding, although different jockeys have their own favoured exercises which are designed to simulate the effect of a race. Eph Smith, for example, was fond of shooting, but it was hiking over the countryside through the winter training his dogs that built up his leg muscles. However building muscle also puts on weight. It used to take Eph about three months of the season to get back to his lightest riding weight. You might expect cycling and running to have the same drawback but I never noticed it – perhaps I didn't do enough of it! I chose that way of exercising to help clear my wind. I always felt you must make yourself blow to achieve race fitness. It was a bit of a chore, but it was better to do the hard work at home than to lose a race or two early on that I should have won.

There is much more to winning races than simply being a good rider, and if you want to stay up with the leaders you have to be prepared to give a lot of thought to strategy in race-riding. While other jockeys have become known for their riding styles or brilliant finishes, I came to be thought of by many people as a tactician.

For me tactics meant any legitimate way by which I could create an advantage for my mount. Of course, the most important tactic of all was getting on to the right horse in the first place, which was why 'homework' played such an important part in my life right through my career. Everywhere I went I carried a doctor's bag containing a form book, a racing calendar, Timeform and the day's racing newspapers. It was a standing joke among the other jockeys that I also kept a telephone in that bag. If it had not been before the days of portable telephones they would probably have been right!

Many jockeys would say primly that they never ring for rides but if this is so, in my opinion it is for one of two reasons; either they have lost heart after being rebuffed and turned down on the 'phone once too often, or they are not paying enough attention to the job of riding winners. Finding the best ride is half the battle and they rarely come looking for you. Tom O'Ryan recently described me as '. . . the man who never missed hearing even the faintest sound of opportunity knocking', one of the best compliments I have been paid.

In my study of the form and the quest for good rides one of my best allies was Walter Glynn, who worked as a handicapper for *Raceform*'s 'yellow book'. I would ring him up to find out the four-day declarations and knock-outs before they appeared in the following day's news-papers and he would let me know of any trainers he had heard were looking for jockeys.

Over the years I developed a system of checks to be made when I arrived at a racecourse. My first task was to check the flags on the roof of the stands to see whether there was a strong wind, and whether it was a head-, tail- or side-wind. I had to bear in mind that the wind on the course was not necessarily the same as that at the top of the stand, but the flags were useful as a guide. The wind could definitely affect the way I rode a horse. In theory, the stronger the head-wind the more important it is to cover up your mount, but I also learned that if it was very strong, a horse coming out of the pack and feeling it for the first time would often react by hesitating in its challenge. It could thus take longer to quicken up than normal so, anticipating this, I would make my challenge at an earlier stage in the race than I would on a calm day. If there was a strong side-wind and I found myself with a choice, I would obviously prefer to make my challenge on the side away from the wind.

Another factor I assessed before the first race was whether the grass on the track was striped, which indicated that it had been recently rolled or harrowed in alternating directions. There were a few tracks where this often happened and you could use this knowledge to your advantage, particularly if the grass was long. The secret was to race on the light strip, on which the grass was facing away from you. It was easier to gallop through than the grass on the dark strips which was leaning towards you. It might only make a miniscule differ-ence to your horse, but if that slight difference made you first instead of second, it was worth having.

At some courses, like Beverley and Ripon, the betting odds were always displayed close to the track where they could be seen by the jockeys on their way to the start. People who may have seen my head twist round as I assessed the market can rest assured that it was not because I had £100 on my own mount – it was just to check that something I had not previously considered a danger was being heav-ily supported in the market. If that was the case I would make sure I kept an eye on it during the race whereas otherwise I might have ignored it.

One of the items that my doctor's bag always contained was an adapted walking stick, cut in two sections to fit into the bag, and marked off in inches. If the course had been watered, and especially if it had rained on top of watered ground, I would walk the course before racing and test the going by digging the stick in at intervals at three points across the track. In this way I could familiarise myself with any differences in the going and decide if it was worth crossing the track to find faster ground. There's no doubt I won races by this ploy. As early as 1954, when riding Father's Happy Circle at Haydock after heavy rain, I realised as I cantered down to the start that the stands side was faster than the hitherto favoured far side. Happy Circle's victory stressed to me the importance of seeking out the better ground, and I repeated the tactic many times.

Although some people, for example Alex Bird, agreed with my thinking, there was a lot of prejudice in my early days against crossing the track and taking the longer way home. It always looked as though you were asking your horse to run much further than the other horses. Mr Bird believed this to be an optical illusion and proved it at Haydock one day with a length of clothes-line. By tying this line between various points on the track he demonstrated to his sceptical trainer, Towser Gosden, that if a horse crossed the track on a diagonal line taking 100 yards to make the switch he actually travelled only an extra length and a quarter at Haydock. If the going is faster on the other side you should be able to give that away with no trouble, and in fact Alex Bird's own horse, Orthopaedic, did just that on the afternoon following the clothes-line demonstration. It took a while to convince other trainers and jockeys of this piece of simple geometry, but eventually most people conceded that he and I were correct and these days at Haydock it is common practice to swing over to the stands side after rain.

Both York and Newcastle are tracks where the sprinklers water only the inside two thirds of the course on the back straight. One result of this is that when rain falls soon after the course has been watered the going is much faster on the outside of the track. For the horses on the inside, it is like racing in a ploughed field against a competitor running on the road. I remember using that knowledge to the benefit of my mount on at least three occasions; once on Jack Hanson's Emerald Emperor at York and at Newcastle on Bruce Hobbs' Epilogue and Andy Geraghty's Brother Kempinski. In all three races, after heavy downpours I raced on the wide outside around the back before switching back to the inner turning for home. In those cases, it possibly did mean covering quite a lot more ground, but we won because the path we had followed was so much less testing. In fact, on each occasion my mount was the only one still on the bit coming into the straight.

At Doncaster at one time you could only win races down the stands side and I once rode Tudor Jig to win there, even though he was unfavourably drawn, by dropping him right out to last place at halfway and then tacking across to the favoured stands side. Now the draw advantage seems to vary from meeting to meeting on the Town Moor and the Lincoln is usually won by a horse drawn on the far side.

You must be on the right sort of horse to adopt these tactics. If your mount needs covering up it's obviously no use ploughing a lone furrow looking for the better ground. In such an instance, I would try to get the two or three horses I was drawn alongside to come with me, as long as I didn't think they included one that could beat us! Doing the unorthodox takes a certain amount of courage since while it might look clever when it comes off you can look pretty foolish when it doesn't. Once, at Beverley, I was riding a filly called Love Beach for Barry Hills, and turning into the straight I came over to the faster ground on the stands side but managed to finish only fourth. John Lowe and Catchword had come across with me and went on to be beaten a short head. Unfortunately the stewards took the view that I was to blame for carrying John across and they gave me four days for my troubles! I wonder if anything would have been said if John had won? I was beaten at York in similar circumstances on a horse of John Winter's, much to the disgust of one irate punter who was heard to say, 'I expected Hide to look for the better ground but I didn't think he'd go round by the city walls trying to find it!'

One idea I had fostered ever since my Cesarewitch win with Prelone was the benefit to a horse of having the weight taken off its back before the race – the old bucket-of-water theory. Consequently, if I found myself in the stalls when there were still a number of runners to load I would make a point of taking one foot out of the stirrup and putting my weight on the ledge of the side of the stall. Sue claimed she always watched the starts of my races with her heart in her mouth because she feared that one day I wouldn't get my leg back in the iron in time and would be left standing in the stalls as the horse jumped out without me. Fortunately, that's one embarrassment I managed to avoid!

Different courses demanded different riding tactics. In all, I rode 142 winners at Catterick, a sharp left-handed undulating track where it is essential to keep a horse balanced. Catterick came to be regarded as one of my most successful tracks. The run-in after the last bend is quite short and experience soon showed me that unless the pace was suicidal, it was difficult to come from behind to win however well your horse seemed to be going. Possibly the reason for this was that the camber at Catterick in those days was all wrong. Horses would scramble round the bend and were often unable to regain their balance in time to make a successful challenge. Whenever I could, therefore, I tried to poach a lead before I turned into the straight at this course, and it was amazing how often this worked for me.

Chester, another sharp track, is flatter than Catterick but again, because the course is almost totally on the turn, balancing your mount is essential. More than most tracks, it is one where you need luck in running since the field is often closely bunched on the inside. To compensate, I found that for some reason there would always be one or two setting a good pace, which meant that sooner or later there would be tiring horses going backwards, and you'd usually get your run. Even so, if you had a bad draw and wanted to avoid traffic problems and guarantee a run at the Roodeye, you were almost forced to take a wide course although it cost you valuable ground. The only alternative if you were drawn on the outside was to get out of the stalls quickly, and show enough early speed to cross over to the inside well in front of the other runners. I was by no means the only rider to use this technique at Chester. On one occasion it paid off in a six-furlong race at the September meeting in 1968. I rode Dashing Dane, who was drawn on the wide outside, for Joe Hartigan and after crossing to the rails we just held on by a neck.

The reason that race holds a special place in my memories is that Joe calculated it to be my 50th winner for him and a little later he presented me with an inscribed St Christopher key-ring. I don't recall ever receiving mementoes from any other trainer and I was touched by his thoughtful gesture. Levitation, a sprinter of Joe's was an old favourite of mine. Towards the end of his career his near-fore joint was so swollen it resembled a battered football and I used to avoid looking down when I was about to mount as I didn't want to see it. It didn't appear to affect him and he always ran his heart out.

Early on in my career, Father gave me two pieces of sound tactical advice which stood me in good stead. One was, when possible, not to make ground when going uphill or on the outside around a bend. The second was to keep in touch with the leaders in a slowly-run race. If you wait, when they quicken in front of you you have to go twice as fast to get by them. Common sense, maybe, but worth remembering. Another of Father's gems of wisdom was that there was no need to give a good jockey orders because he wouldn't need them and there was no point in giving a bad jockey orders because he couldn't follow them!

Whenever I was not riding in a particular race I always watched it from the stands. Apart from familiarising owners and trainers with your face you also got to know the horses. The jockey that knows the characteristics of many horses has a considerable advantage. All racehorses are different: some are better suited by soft ground, some by fast; some do best on a galloping track with a long straight, while some only show their best form on a sharp course with a short run-in. Some have good finishing speed, others need to be ridden up with the pace if they're to have a chance. A jockey must take advantage of his knowledge of a horse's assets to win races and also make use of his opponents' weaknesses on occasion. You would never track a doubtful stayer for example. A horse you had seen go to the front two from home looking all over a winner only to be beaten might come into that category. If, in a race on another occasion, you found your-self riding that horse you would try and get a lead for longer so that you didn't find yourself in front as early.

If I rode against a horse I knew to be lazy I would always try to challenge wide so as not to encourage it to battle. Horses differ even in the way they respond to encouragement: if you are riding against a horse you know is of doubtful courage plenty of vocal support for your own horse when battling out a finish can gain you the victory. Some horses will find extra when given a smack with the whip, others will curl up and come back under you. Occasionally, a horse might appear to have nothing more in reserve, but if I pulled my whip through to the other hand, even if it was running straight and there appeared to be no need to change, it would often find a little extra. I wondered about this and put it down to the fact that most jockeys, and indeed most lads, are right-handed, so if a horse is hit at all it is most likely to be hit on the right side. Thus, if it is hit on the left it is simply surprise that makes it briefly react with an extra surge.

If I was beaten in a race there were obviously no second chances, but I would always look ahead to the horse's next race and try to think what I could do differently to give me a chance of winning then. Perhaps the horse needed a different track, distance or going? Did it want holding up? Making more use of? Covering up? Being allowed to see more daylight? If it did win, though, I didn't necessarily assume it should always be ridden the same way in future races – maybe it would have run even better if I'd ridden it differently. While perhaps 95 per cent of races are won by the jockey who is on the best horse there are still many ways in which an incompetent rider can get himself beaten. The easiest are to go too fast too early or to do what Father warned me against and lie out of your ground in a slowly-run race. Outside influences, such as interference or accidents do, of course, befall the competent and the inexperienced alike, but the more adept jockey can often minimise their effects by forseeing trouble and taking evasive action.

Perhaps the most important point about riding tactics is that you should be able to change them on the spur of the moment, depending on how the race develops. The jockey who decides beforehand how he is going to ride his horse and who he is going to track, and then sticks to that plan come hell or high water, is not going to get very far. The art of race-riding lies in reacting and adjusting to constantly changing circumstances, and in doing it quicker than the next chap. The timing is split-second. In a five-furlong race you can have less than 60 seconds to make all the right decisions. This is an example of how pre-conceived plans may go adrift: if you are on a horse which likes to make the running and you plan to let him do just that, you may suddenly find yourself upsides another front-runner. If they take each other on they will cut their own throats so you must revise your plans, probably deciding to tuck in behind. If, on the other hand, you are on a horse you know is possessed with some finishing speed and you reluctantly find yourself out in front you should, set a pace a stride slower than normal so that when you quicken those behind you will have to find a lot more to get past you.

If possible you should always quicken at a point when the other riders are least expecting it, and try to avoid making it obvious that you are asking your horse to go on. That is easier said than done. I found it very difficult not to drop lower in the saddle when I wanted my mount to quicken. Lester though, could put his foot on the 'go' pedal apparently without moving a muscle. If you were tracking him you could watch him like a hawk but there would be no visible signs that he was doing anything different. Suddenly his horse would lengthen its stride, and by the time the rest of the field had realised what was happening he had often gained that vital length or two.

If you asked me what qualities it took to be a successful jockey I would say ability, ambition, dedication and diplomacy. Perhaps the last attribute is not always there but it can be a valuable one, particularly when dealing with owners, who are in the main very sensitive people when it comes to their horses. Many would tolerate insults about their wives or husbands rather than hear unsavoury things about their beloved animal! So after a race I would try to be as tactful as possible, especially if I didn't know the owner, in my remarks and in communicating any disagreeable suggestions such as the fitting of blinkers. Often I'd wait to discuss my proposals first with the trainer. Although I aimed never to mislead owners about their horses, I always tried to behave as part of a team and to avoid showing any disloyalty to the trainer. For instance, if I felt that a horse wasn't fit enough and had felt it 'blow up' during the race I wouldn't comment on it after unsaddling unless the owner realised his animal needed the run.

Perhaps, in the end, the most important quality for any jockey is common sense, though they do say that is the rarest sense of all! Edgar Britt once said of Sir Gordon Richards that it was his intelligence and perseverance that made him great, along with a willingness to learn, even at the end of his career. The latter quality at least is one I always strove to emulate.

– 24 –
Reflections

YOU can't ride racehorses for more than three decades without form-
ing some pretty definite opinions about the way racing is run in this
country. Perhaps this is the place to unfold one or two of my ideas.
A topic about which I feel strongly is the apprenticeship system – or
rather, the current lack of it. After all, the way that apprentices are
trained determines the standard of the next generation of jockeys and
so I feel the subject deserves more attention than it is given by both
the press and the authorities. One factor about apprentices I think
has been ignored for too long is that they are getting heavier. Since
the welfare state came into being and the supply of skinny, under-
nourished boys from deprived areas thankfully began to dry up, it has
become harder and harder to find true lightweight jockeys. Apparently, in boxing the same effect has been seen in the flyweight division, where in contrast to 30 years ago when there were around 40
fighters at that weight there are now only a handful.

To my mind, there is a strong argument for raising the weights all
round by at least half a stone to reflect the true weights of today's
healthy youngsters. But I fear it will be a long time before such action
is taken, since most trainers seem far more frightened that their
horses might be damaged by carrying extra weight than that their
jockeys might suffer by half-starving themselves. The instances of
both apprentices and jockeys collapsing after overdoing the wasting
certainly seem more frequent now than I remember.

One thing I regret is the abolition of the old-fashioned indenture
system of apprenticeship. Although I appreciate the intention of
avoiding the evil of 'slave labour' in stables I am convinced that those
who will suffer most from the change will, in the end, be the apprentices themselves. After all, what trainer is going to invest in teaching
youngsters the ropes properly if at any moment they can walk out
and take their expensively-acquired knowledge to someone else's
stable? It's just not worth a trainer's while to give the training if he

ends up with no rights to retain his own apprentice at least for a couple of seasons. Some people seem to think that training an apprentice is just a matter of giving him the odd ride now and then on one of the stable's no-hopers. Nothing could be further from the truth. To educate an apprentice in race-riding in the traditional way takes a lot of money, a lot of time and a lot of hard work on the part of the trainer. It means he has to keep at least one or two horses of his own for him to ride, since few owners are sufficiently philanthropic to give an educational ride to an inexperienced lad or lass, particularly when it will cost them the same riding fee as putting the Champion Jockey up. In the beginning, while the apprentices are learning, there is no question that it is going to cost the trainer a race or two. What is the incentive for him to bother if at any moment they can say Thanks guv'nor, or perhaps not even that, and disappear?

In the 1950s and 60s some trainers used to specialise in producing apprentices. Sam Armstrong was recognised for it. In 1957 he had four stable jockeys and 12 apprentices. Among the many to emerge from his stable were Wally Swinburn, Paul Tulk, Josh Gifford and 'Kipper' Lynch. Sam used to turn his lads out looking immaculate and their manners were impeccable. Ernie Davey was another master at training likely lads. Among his protégés were Jimmy Etherington, Lionel Brown, Jock Skilling, Ron Sheather and Johnny Seagrave. He always had at least four or five boys on the go. These days, the only man who springs to mind as a specialist in bringing on youngsters is Reg Hollinshead.

It makes you wonder where the next generation of jockeys and good stable staff is going to come from. The apprentice schools are doing a good job, but their function is limited and a short course is no substitute for a good trainer. I suppose the exceptional lad or the one like me, whose family can supply him with rides, will still survive, but for the ordinary youngster it has never been more difficult than it is now to become a jockey. Those with ambition but no strings to pull are really up against it. Perhaps it's time somebody thought about this. After all, the old saying that a jockey can't come without the horse is equally true in reverse.

If I were asked to give advice to any aspiring jockey it would be this. Write a letter to the trainer of your choice, saying 'I want to be a jockey, I want to commit myself to working for you. If you take me on I promise to stay with you for at least three years'. If you can convince him you mean it, you might have a chance – otherwise, these days, you will be fighting an uphill battle.

The introduction of the camera patrol film has been one of the most significant developments during my racing career, and has probably done more than any other single innovation to clean up racing's image. First and foremost, it instantly made it more difficult to get away with not running a horse on its merits. In addition, jockeys had to become more gentlemanly in their behaviour towards each other! In the days before races were recorded it was by no means uncommon for jockeys to take the administration of justice into their own hands, and frequently they would respond to being hampered or bumped by retaliating in later races. Fortunately, few took it to the same extremes as Charlie Spares. Charlie, who had won the Derby on Arctic Prince in 1951, was notorious for his short fuse. I was riding one day in a Doncaster sprint when I witnessed him in midfield virtually removing his hands from the reins in an all out attempt to push the jockey next to him off his horse. Luckily, for both of them, he didn't succeed.

There was another jockey who never said a word when an incident happened but stored up the grudge, biding his time until he thought the moment was right to retaliate. The most vicious example I saw of his revenge happened one day at Manchester, when he rode straight at an apprentice, turning his horse half-round with the impact and causing him to cannon into the rails. The apprentice survived unscathed apart from a nasty jolt to his nervous system, but it was no thanks to the jockey concerned.

Some of these incidents had their lighter side. At York some years ago, I got in Eph Smith's bad books after he felt I'd hampered him in a race. The next day, in a long distance race, we had reached the wood well away from the stands when Eph saw his opportunity to even the score. He cut sharply across in front of me. Luckily, I was awake enough to see what was coming and took avoiding action. Eph's brother, Doug, who was tracking me, struck into my horse's heels and nearly came down. Upon returning to the weighing-room Doug was most put-out and set upon Eph. 'I don't mind you doing him,' he said, pointing to me, 'but all through the war when you wrote to me, you signed your letters "Your loving brother, Eph", and now you try to kill me!'

Since the introduction of the camera patrol film you are certainly safer from incidents of rough justice, although it's possibly true that you learned more then, and the system probably produced a tougher, sharper jockey than today's. You didn't make the same riding mistake twice in those days. There is no faster way of learning a lesson than knowing that the penalty for not learning it will be physical and unpleasant! Self-preservation was probably as effective in making you abide by the Rules of Race-riding as the threat of being caught out by the camera does now. Even so, the camera has its uses. In his summary of the racing year of 1960 Tom Nickalls of the *Sporting Life* described the patrol film as an instant success in assisting the stewards in difficult cases, predicting that the innovation would soon be standard on all important courses. He was proved right, of course, and in recent times a colour video film replaced the earlier black and white version. The stewards can now view and review all races on a large television-sized screen – it would be even better if funds allowed them the same facilities as the Disciplinary Committee at Portman Square, where they have a much larger screen to aid them.

In spite of its benefits, however, the patrol film is not infallible. In October 1981 at Redcar I was fined £50 for supposedly not riding out for a place. I had absolutely no chance of finishing in the first four, had not been hard on my mount and crossed the line in ninth place, beaten about a dozen lengths. When the stewards showed the 'head-on' patrol film, which was all they had to go on, it looked as though I had been right on the heels of the leaders when I stopped riding hard. The camera lens had foreshortened the distances quite dramatically. They say that the camera doesn't lie, but a telephoto lens can certainly distort the truth. This greatly perturbed me; I realised that the stewards could not possibly glean a true picture of a race by viewing only a head-on film. It was the second time this point had been made forcibly to me. In 1976 at York, Empress Regent and I passed the leader and pacemaker Lochranza, ridden by Lindsay Charnock, who was then a 5 lb-claiming apprentice. About three furlongs from home, I crossed to the rails in front of Lochranza. I was a good three lengths clear of him at the time but just as I came across Lochranza put his foot in a hole and stumbled. Lochranza's connections persuaded Lindsay (against his better judgement) to object. On the head-on film it looked bad. The foreshortening effect made it look as though I had crossed too soon causing Lochranza to stumble through clipping my heels. However, I remained confident since I knew that the side-on film would show the three-length distance between us. At this stage Lindsay, as he told me afterwards, was thinking 'This is where I get a month's suspension for making a frivolous objection'. But it transpired that the side-on camera had broken down, and Lindsay was awarded the race on the evidence of the head-on film. On the basis of what they'd seen, taken at its face value, I couldn't blame the stewards for their decision, but I was in no doubt that it was unjust. Unfortunately, they seemed completely unaware of the misleading properties of the telephoto lens.

After the second incident I was determined to demonstrate my point to the powers-that-be, and I enlisted the help of Alec Russell, the racecourse photographer who has lived in the cottage on my farm for some years. He and his daughter Joanna took two photographs of each race one day at Doncaster. One of these photographs was taken from head-on with a telephoto lens, the other was taken simultaneously from the side. To back up our argument we took another pair of complementary photographs at home, this time using three stationary cars, which we arranged in a staggered line in a field so that although from the side they appeared to be in a row and were obviously several yards apart, a head-on telephoto shot made them appear to be parked side by side. The consequence of this sort of camera deception in an inquiry into a race incident was we now felt, self-evident. If you couldn't tell how close the horses were to each other, how could you possibly detect interference with any certainty?

At first, it seemed that we had made some headway in convincing the Jockey Club of our argument. In February 1983 I showed both sets of photographs to Lord Vestey, who was later to be appointed Chairman of the Disciplinary Committee. He was very sporting and had a go at guessing the distances involved by looking at the head-on pictures, both of the races at Doncaster and of the cars. In each case he was a long way out and was so impressed by our demonstration that he expressed his wish to use the photographs at the forthcoming seminars for race-day stewards. Alec duly sent off copies of his prints for this purpose. The stewards' seminars are held at four different venues each year and all the race-day stewards are expected to attend at least one of them to ensure that their standards of adjudication are kept up to the mark. At the seminars the stewards are shown an incident on film on which they have to give a verdict. They then have to justify their decision if it differs from that of the Jockey Club. There is no doubt that such in-service training is beneficial. It would be even better if there were more courses, but obviously, since stewards work on a voluntary basis, the time they can reasonably be expected to devote to such courses is limited.

I anticipated that my photographs would prove of some use to them. However, I was surprised and disappointed to learn from a friend who has attended these functions for the past four years that he has yet to see these pictures. I have recently been told that all stewards are 'made aware' by the Stewards' Secretary of the properties of telephoto lenses, but surely a visual aid such as our photographs would help them in this awareness? Let's hope they come up on the agenda soon.

While I have emphasised the importance of the side-on film in helping the stewards to come to a fair decision I do not believe that even these are infallible. My main criticism is that the side-on film is in fact very seldom truly side-on to the incident the stewards are considering. A camera stuck on the end of the stand or a scout camera placed down the course rarely gives a clear picture of an incident because of the distortion caused by the angle of viewing. An improvement would be, if enough money became available, to position more cameras round the course.

While on the subject of patrol films, another of my 'hobby horses' is the belief that in an inquiry the film of the incident should be shown to all concerned before any questioning starts. At present the

Stewards' Secretary interrogates the jockeys involved before showing them the film, which seems pointless since the film is the deciding factor. Time is always crucial when both jockeys and stewards have to be available for the next race and it would surely speed up the inquiry considerably to show the film first, if only because jockeys' memories of events which happened in a split second may not always be clear. To see the incident first would make describing it easier and save so much time. I can only think the present system is a legacy from the days before the patrol film.

In the autumn of 1982, Yorkshire Television screened a documentary called 'Stewards' Inquiry' which gave the public a glimpse of the inner workings of the Jockey Club. One scene showed the York stewards conducting an inquiry into the William Hill Handicap in which I was disqualified after passing the post first on my brother's Celestial Dancer. The film caused a public outcry as both Willie Carson and I were shown standing to attention in front of a panel of seated stewards, who curtly addressed us by our surnames while we called them 'sir'. We were treated like errant schoolboys on trial in front of their teachers, which was the humiliating situation jockeys had come to expect as the norm in a stewards' inquiry. On one occasion, years before, at Sandown I was literally hauled, by the shoulder, in front of the Chief Steward by the Stewards' Secretary, who then pushed me to one side as he informed the panel of my name and supposed misdemeanour. The other rider involved received the same treatment.

As a result of the controversy stirred up by the Yorkshire Television film the Jockey Club adopted the courtesy of calling all jockeys 'Mr' from the following month. This was definitely a step in the right direction away from the master-servant relationship. Nevertheless, it took a little while for some of the officials to change their feudal ways. Their attitude may have been rooted in the days when jockeys were the paid servants of their masters and wore their livery just as hunt servants did. I don't know if hunt servants today suffer from the same unwillingness on the part of their employers to recognise the arrival of the 20th century. John Francome, never one to suffer fools gladly, was hailed one day by a Stewards' Secretary with the words 'Francome! The stewards would like to see you'. The irrepressible John responded 'I'm not moving an inch until you call me either John or Mr Francome'. He made his point.

From a jockey's point of view, one of the most disliked rulings was the totting up-system, whereby if a jockey committed a second offence within a year of his first, the sentence imposed had to be more severe than the initial one. I fell foul of this ruling at Pontefract in April 1983. I had ridden a horse called Streamon to win a seller. An hour or more after the race John Lowe and I were summoned to appear before the stewards. Neither of us knew why we were being called in or which race they were inquiring into. It turned out that the stewards had spotted an incident just over half a mile from home of which neither of us had been aware. As a third jockey was involved and had by that time left the course the inquiry was postponed until Thirsk races a week later. John told the inquiry that the incident did not affect his chances but I was suspended for 'careless' riding.

The incident was very minor indeed but because it was my second in 12 months – I had been stood down for ten days for the first 'offence' – I received a 12-day suspension; a stiffer sentence for a lesser offence. The penalty was out of all proportion to the 'crime' and showed the absurdity of the totting-up rule. That June, Joe Mercer, Tony Ives and I went to speak to the Jockey Club Disciplinary Committee about this and, to their credit, soon afterwards they dispensed with the whole ridiculous system.

The way the Rules are administered is always a good topic for debate in any sport and racing is no exception. The Jockey Club stewards in this country have an unpaid and pretty thankless task, and in the main are hard-working, honest men who do their best for racing. They often find that whatever decision they make someone will think it unfair, but that should not mean they are above criticism or indeed in some cases suspicion! Perhaps it was in trying to recoup some of his expenses as a steward that one gentleman I knew of, who sat in judgement on me on more than one occasion, became well-known for his love of a bet. When a trainer friend of mine had a horse demoted to second after a stewards' inquiry, he was asked by a fellow trainer if he had tipped the horse beforehand to the same steward. He hadn't, he replied. 'You should have done', commented the other trainer knowingly, 'then you'd probably have kept the race!'

On a more serious note, it is impossible for either the stewards or the jockeys to get it right all the time. The recent new whip guidelines are an example: a whip is used either to hit a horse or to threaten it, and it is up to the stewards to differentiate between the two and decide what is excessive and improper and what is not. I abhor seeing a horse knocked about when its chance has obviously gone, and jockeys guilty of that deserve to be jumped on. However, I do feel strongly that the people who commentate on television and report races for the newspapers are responsible for encouraging jockeys to use the whip. When they say, as they frequently do, that a horse wins 'under hands and heels' they give the unfortunate impression that if the jockey had hit his mount it would have run even faster or won by a greater margin. This is seldom the case. Many free-running horses will find virtually nothing under the whip; indeed quite often will do the opposite and 'curl up'. Race-goers often don't realise this and a jockey always has it at the back of his mind that if he is beaten and is not seen to be riding a strong finish and using his stick some people will blame him for not doing enough on the horse. Maybe if racing writers more frequently publicised the 'stopping' effect the whip can have jockeys would feel less compelled to use the stick to keep the connections happy.

Many of the complaints about over-use of the whip come from the non-racing public who have reacted to seeing a bit of hard riding on television. I was among the jockeys who were instructed once by the Stewards' Secretary before racing at Ayr to be careful about our use of the whip in the televised races because of recent criticism from viewers. The first of my rides was a green two-year-old who was unable to gain a challenging position, and so I obediently refrained from even pulling my stick out. After weighing-in I was surprised to be called in by the stewards for making insufficient effort. When I tactfully pointed out that I was merely doing what I had been requested to do beforehand my explanation was accepted. Later the Stewards' Secretary, obviously feeling rather awkward, said to me, 'You must realise, Edward, that you had us by the short and curlies in there. Please be a little more careful in future'!

In spite of these few complaints, I don't really think there is too much to criticise about the way racing is administered in this country. The system has been tried and tested over many years and there is little doubt that it is the best suited to racing in England. I do feel that the Stewards' Secretary should have more authority – at present he acts purely in an advisory capacity. But, having experienced at close quarters the professional monopoly of stewarding in Hong Kong, I wouldn't rush to say it would solve the problems we have here. My greatest worry for the future is how long the right sort of person will continue to be available for stewarding duties. There are not too many people who can afford the time to act as an unpaid official at their local meetings. There is a lot of pressure on stewards these days, from the professional sector and the public alike. How much longer will they be prepared to do the job for nothing when they are open to so much criticism? With instant replay and the beaming of racing into thousands of betting shops there is now often what amounts to trial by television over every decision, and it must put a great strain on stewards just as it does in the case of cricket and tennis umpires and football and rugby referees.

My main hope for the future is that these growing administrative difficulties do not ever have to be resolved by the introduction of centralised racing. One of the chief attractions of English racing for owners, trainers, jockeys and the public is the wide variety of courses. We have left- and right-handed tracks, short, sharp, undulating courses and long, level, galloping ones. This enormous variety provides scope for any horse to be given the chance to be suited, and it would be a sad day if we ever lost that choice. Having seen racing in many other countries I still have no doubt that English racing is the best in the world, despite my occasional grumbles and grouses. Since 1950, when I had my first ride, I've seen many changes, and most of them have been for the better.

Away from the racetrack I have watched the introduction of betting shops, and recently, of the satellite television service, and I have seen the racing world shrink as better communications and the development of horse transport by air have made international competition almost commonplace. On the course itself I have witnessed the introduction of starting stalls, photo finishes and electrical timing. Since I started, television coverage, films and video recorders have revolutionised racing so that every television viewer with action replay and hindsight can be an armchair racing critic. This includes every owner's friend who, on the evening after a race, can play and replay the recording of it and explain just why his horse didn't win and what the jockey was doing wrong!

One quite far-reaching change was brought about when overnight declarations and the draw were brought in in 1961. Prior to this, the draw had been made by the Clerk of the Scales shortly before the race using a canvas bag containing numbered ivory discs. I am sure this was always above board, but there was certainly scope for skulduggery in the system, as was illustrated by a tale Grandpa Edwards liked to tell.

He was once called upon to attend a draw at the local village inn. The draw took place, year after year, in full view of all those who had bought tickets or in this case metal discs. And, year after year, the inn-keeper and the numerous members of his family invariably drew winning tickets. This was generally agreed too amazing to be coincidental, but no one could come up with an explanation. On the night that Grandpa attended the draw the inn-keeper's youngest child was, as usual, drawing the discs. He picked one disc at a time out of a tub, the inside of which he certainly could not see. As usual, the family were taking most of the prizes that were worth winning. In fact, only one child had not yet won when the little boy, his hand buried in the discs, suddenly called out 'Mother, I can't find another hot one'. It was as simple and as clever as that: just before the draw the discs representing the family members had been well heated in the oven!

Since I started riding I have seen the closure of 11 racecourses, but most of these have been urban tracks on land of enourmous value to developers and I don't think the closures necessarily reflect a decline in attendance at race meetings. On the contrary, in view of the introduction of evening meetings, racing is probably as popular as it has been for years. On the financial side I have seen the development of sponsored races which have provided a valuable injection of money. My only slight criticism of that development is that it is a pity so much sponsorship money goes towards owners' prizes in top races like the Derby, where the prize-money is really insignificant to the owner of an animal who is now worth millions at stud. Surely it would be better spread around lesser races?

I have seen the cost of keeping a horse in training rise from £5 a week to nearly £200, while the price of the best-bred yearlings at auction has rocketed from the days when £20,000 was a remarkable price to the bloodstock boom of the 1980s, when a yearling sub-sequently named Snaafi Dancer fetched over $10 million – and, incidentally, never even made it to the race-course!

There is no doubt that racing is many times safer now than it was when I started. Crash helmets and riding goggles have been introduced, plastic rails installed and the old lethal concrete posts phased out; banking has been built into bad turns and gradients changed in response to jockeys' complaints – often mine! The fact that jockeys' views are noted and acted upon these days is another major innovation. Both training and racing surfaces have improved with the introduction of all-weather gallops and the regular watering of courses. This latter development has meant that these days 'hard' going is a rarity, and this undoubtedly reduces the number of stress fractures and break-downs. I feel it also helps explain the much-discussed fact that race-times have shown so little improvement in the last 50 years. Course records are usually set on extremely firm going and watering has virtually eliminated this on most courses.

There has been much debate recently about whether thorough-bred performances can be improved any further. It seems strange that while human race-times have improved so much in the 35 years since the first four-minute mile was run, racehorse times have stood still. Surely the sort of modern training techniques that have cut the record time for the mile by nearly 14 seconds in that period could be adapted somehow and applied to racehorses? I read an interesting article in *The Sunday Times* recently in which Professor Allen Goodship of Bristol University stated his intention of doing just this. He claimed that racehorses at present do only about one sixth of the physical exercise and training for races that their human counterparts undertake. Years ago, one man did relate human concepts of fitness to his horses. Tom Coulthwaite, an athletics coach with little experi-ence of racehorses switched to training jumpers in the Midlands and made a very successful job of it. But he was an exception – in general people who have tried to introduce modern athletics training regimes to thoroughbred racing have met with little success.

Having watched various new ideas being tried and discarded over the years I reluctantly have to agree with the majority conclusion, that improved training programmes can only have a limited effect where racehorses are concerned. Interval training and other innovations may have worked wonders for Steve Cram and his contemporaries but where human athletes differ from horses is that they are motivated to train and to keep on training. They don't become bored, or sour, because they can hold a goal, an incentive in their minds. The mere idea that one day, maybe years in the future, they might be awarded a gold medal on a piece of ribbon is enough to keep them going, to encourage them to endure the discomfort, the pain and the sacrifices. How do you create similar inspiration in a horse? Try persuading a horse that it will be worth his while to get his head in front, even though his lungs are searing and his legs are turning to jelly, because his owner will get a nice trophy and will give him a grateful pat in the winners' enclosure? Even if you could get him to understand you it wouldn't work. There is no way you can motivate a horse beyond his natural urge to lead the herd.

Unfortunately, though, you can very easily de-motivate him. Overdo the training, hit him once too often or too hard, make him run before he has recovered from his last race, or in any other way give him a reason to think that racing is unpleasant and you have blown it. That urge to win – that small, easily crushed natural impulse to beat the next horse, is all you have to work on. If you lose that fragile instinct through insensitive handling it doesn't matter how good his pedigree, or how fit his muscles, or how brilliant his action, he won't win another race. You have to nurture that spirit and guard it in the same way you would guard a flickering flame when there are no more matches. The ability to do that, to my mind, is what makes a great trainer, far beyond any fancy training surfaces or exercise machines or other aids introduced in an effort to emulate the training of human athletes. That ability is one quality that has existed since men first started training racehorses. There are trainers that have it and there are those that don't. That is one thing that will never change whatever new developments there are in the next 35 or indeed 100 years.

One of the trainer's most important allies in this psychological game with the horse is the jockey. It is into his care that the horse's love of racing is entrusted every time it runs, and by his handling of the horse duirng those brief moments he helps decide in what frame of mind it will go racing the next time. It's a great responsibility but few jockeys would change it for any other job they could think of.

I have a lot to thank my career for. It has given me the chance to travel all over the world and to meet people from all walks of life. It has given me enormous satisfaction. I have very few regrets, although if I had been given the chance to alter anything by some fairy god-mother I would have swapped a few of my Northern Championships to have headed the overall list just once. And, while we're talking of exchanges, perhaps I would have given up one of my 1,000 Guineas in return for a 2,000 Guineas, which would have given me a 'full house' as far as the classics were concerned.

I only ever had one aim in life – to become a Flat race jockey – and I have to be grateful that I possessed enough ability and remained small and light enough to make my dream come true. To be able to make a living at something you love doing is a privilege granted only to a few lucky people. I sometimes ponder how differently my life might have turned out if my ambition had been to become a top golfer or tennis player. I enjoy both sports as hobbies but I would not have stood the remotest chance of making the grade. Fortunately, providence ordained that my talent should coincide with my ambition. If I had to name one secret of whatever success I achieved it would perhaps be that, because of my family and my upbringing, I was always a horseman first and a jockey second. In other words, my commitment was to all aspects of the job of getting horses to win races rather than to being spectacularly brilliant in the saddle. I never thought I was marvellous – I just marvelled at the opportunities that came my way!

British Career Statistics

Date	Winners	2nd	3rd	Rides	Position in Jockeys' Championship
50	0	0	0	3	
51	1	0	2	16	
52	6	8	7	66	
53	25	40	18	281	
54	53	41	48	386	Champion Apprentice
55	43	36	58	368	
56	75	80	68	537	7th, Champion Apprentice
57	131	103	103	716	2nd, Cock of the North
58	116	107	87	665	4th, Cock of the North
59	118	95	83	623	4th, Cock of the North
60	90	82	69	591	6th
61	92	66	68	529	4th, Cock of the North
62	88	96	76	546	5th, Cock of the North
63	68	67	65	508	10th
64	72	69	53	480	7th
65	78	59	58	496	6th, Joint Cock of the North with J. Sime
66	59	63	61	498	10th
67	56	71	53	486	11th
68	52	46	43	397	12th
69	71	74	48	483	9th
70	66	60	53	513	11th
71	84	86	77	561	6th, Cock of the North
72	105	90	89	610	3rd, Cock of the North
73	107	107	90	657	5th, Cock of the North
74	137	109	83	753	3rd, Cock of the North
75	78	59	51	444	8th, Cock of the North
76	103	93	101	675	4th, Cock of the North
77	111	99	108	785	3rd, Cock of the North
78	88	77	73	640	8th
79	53	62	67	644	
80	106	92	102	707	4th, Cock of the North
81	105	85	85	685	4th, Cock of the North
82	65	66	69	525	11th
83	53	70	65	512	12th, Cock of the North
84	26	31	28	247	
85	10	14	8	67	
GRAND TOTALS					
	2591	2403	2217	17700	1 in 2.45 were placed

WINNERS BY TRAINERS

Trainer	Wins	Trainer	Wins	Trainer	Wins
N. Adams	1	R. Colven	2	W. Hall	11
T. Ainsworth	1	W. Combs	1	B. Hanbury	5
P. Alden	1	A. Corbet	4	R. Hannon	2
N. Angus	16	T. Corrie	12	J. Hanson	2
F. Armstrong	9	H. Cottrill	5	J. Hartigan	55
G. Armstrong	1	C. Couch	1	G. Harwood	1
R. Armstrong	6	H. Cousins	1	D. Hastings	1
P. Asquith	1	V. Cross	4	P. Hastings-Bass	2
W. Atkinson	1	N. Crump	5	W. Hastings-Bass	9
A. Bacon	2	L. Cumani	10	N. Henesey	1
P. Bailey	1	F. Cundell	9	W. Hern	10
A. Balding	1	K. Cundell	3	A. G. Hide	11
G. Balding	1	R. Curren	3	W. Hide	136
A. Barclay	2	L. Dale	1	C. Hill	5
H. Barclay	5	T. Darling	1	B. W. Hills	49
E. Barker	1	E. Davey	8	J. Hindley	5
R. Barnes	3	P. Davey	2	B. Hobbs	39
L. Barratt	7	J. Davis	1	R. Hobson	1
T. Barron	4	M. Delahooke	1	W. Holden	1
A. Bastiman	1	J. Dennistown	1	R. Hollinshead	2
J. Beary	1	T. Dent	3	D. Holmes	1
P. Beasley	27	A. Dickinson	2	R. Houghton	14
G. Beeby	3	Mrs L. Dingwall	1	F. Hudson	1
C. Bell	1	P. Doherty	1	G. Hunter	5
W. Bellerby	4	D. Doyle	1	S. Ingham	3
W. Bentley	3	E. Duffey	1	K. Ivery	1
J. Berry	1	J. Dunlop	17	A. Jarvis	1
J. Bethell	3	F. Durr	1	J. Jarvis	2
H. Blackshaw	11	W. Dutton	24	M. Jarvis	5
G. Blum	1	M. H. Easterby	15	R. Jarvis	8
R. Boss	2	M. W. Easterby	115	H. B. Jones	25
C. Bowser	2	W. Easterby	1	H. T. Jones	8
G. Boyd	5	C. F. Elsey	165	P. Kelleway	8
C. Boyd-Rochfort	5	W. Elsey	307	J. Kenneally	1
A. Breasley	1	L. Elwell	7	D. Laing	2
K. Bridgewater	1	J. Etherington	20	E. Lambton	1
C. Brittain	81	S. Everitt	11	H. Leader	1
A. Budgett	18	T. Fairhurst	2	T. Leader	1
B. Bullock	1	J. Faucus	2	D. Leslie	1
J. Byrne	1	M. Feakes	1	C. Lloyd Jones	1
N. Callaghan	7	R. Fisher	2	Mrs R. Lomax	1
J. Calvert	12	J. Fitzgerald	24	W. Lyde	2
M. Camacho	16	T. Forster	1	D. McCain	1
D. Candy	2	B. Foster	1	P. Makin	1
H. Candy	1	W. D. Francis	5	R. Mansfield	1
E. Carr	2	N. Gaselee	1	D. Marks	3
F. Carr	9	A. Geraghty	1	W. Marshall	5
W. Carr	14	E. Gifford	2	J. Mason	1
R. Carter	2	E. Goddard	1	R. E. Mason	1
P. Cazelet	2	J. Goldsmith	1	T. Masson	1
H. Cecil	4	A. Goodwill	2	H. Maw	5
D. Chapman	1	J. Gosden	9	F. Maxwell	4
D. Charlesworth	1	T. Gosling	1	S. Mercer	19
F. Clark	1	W. Gray	3	C. Mitchell	1
H. Clarkson	1	R. Greenhill	1	T. Molony	3
J. Clayton	4	W. Guest	1	S. Morant	5
P. Cole	4	D. Gunn	1	D. Morley	2
W. Colley	1	W. Haigh	1	J. Mulhall	2
R. J. Colling	9	S. Hall	14	N. Murless	2
E. Collingwood	1	Miss S. Hall	3	R. Murphy	1

M. Naughton	2	E. Reavey	4	J. Tree	2
A. Neaves	2	G. Richards	42	B. Van Cutsem	6
C. Nelson	3	G. W. Richards	12	A. Vasey	6
P. Nelson	40	F. Rimell	4	J. Vickers	2
S. Nesbitt	5	P. Robinson	3	N. Vigors	1
W. Nevett	1	R. Robson	5	S. Wainwright	1
W. Newton	10	P. Rohan	20	I. Walker	3
W. Nightingall	1	L. Shedden	62	P. Walwyn	6
S. Norton	1	J. Sirett	1	R. Ward	9
V. O'Brien	3	A. Smith	1	J. Waters	1
W. O'Brien	2	Denys Smith	10	F. Watson	2
H. O'Neil	2	Doug Smith	10	J. W. Watts	160
J. Ormston	7	H. E. Smyth	2	W. C. Watts	2
J. Oxley	12	W. Stephenson	2	T. Waugh	7
S. Parker	4	W. A. Stephenson	20	J. Weston-Evans	2
K. Payne	1	A. Stevens	1	E. Weymes	25
H. Peacock	4	H. Storey	1	J. Weymes	1
J. Peacock	1	M. Stoute	94	W. Wharton	20
R. Peacock	54	R. Sturdy	7	D. Whelan	1
J. Pearce	1	J. Sutcliffe	1	H. Whiteman	1
A. Pitt	3	J. Sutcliffe Sen.	2	W. Wightman	34
M. Pope	1	M. Tate	2	C. Williams	1
J. Powney	1	F. Taylor	1	D. Williams	11
C. Pratt	1	P. Taylor	57	H. Williams	2
W. Pratt	1	D. Thom	11	W. H. Williams	2
P. Prendergast	2	A. J. Thomas	5	J. Winter	12
M. Prescott	7	C. Thornton	5	G. Wragg	1
H. R. Price	4	N. Tinkler	3	H. Wragg	7
G. Pritchard-Gordon	8	R. Titterington	1	J. Yeomans	2

MILESTONES

First Ride	Copper Wire	Birmingham	29 August 1950
First Winner	Ritornello	Chepstow	22 September 1951
1000th Winner	Three Six	Ayr	15 May 1965
2000th Winner	Triple First	York	10 May 1977
2500th Winner	Chrome Mag	Edinburgh	3 November 1982
Last British Winner	Hi-Tech Leader	Nottingham	13 August 1985
Last Ever Winner	American Liberty	Sha Tin	18 May 1986

Winner of the Horse Writers Association award as the Flat Jockey of the Year December 1972
Winner of the Timeform Personality of the Year   10 June 1977

WINNERS BY COURSES

Alexandra Park	4	Folkestone	2	Nottingham	77
Royal Ascot	18	Goodwood	26	Pontefract	126
Ascot	19	Hamilton	75	Redcar	193
Ayr	153	Haydock	125	Ripon	109
Bath	13	Hurst Park	2	Salisbury	14
Beverley	115	Kempton	14	Sandown	12
Birmingham	29	Lanark	33	Stockton	67
Bogside	20	Leicester	64	Teesside	23
Brighton	18	Lincoln	21	Thirsk	143
Carlisle	51	Lingfield	8	Warwick	30
Catterick	142	Liverpool	41	Windsor	18
Chepstow	9	Manchester	43	Wolverhampton	72
Chester	29	Newbury	8	Worcester	6
Doncaster	142	Newcastle	142	Yarmouth	18
Edinburgh	86	Newmarket	97	York	116
Epsom	18				

Index

INDEX